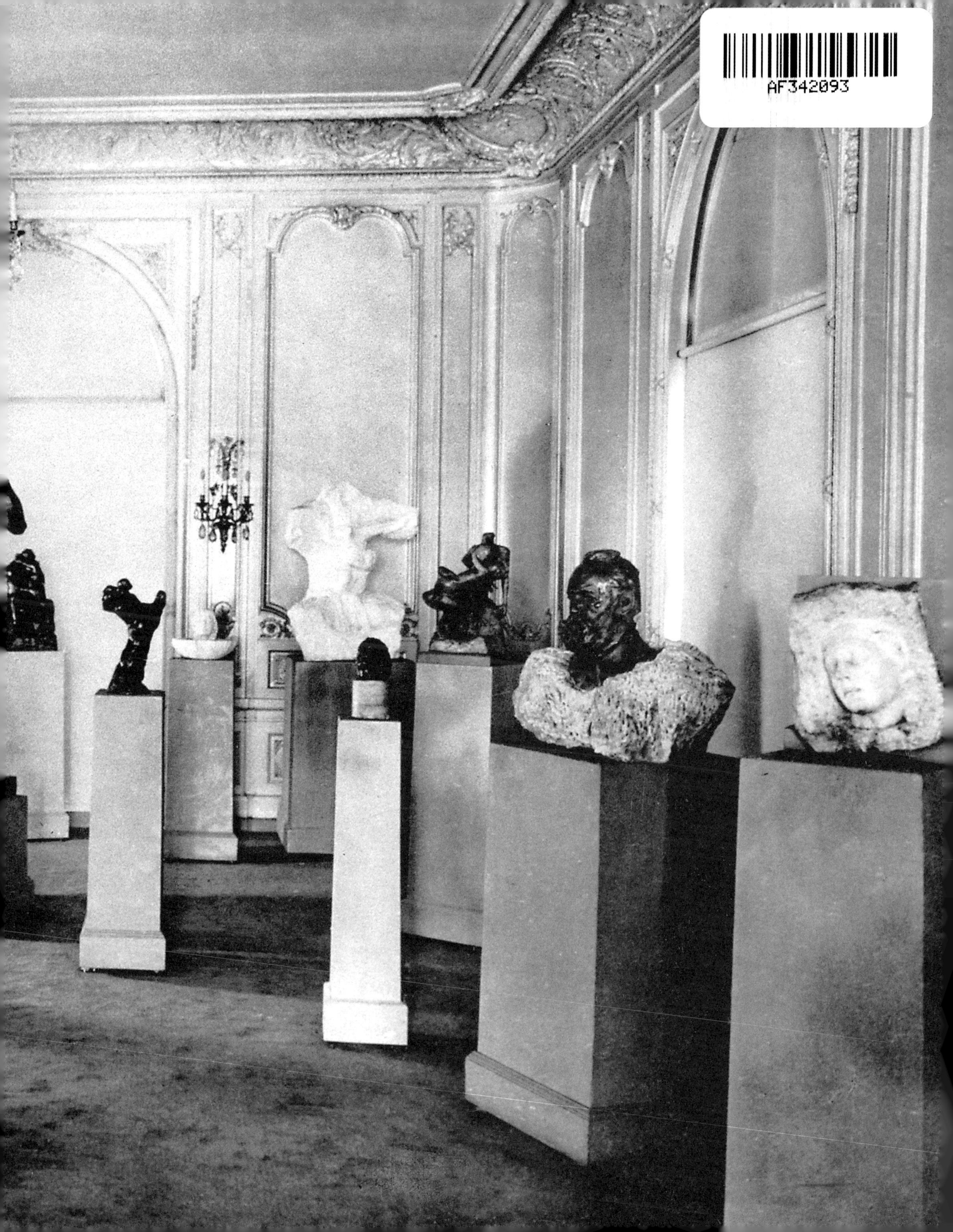
AF342093

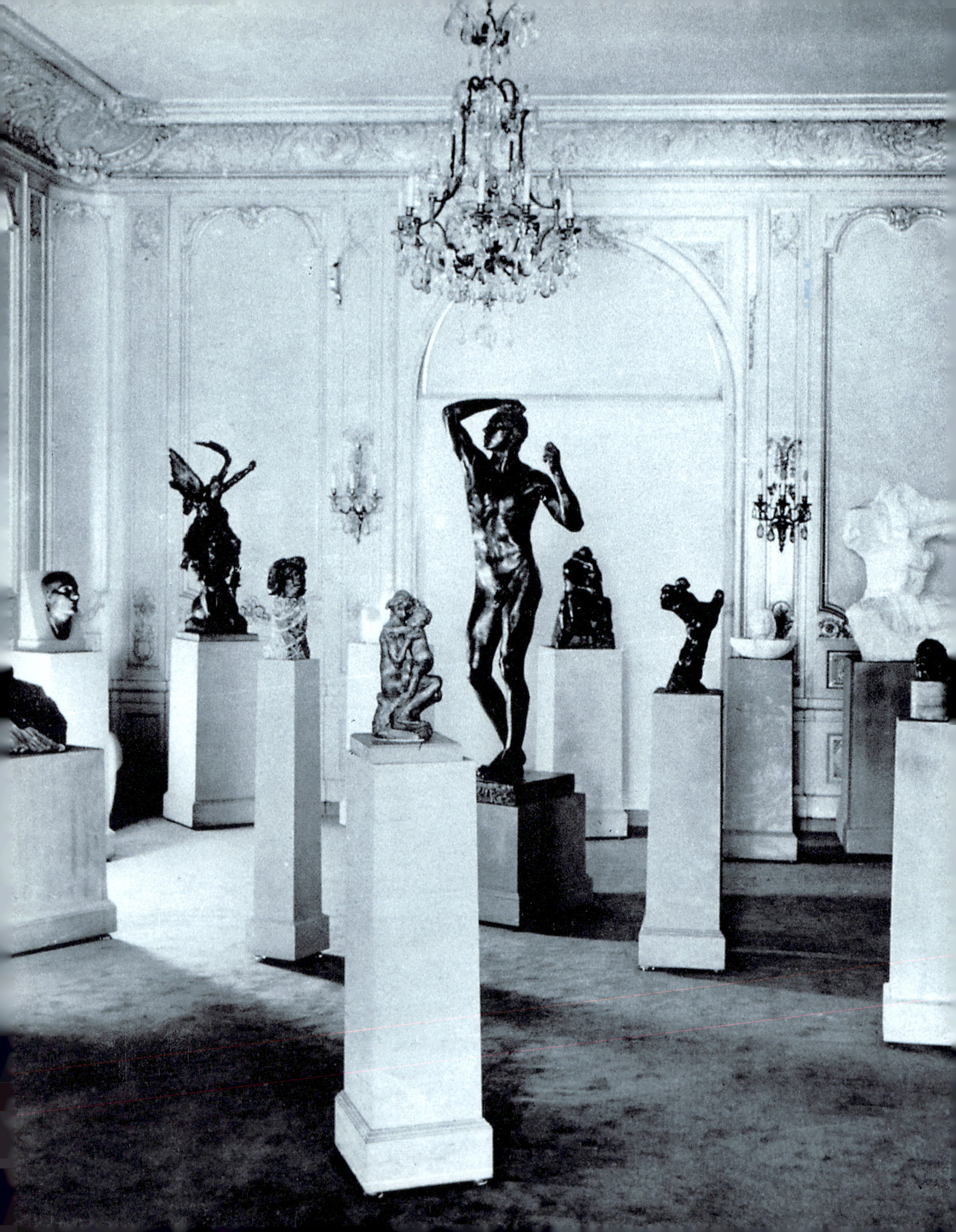

THE SCULPTURE OF

AUGUSTE
RODIN

AT THE LEGION OF HONOR

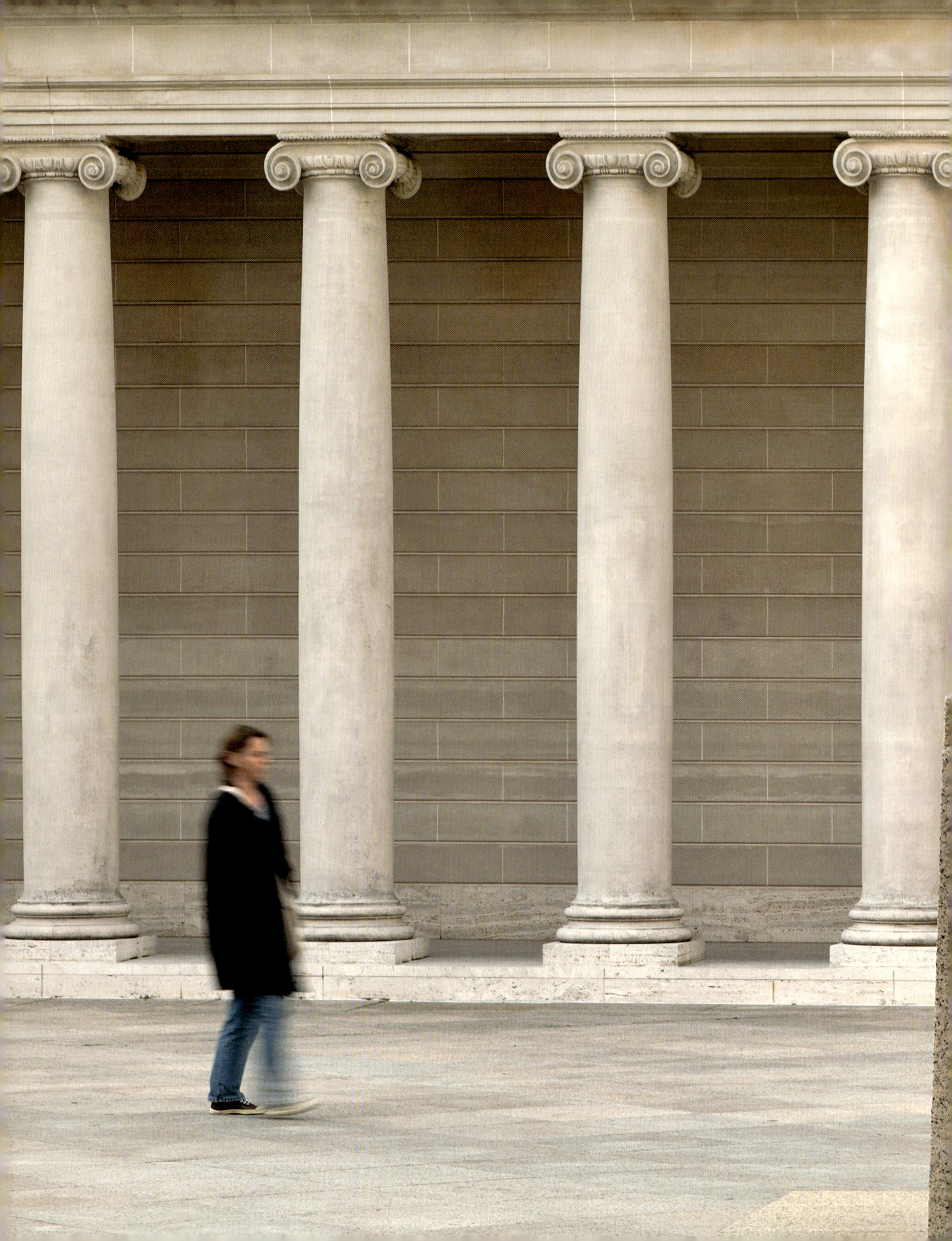

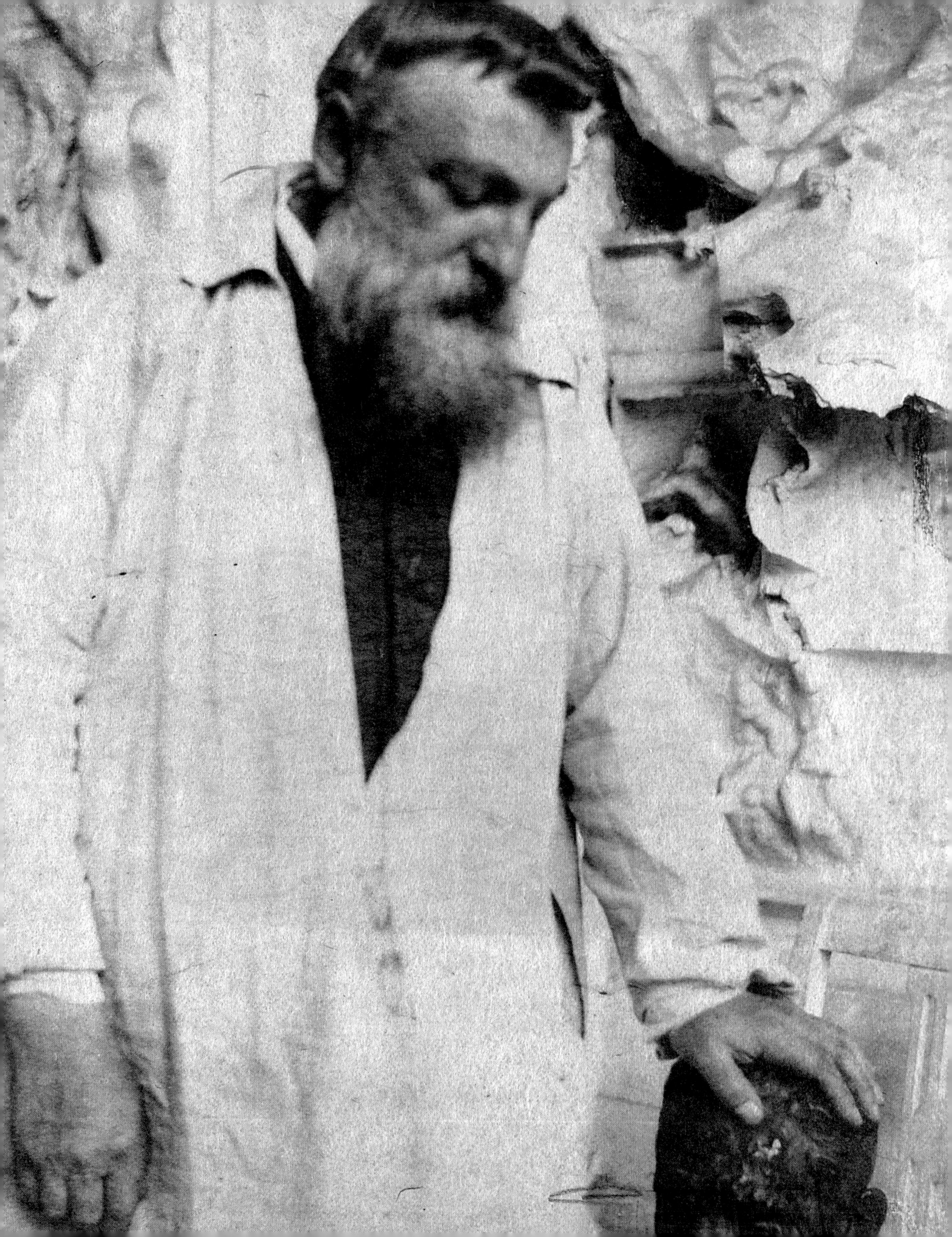

CONTENTS

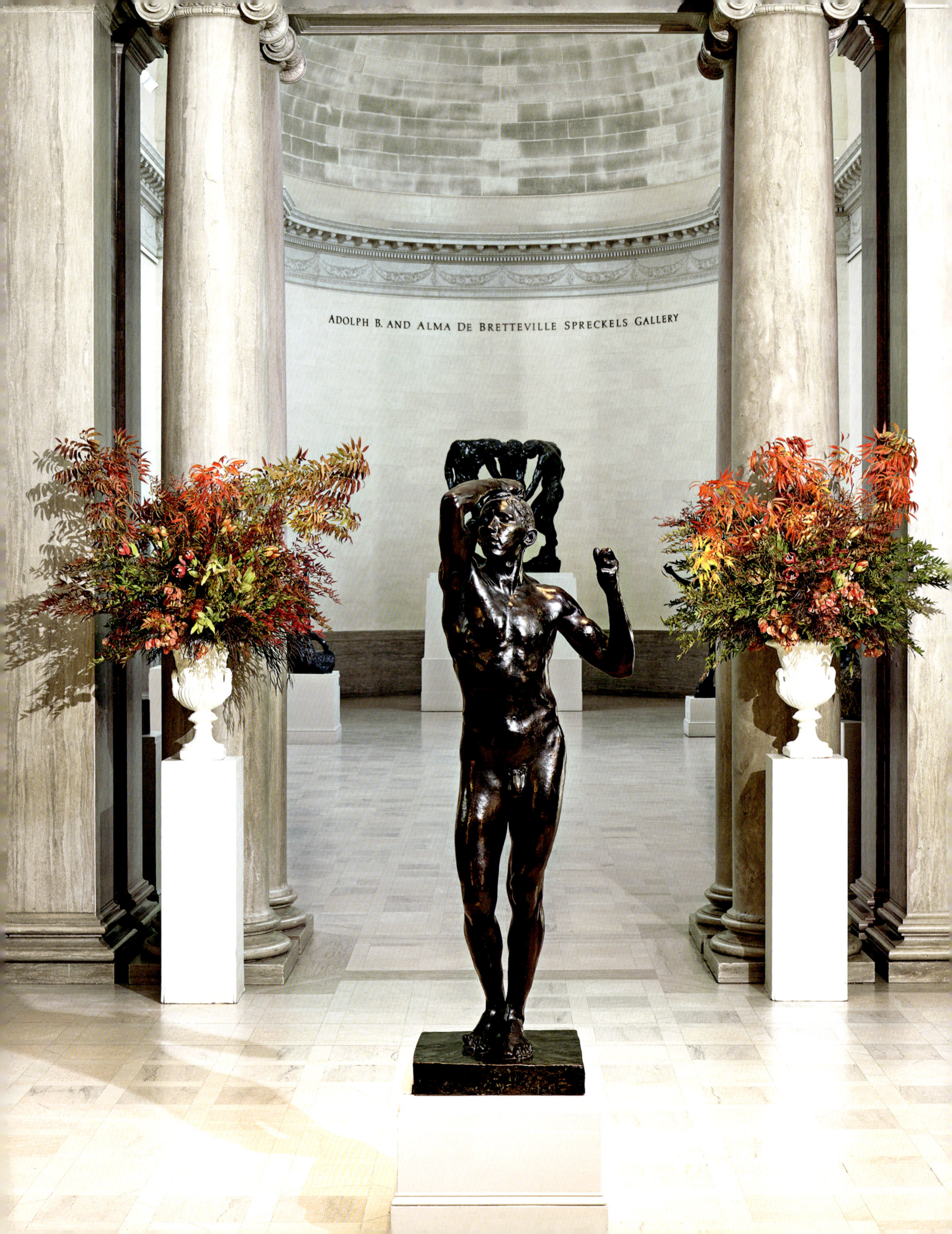
ADOLPH B. AND ALMA DE BRETTEVILLE SPRECKELS GALLERY

FOREWORD

MAX HOLLEIN

DIRECTOR AND CEO

FINE ARTS MUSEUMS OF SAN FRANCISCO

Auguste Rodin broke the rules of academic training in Paris in the late nineteenth century, dispensing with traditional aesthetic boundaries to find new vocabularies and create a powerful agenda for sculpture in the modern world. After struggling to achieve recognition in his early career, by 1900 Rodin was the most famous sculptor in the world. His acclaim did not go unnoticed in San Francisco. Due to serendipitous circumstances, Alma de Bretteville Spreckels, who would later found the Legion of Honor, was introduced to the artist and became an important collector of his work.

Originally assembled in 1915 by Spreckels and her husband Adolph, their personal collection, which included pieces acquired from the sculptor before he died, formed the core of the Legion's holdings—which grew to become one of the most significant repositories of Rodin's works in the United States. *The Thinker*, placed in the Court of Honor since the Legion's founding in 1924, has become emblematic of the museum, and other significant works by Rodin greet our visitors as they enter the building, including the poignant *The Age of Bronze* in the Rotunda.

There has not been a publication on our Rodin works since Jacques de Caso and Patricia B. Sanders published their excellent catalogue in 1977. With the 2017 centenary of the sculptor's death, it is a fitting moment for the Fine Arts Museums of San Francisco to produce a fresh volume on Rodin's achievement as it is reflected in our holdings.

We acknowledge and thank John A. and Cynthia Fry Gunn for their generous support of this presentation. Our Board of Trustees, led by Diane B. Wilsey, president, has provided its advocacy and made this project possible. Further gratitude is extended to Martin Chapman, curator in charge of decorative arts and sculpture, for his sensitive oversight of this project, and to the entire staff of the Museums, who uphold and maintain our robust programs.

We hope that this book will not only serve as a guide to the work of Rodin at the Legion, but that it will offer vibrant approaches to his art for a new generation of enthusiasts. For this centenary—and to demonstrate the enduring qualities of Rodin's work—we are redisplaying the collection in our galleries and introducing dialogues with contemporary artists. It is our wish that these interventions will expand upon the horizons of sculpture, just as Rodin did in his lifetime.

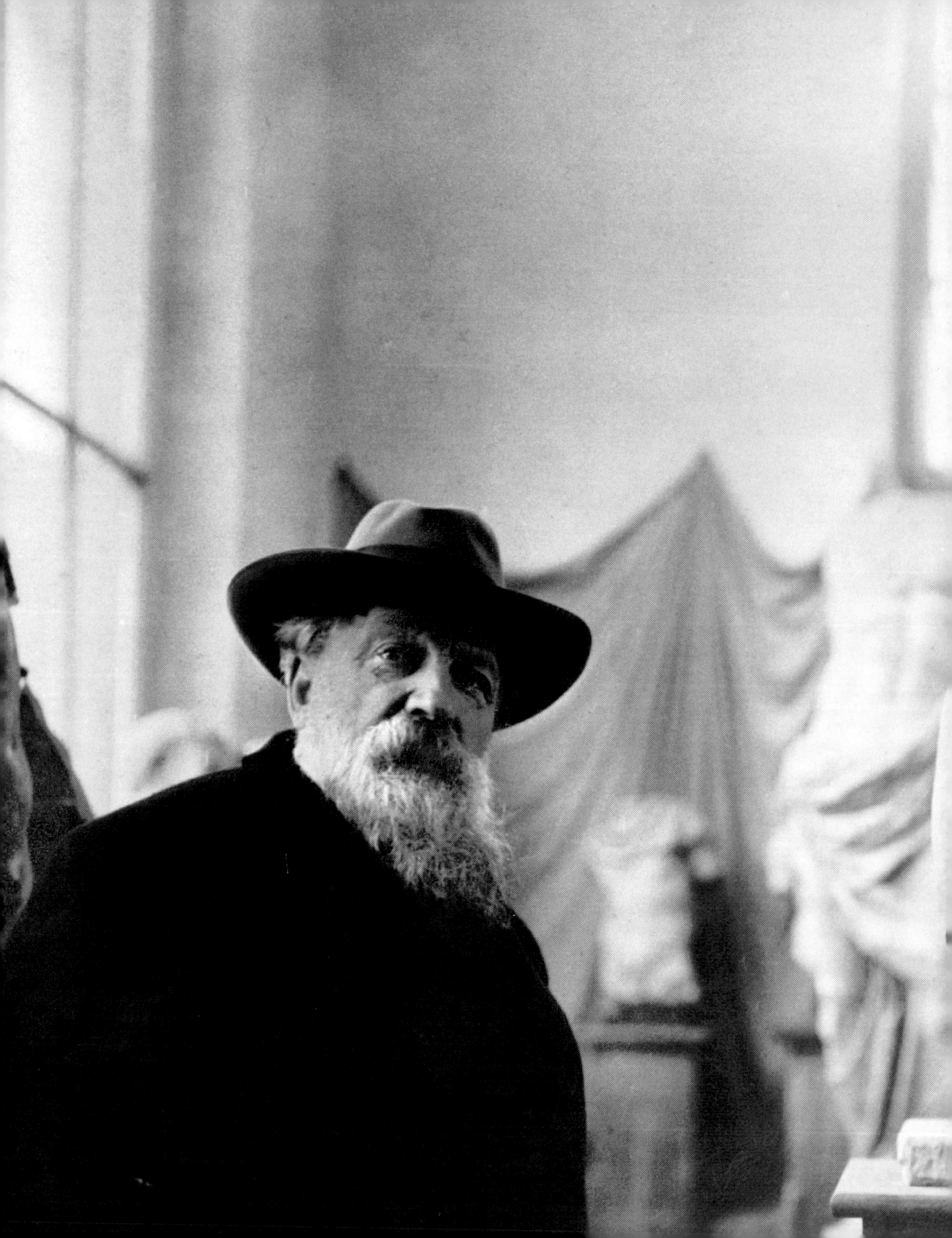

INTRODUCTION

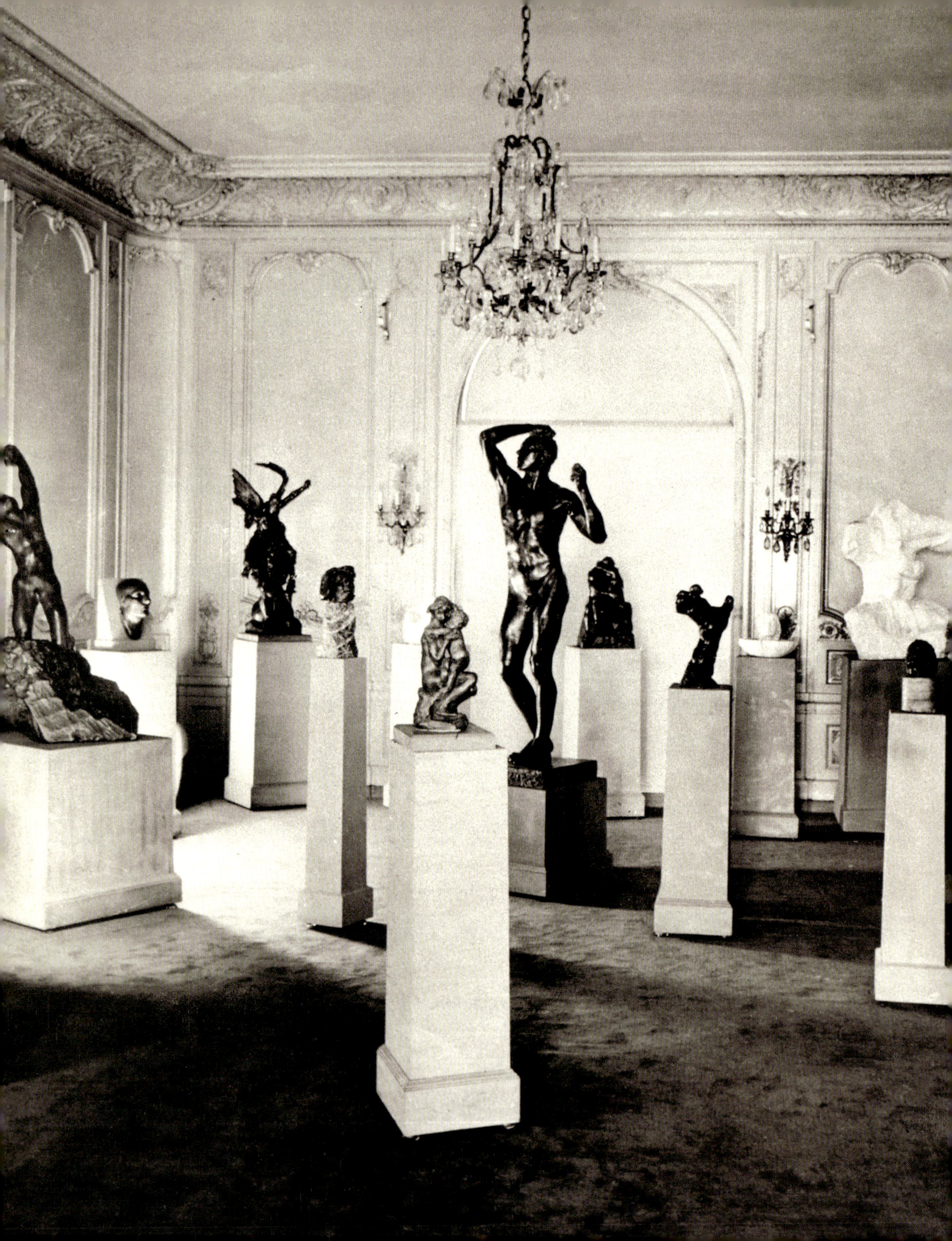

THE HISTORY OF THE SPRECKELS RODINS

MARTIN CHAPMAN

"The greatest collection of perfect Rodins in the world."

— LOÏE FULLER, 1927

The work of the French sculptor Auguste Rodin (1840–1917) lies at the heart of the Legion of Honor. His art is in evidence as soon as visitors arrive at the museum, where the massive statue *The Thinker* dominates the Court of Honor (pp. 2–3 and pl. 12). Entering the building through the main doors, guests immediately discover the full range of Rodin's sculpture in galleries radiating from the Rotunda and stretching to the back of the museum. Included are his most famous works, such as *The Age of Bronze* (pl. 1) and *Saint John the Baptist Preaching* (pl. 4), that established his reputation, through to *The Kiss* (pl. 13) and *The Burghers of Calais* (pls. 23–30) that heralded him as "the father of modern sculpture." The majority of the bronzes and marbles were produced for the sculptor during his lifetime, which alone makes the collection impressive. However, when the museum's wide spectrum of his plasters, models, and fragments is added into the mix, the Legion is arguably one of the most comprehensive holdings of Rodin's works in the United States.[i]

The collection was first assembled by the museum's founder, Alma de Bretteville Spreckels (American, 1881–1968; fig. 1), the wife of the sugar baron Adolph B. Spreckels (American, 1857–1924). She was inspired to collect art following a chance encounter with the American dancer Loïe Fuller (American, 1862–1928; fig. 2), whom she met at a dinner in Paris in 1914.[ii] Fuller, a pioneer of modern dance, met Rodin in 1898, and they became fast friends and mutual admirers of each other's work. She effectively became the sculptor's agent in the United States thereafter, championing Rodin's work to the many potential patrons among the barons of the Gilded Age. Although she failed in her first attempt in 1903 to show his work in New York—where not a single piece found a buyer[iii]—by 1914 the tides had turned and American collectors joined the international band of admirers of the artist by acquiring his work.[iv] Fuller's persuasive skills ensured that Spreckels would become one of Rodin's most important American patrons during his lifetime. The dancer brokered all of the early acquisitions with the intention that the Spreckels sculpture would be "the greatest collection of perfect Rodins in the world."[v]

Fuller introduced Spreckels to Rodin on the collector's first and, as it turned out, momentous visit to France in 1914 with the ambitious claim that Spreckels was going to open a museum in San Francisco. To encourage Rodin to sell some of his most important sculpture, Fuller showed "the Master" (as she referred to Rodin) a photograph of the Spreckels mansion to give the—incorrect—impression that it was to be the new museum (fig. 3).[vi] Rodin promised some significant works that were on show in London at the time, although eventually a different group was sent to San Francisco.[vii] In the end, Spreckels did, indeed, keep some of her collection of Rodins on view in her private mansion, even long after the opening of the Legion in 1924. However, it was with *The Thinker* prominently placed in the Court of Honor and the majority of the Spreckels collection temporarily displayed in the galleries that the museum held its opening ceremony (fig. 4).

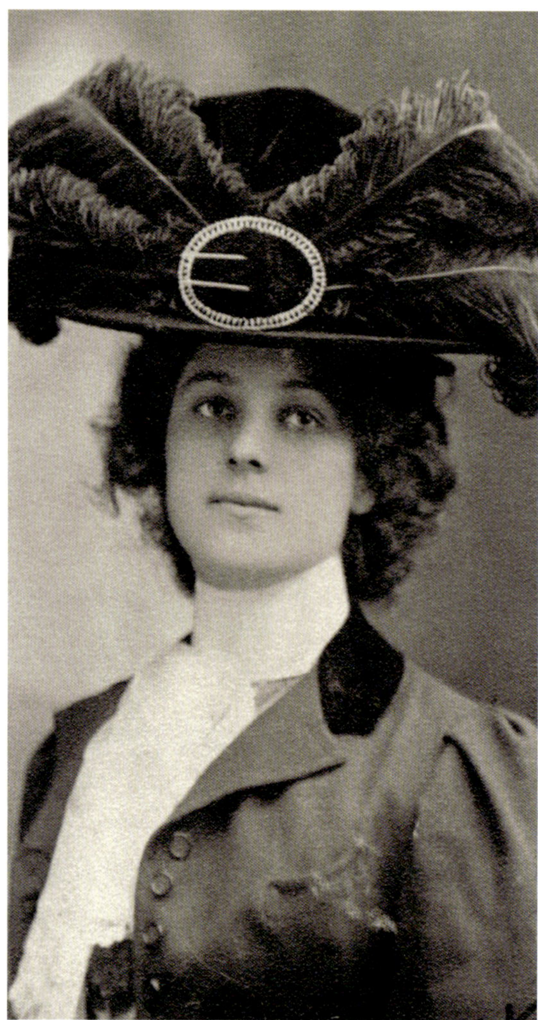

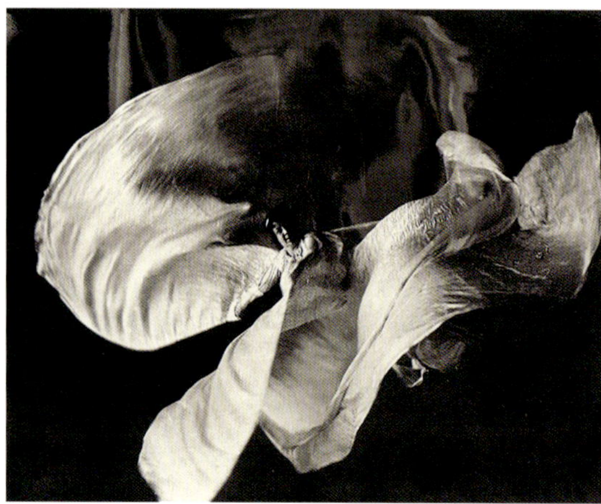

The first opportunity for the Spreckelses to show their newly acquired Rodins was at the Panama-Pacific International Exposition (PPIE), which was held in San Francisco in 1915 to celebrate the recovery of the city after the disastrous earthquake of 1906 and the opening of the Panama Canal. From Alma Spreckels's point of view, the fair was an occasion to prove to the citizens of San Francisco that she was a serious collector of art. Fuller actively supported her in this venture by securing the Rodins for the exposition and, ultimately, the Spreckels collection.[viii] She also encouraged Spreckels's dream of building a museum.[ix] At a critical time during the First World War, when the Germans had already invaded France and Belgium, Fuller badgered the French authorities to release the pieces of sculpture that she had acquired directly from Rodin for the exposition.[x] Fuller shipped the principal works in December 1914, and they arrived in San Francisco via the Panama Canal in March 1915.

The Rodins—six of which were later acquired by Spreckels—were set up in the French Pavilion of the exposition, where they made an impressive splash in the central gallery (fig. 5).[xi] The French Pavilion, fashioned after the Palais de la Légion d'Honneur in Paris, was specifically chosen for its symbolism of patriotism at a time when France was seeking popular sympathy among Americans and before the United States had entered the War. This structure, originally built in the 1780s as the private town mansion for the Prince Frederick III of Salm-Kyrburg, had been transformed into the home for Napoleon's order of chivalry, the Légion d'Honneur. It was, therefore, regarded as an important French national landmark, further appealing because of its striking but restrained neoclassical facades that, to Spreckels and her peers, gave an impression of dignity and taste.

The design of the French Pavilion so impressed Spreckels that she chose this same model for her new museum, a project that she could not realize until the hostilities ceased. The Francophile nature of the new museum was important to Spreckels, who claimed distant but distinguished French aristocratic ancestry. This declaration was despite the fact that her husband's much more recent origins were German, meaning that the funding for the museum was coming from a German-

Fig. 1 Alma de Bretteville Spreckels, 1904

Fig. 2 Nadar, *Loïe Fuller*, early twentieth century. Gelatin silver print, 7 ⅛ x 9 ½ in. (18 x 24 cm). Fine Arts Museums of San Francisco, Museum purchase, Nancy van Norman Baer Memorial Fund, 2007.17.10.2

American source. This dichotomy of allegiances at such
a critical time just after the First World War (fought
principally between France and Germany) was settled
by making the museum a memorial to the California
war dead. The somewhat protracted (and confusing)
original title of the institution—the California Palace of
the Legion of Honor—refers not to the French Légion
d'Honneur but to the Californian branch of the American
Legion (founded in 1919) that serves war veterans. Even
so, Spreckels's primary interests remained rooted in
French art. Beyond the architecture, the French identity
was still to the fore when the museum opened with an
exhibition of paintings lent by the Musée du Louvre,
Paris, and a display of the permanent collection with the
Rodin sculptures as its centerpiece (fig. 6).

The history of the acquisition of the Spreckels Rodins is
somewhat hazy as the collector kept scant information
about her purchases of sculpture. Possibly she did
so intentionally to hide monetary figures from her
husband—her initial rashness to secure the promise
of her first purchases from Fuller in 1915 caused
Adolph Spreckels to impose a tighter rein on his wife's
spending on art.[xii] Even after her husband died, just
before the opening of the Legion in November 1924,
Alma Spreckels remained reluctant to reveal the details
about the origins—and costs—of much of her art. Some
of this information was confided to her assistant Jean
Frickelton, who was intending to write a biography that
never materialized. Unfortunately, Frickelton destroyed
many of these papers before she died in the 1970s and,
therefore, important details about the acquisition of the
Rodins have been lost.[xiii]

The general collecting pattern can be reconstructed,
however. Initially, Alma (and Adolph) Spreckels bought
six of the Rodins sent by Fuller to the PPIE, including
some of the most impressive pieces in the collection:
The Thinker (fig. 7), *The Age of Bronze*, and *Saint John
the Baptist Preaching*.[xiv] Spreckels also acquired *The Call
to Arms* (pl. 2) to raffle at a tombola in aid of French
war relief, although it still remains in the Legion's
collection.[xv] She continued to acquire pieces, but at a
slower rate due to America's entry into the war. For
the opening of the museum she gave only two works

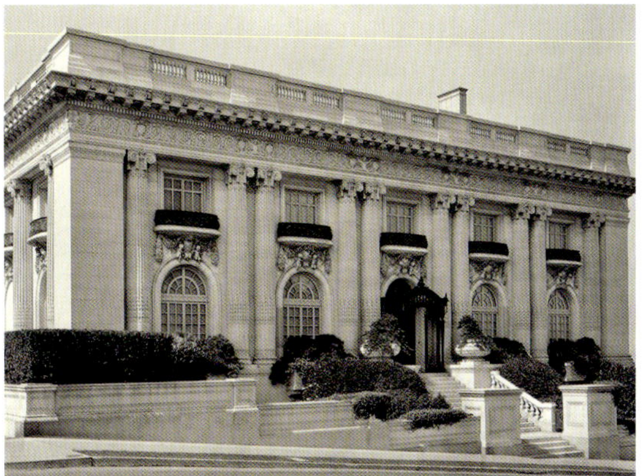

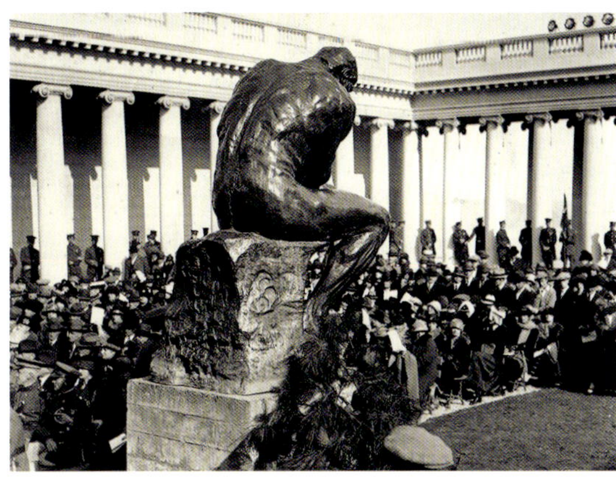

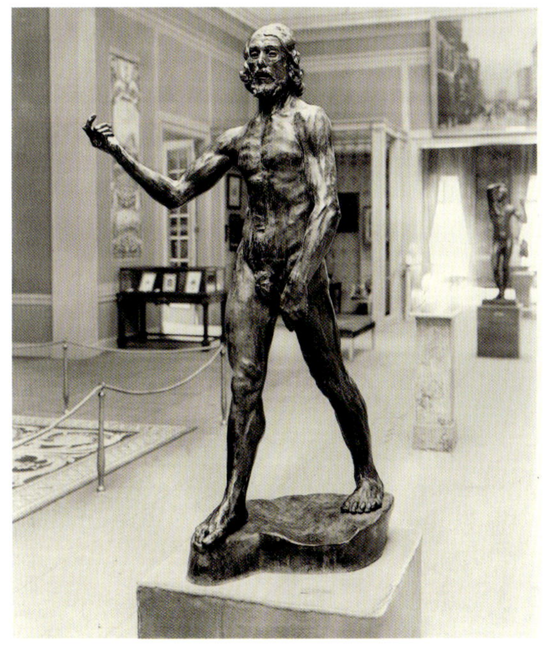

Fig. 3 The Spreckels mansion at 2080 Washington Street, San Francisco, ca. 1925

Fig. 4 *The Thinker* (pl. 12) in the Court of Honor at the Legion of Honor, San Francisco, on the museum's opening day, November 11, 1924

Fig. 5 *Saint John the Baptist Preaching* (pl. 4) with *The Age of Bronze* (pl. 1) in the French Pavilion, Panama-Pacific International Exposition, San Francisco, 1915

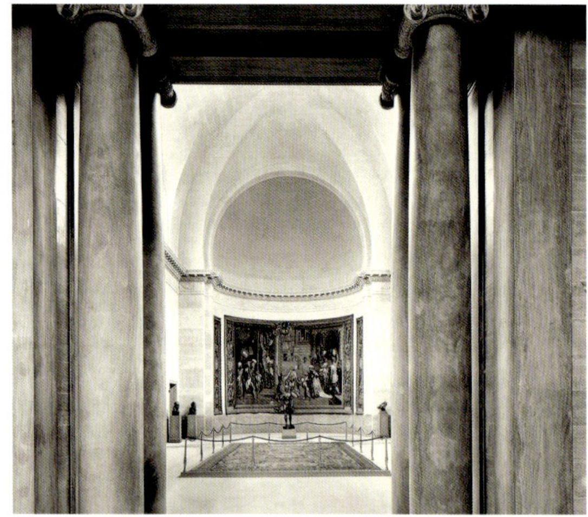

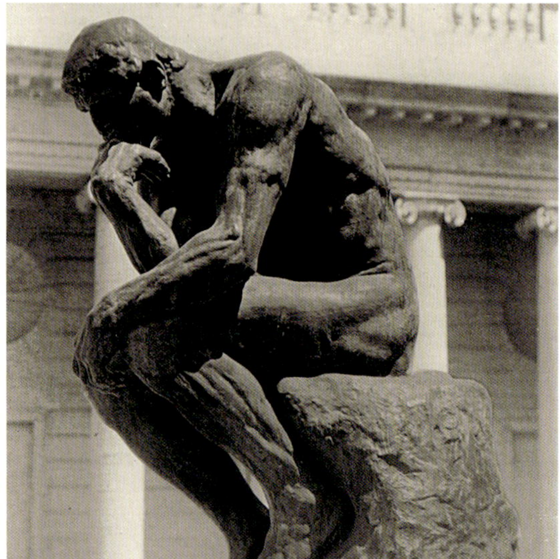

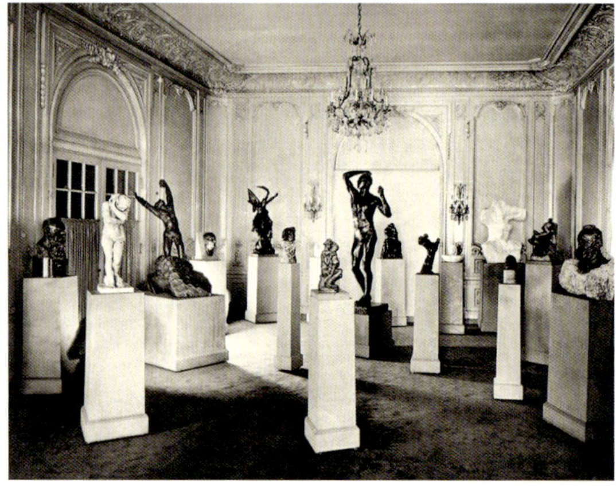

outright, *The Thinker* (which had been paid for by her late husband) and a plaster, *Brother and Sister* (pl. 43). In the following years she lent most of her Rodins to the Legion, apparently switching them in and out of her home on Washington Street at whim (fig. 8). In 1933 she gave the first larger group of Rodin's work, mostly plasters acquired from Rodin's bronze founder Eugène Rudier, to the museum in the name of her son, Adolph Jr. (fig. 9).[xvi] But it was not until the early 1940s that Spreckels donated the bulk of her Rodin sculpture to the Legion. These gifts comprised the principal pieces from the Spreckels collection, including *The Age of Bronze*, *Saint John the Baptist Preaching*, *The Call to Arms*, *The Burghers of Calais*, and *The Kiss*.

By the time of her death, in 1968, the collection added up to more than ninety pieces of the artist's sculptural work. In addition, Spreckels gave some works on paper that served as the base of the collection of prints, drawings, and photographs associated with Rodin in the Legion's Achenbach Foundation for Graphic Arts (figs. 10 and 21), which would grow into a complementary asset to the sculpture collection.

From the time of the opening of the museum, the Rodins were displayed as they are today in the impressive main gallery with its handsome vaulting and apse and, originally, set against a background of tapestries. In November 1974, the fiftieth anniversary of the Legion, this primary display space was designated as the Adolph B. and Alma de Bretteville Spreckels Gallery. The architectural work was completed by the Spreckels's grandson Adolph Rosekrans. This project encompassed the adjacent spaces, including the "garden courts" that were initially intended more for the keeping of potted palms than for the showing of art; these spaces were made more suitable for the display of Rodin's sculpture through the installation of new marble floors and the removal of the trellis on the walls.[xvii] This renovation expanded the scope of Rodin's work in the museum and has ensured that his legacy remains at the core of the Legion of Honor so that visitors can study and enjoy one of the most comprehensive collections of Rodin's work in the United States.

Fig. 6 View of the Rodin gallery at the Legion of Honor, San Francisco, ca. 1925–1930. Photograph by Gabriel Moulin

Fig. 7 *The Thinker* in the Court of Honor of the French Pavilion at the Panama-Pacific International Exposition, San Francisco, 1915. Photograph by Gabriel Moulin from the Charles C. Moore albums of the Panama-Pacific International Exposition views, vol. 3. The Bancroft Library, University of California, Berkeley

Fig. 8 Alma Spreckels's collection of Rodin works assembled at 2080 Washington Street, San Francisco, ca. 1920–1940. Photograph by Gabriel Moulin

Fig. 9 View of the Adolph B. and Alma de Bretteville Spreckels Gallery at the Legion of Honor, San Francisco, 2013. Photograph by Henrik Kam

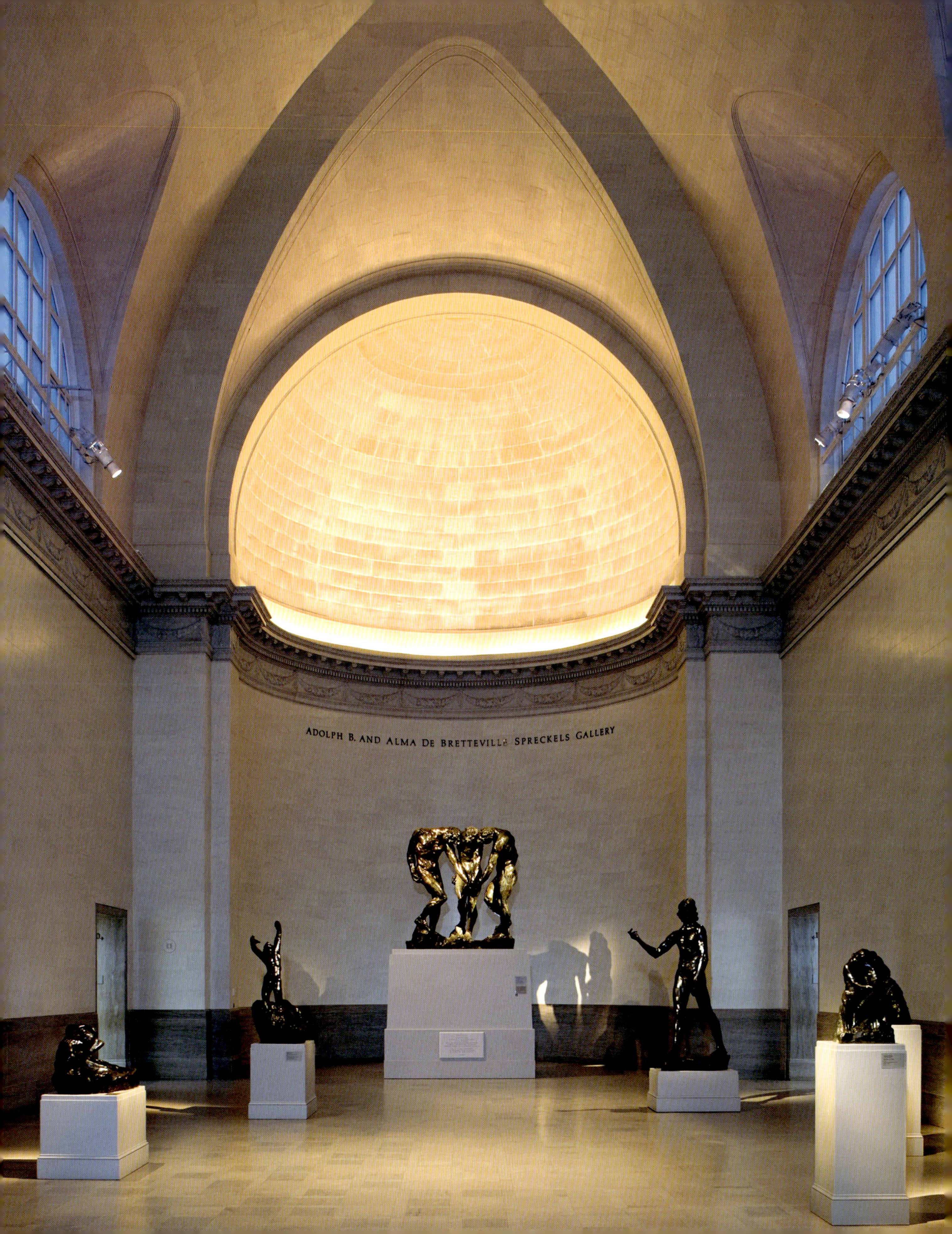

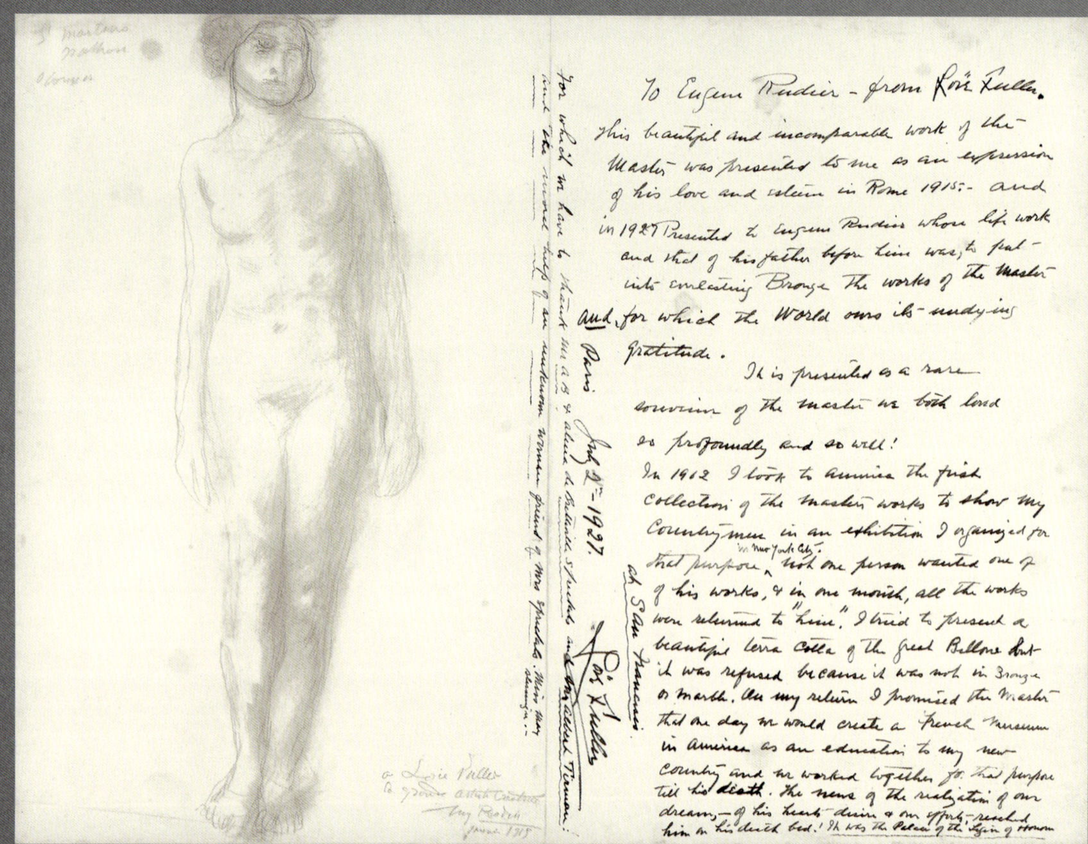

NU FÉMININ DEBOUT

This is the full text of Loïe Fuller's inscription to Eugène Rudier (Rodin's bronze founder) on Rodin's drawing *Nu féminin debout*, which is held in the Legion of Honor's permanent collection. It gives an account of Fuller's promotion of Rodin's sculpture in the United States and her affiliation with the museum.

To Eugene Rudier – from Loïe Fuller.

This beautiful and incomparable work of the Master was presented to me as an expression of his love and esteem in Rome 1915. — and in 1927 presented to Eugene Rudier whose life work and that of his father before him was, to put into everlasting Bronze the works of the Master and for which the world owes its undying gratitude.

It is presented as a rare souvenir of the Master we both loved so profoundly and so well!

In 1902 I took to America the first collection of the Master's works to show my countrymen in an exhibition I organized for that purpose in New York City. Not one person wanted one of his works, & in one month, all the works were returned to "him." I tried to present a beautiful terra cotta of the great Bellone but it was refused because it was not in Bronze or Marble. On my return I promised the Master that one day we would create a French Museum in America as an education to my new country and we worked together for that purpose till his death. The news of the realization of our dream,—of his heart's desire and our efforts—reached him on his death bed! It was the Palace of the Legion of Honour at San Francisco for which we have to thank Mr. A. B. and Alma de Bretteville Spreckels and Mr. Albert Tirman and the moral help of an unknown woman friend of Mrs. Spreckels, May Slessinger.
Paris July 2nd 1927. Loïe Fuller

Fig. 10. Auguste Rodin, *Nu féminin debout*, 1915. Graphite on paper, 17 ⅜ x 23 ¼ in. (44.1 x 56.6 cm). Fine Arts Museums of San Francisco, Museum purchase, Gift of Mrs. John N. Rosekrans, Jr., in memory of her husband, grandson of Alma de Bretteville Spreckels, 2007.49

NOTES

[i] The Rodin Museum in Philadelphia and the Cantor Arts Center at Stanford University are two other American collections that represent much of Rodin's oeuvre.

[ii] The dinner was hosted at Ciro's by the New York dealer French and Co., with whom Alma was working to acquire pieces of furniture for her new mansion. Bernice Scharlach, *Big Alma: San Francisco's Alma Spreckels*, 2nd ed. (San Francisco: Scottwall Associates, 1990; San Francisco and Berkeley: Fine Arts Museums of San Francisco and Heyday, 2014), 73, 75. Citations refer to the 2014 edition.

[iii] See the inscription by Loïe Fuller on Rodin's drawing *Nu féminin debout* (1915, fig. 10), which is in the collection of the Achenbach Foundation for Graphic Arts, Fine Arts Museums of San Francisco. In the inscription, Fuller describes taking Rodin's work to New York in 1902 [*sic.* 1903] and the dream of the creation of the Legion of Honor. For the complete inscription, see this volume, p. 16.

[iv] Rodin's sculpture had already been collected by Americans in Chicago and Boston in prior decades through the efforts of curator Sarah Tyson Hallowell (1846–1924), but Loïe Fuller's exhibition of Rodin's sculpture in 1903 was the first presentation in New York. See Bernard Barryte and Roberta K. Tarbell, eds., *Rodin and America: Influence and Adaptation, 1876–1936*, exh. cat. (Stanford, CA: Cantor Arts Center, 2011), 30–31, 216, 341–342.

[v] Loïe Fuller to Alma Spreckels, September 5, 1927. Loïe Fuller Papers, Dance Collection, New York Public Library, Astor, Lenox and Tilden Foundations, C9–60–5 and C9–60–6.

[vi] Scharlach, *Big Alma*, 81.

[vii] Ibid., 15n9.

[viii] Jacques de Caso and Patricia B. Sanders, *Rodin's Sculpture, A Critical Study of the Spreckels Collection* (San Francisco: Fine Arts Museums of San Francisco, 1977), 26–27.

[ix] Ibid.

[x] Fuller went directly to the French Foreign Ministry to obtain the necessary permission to ship the pieces during the difficult times of war. See Scharlach, *Big Alma*, 89.

[xi] Loïe Fuller Papers, Dance Collection, New York Public Library, Astor, Lenox and Tilden Foundations, C–9–264.13 and C–9–264.14. The invoices from the Parisian shippers Chenue to Loïe Fuller include a case list that describes six Rodins: *The Age of Bronze*, *The Prodigal Son* (pl. 20), *Henri Rochefort* (pl. 35), *The Siren of the Sea* (pl. 11), *Youth and Old Age* or *Triumphant Youth* (pl. 8), and *The Thinker*. *Saint John the Baptist Preaching*, shown at the PPIE, was probably bought by the Spreckels separately after the fair from Fuller or from a representative overseeing the official French submissions. See de Caso and Sanders, *Rodin's Sculpture*, 78. Twelve other Rodins were sent to San Francisco on the USS *Jason* as part of the official French submission. These works may have been shipped directly from Rodin's studio. See Scharlach, *Big Alma*, 90, 95–96.

[xii] Scharlach, *Big Alma*, 86, 95–96, 102.

[xiii] Ibid., 374. There are also some useful provenances derived from the Frickelton papers that cannot be verified today. See de Caso and Sanders, *Rodin's Sculpture*, 10.

[xiv] *Saint John the Baptist Preaching* must have been acquired from the official submission sent by Rodin, rather than from those sculptures shipped by Fuller.

[xv] Scharlach, *Big Alma*, 96–98.

[xvi] Eugène Rudier (French, 1878–1952) was Rodin's preferred founder. After the sculptor's death, Rudier continued to cast bronzes from the models for the Musée Rodin, Paris, until his own death. He also served as an art dealer and sold many bronzes and plasters to Alma Spreckels until the late 1940s. See Antoinette Le Normand-Romain, *The Bronzes of Rodin, Catalogue of Works in the Musée Rodin*, vol. 2 (Paris: Musée Rodin, 2007), 28–31, 47–50. Rudier executed casts using the sand-casting method, rather than the lost-wax process, the latter of which is more common today (see sidebar, p. 103, this volume). He also claimed that he could make bronzes in a single cast, including large versions of *The Thinker*; this, however, was not the way the Legion's cast was made, as the joins of the different molds are visible (fig. 25). These plasters may have been acquired by Rodin's assistant, the American sculptor Malvina Hoffman (1887–1966). I am grateful to Antoinette Le Normand-Romain for this suggestion.

[xvii] De Caso and Sanders, *Rodin's Sculpture*, 10.

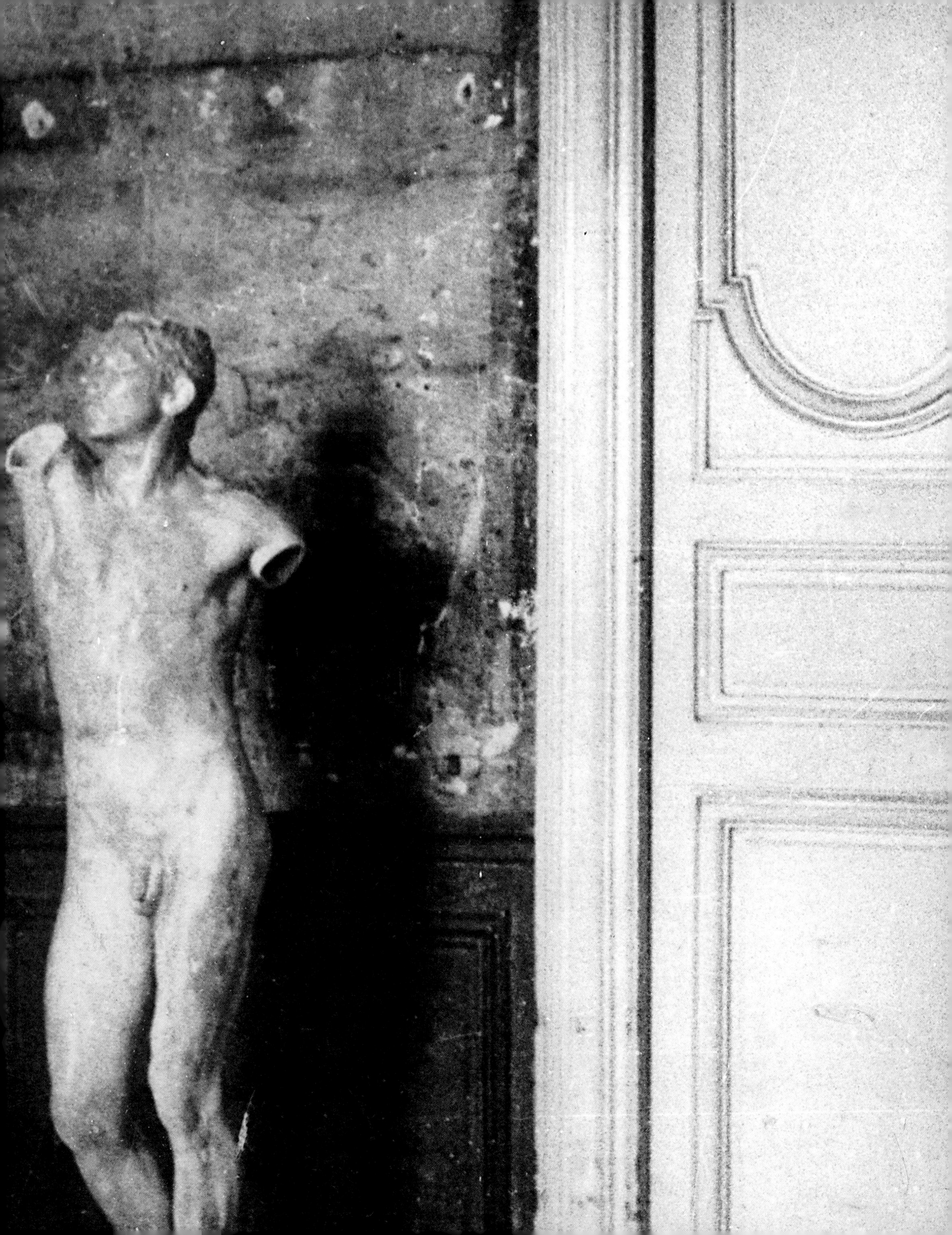

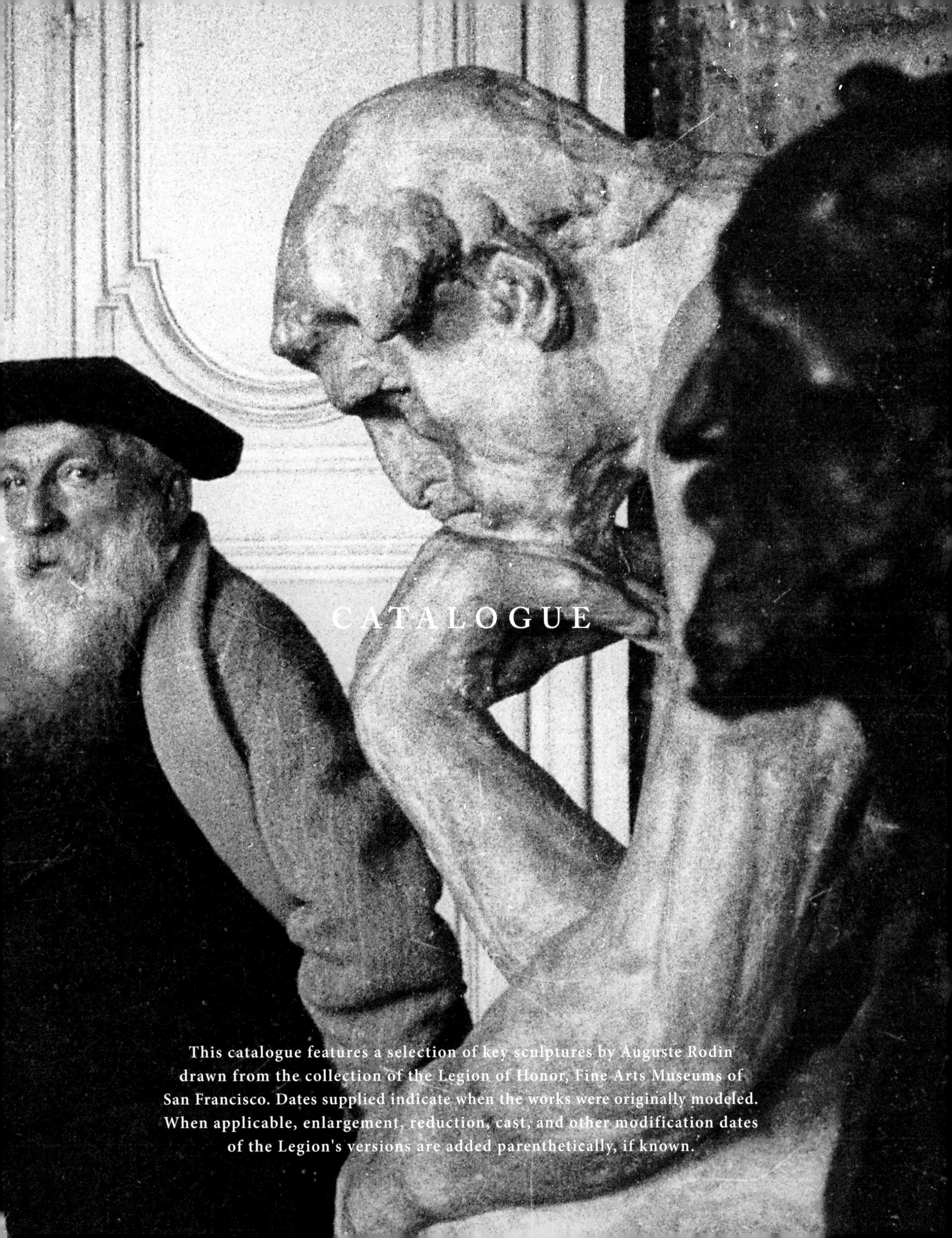

CATALOGUE

This catalogue features a selection of key sculptures by Auguste Rodin drawn from the collection of the Legion of Honor, Fine Arts Museums of San Francisco. Dates supplied indicate when the works were originally modeled. When applicable, enlargement, reduction, cast, and other modification dates of the Legion's versions are added parenthetically, if known.

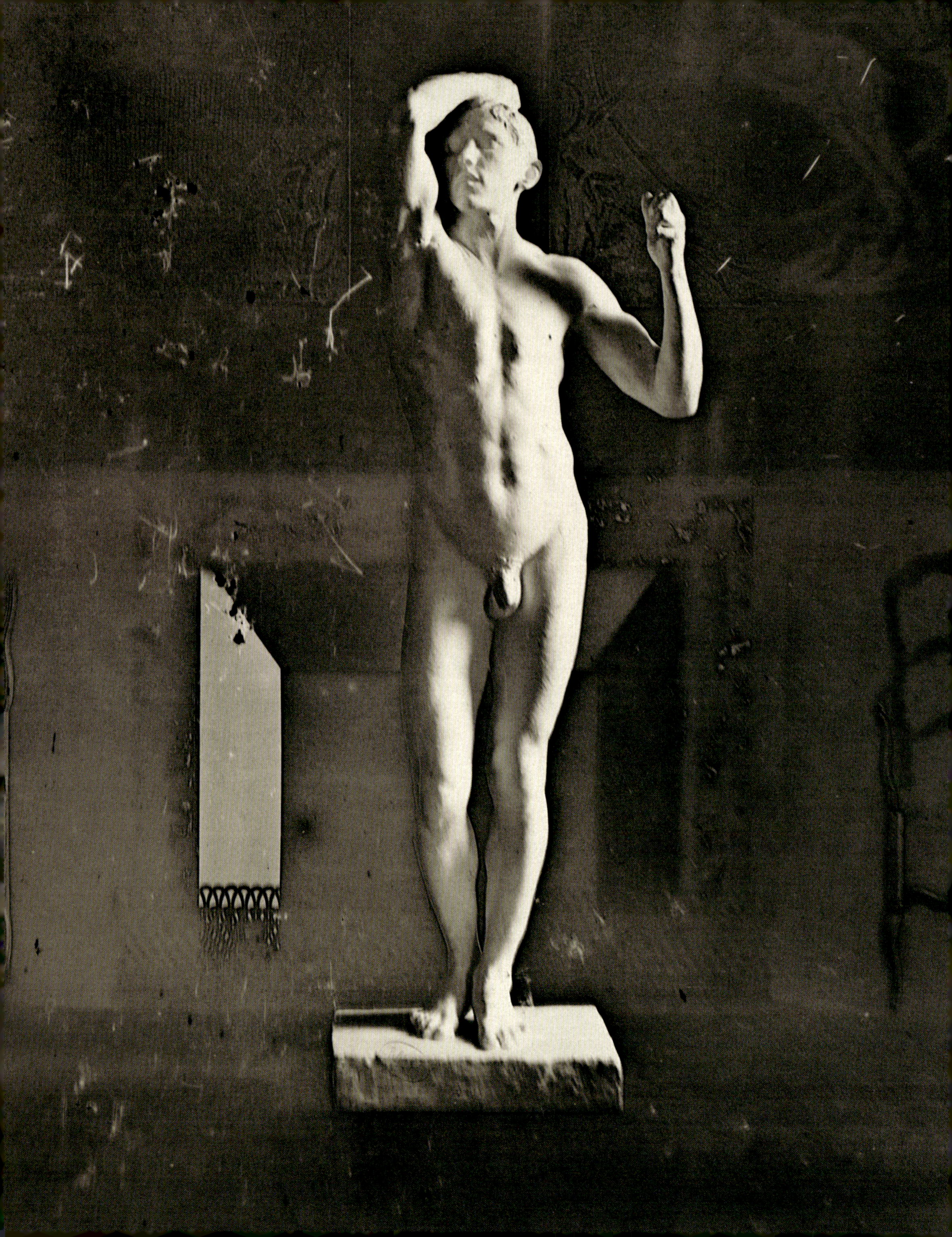

1

EARLY WORKS
The Struggle for Recognition
(1864–1880)

The collection of Rodins at the Legion of Honor reveals a wide range of the sculptor's work from his early days in the 1860s and 1870s when he struggled to gain recognition, through years of adverse criticism, to his heyday in the early twentieth century, when he earned international renown as the artist who had liberated sculpture from the academic tradition. Auguste Rodin's formal education was relatively brief. From 1854 to 1857, he attended the École Impériale et Spéciale de Dessin et de Mathématiques, Paris, known as "La Petite École." However, what he learned from his teacher there was fundamental to his development as an artist. Horace Lecoq de Boisbaudran (French, 1802–1897) taught his pupils to observe closely and to bring their own experiences to their work. Rodin still expressed gratitude for his teacher many years later, and these relatively simple instructions are keys to understanding works the sculptor made throughout his life.[i]

The earliest bronze in the collection and the first sculpture that Rodin regarded as a success is the *Man with the Broken Nose* (pl. 3). Rodin rendered the figure's wrinkled brow and squashed nose based on the features of a local handyman, but its effects were too naturalistic for the Paris Salon, which rejected the sculpture when it was submitted in 1865. The academic canons of art at that time demanded more classically idealized features for sculpture, even though there are allusions to antique prototypes in this bust.[ii] The young Rodin was rejected repeatedly for admission to the École des Beaux-Arts, the prestigious school of fine art in Paris. As a result, instead of following the conventional path of academic training, he found a practical education through his work as an assistant to more established artists such as the sculptor Albert-Ernest Carrier-Belleuse (French, 1824–1887), for whom Rodin apprenticed between 1864 and 1870.

Rodin's freestanding career would only occur after the Franco-Prussian War of 1870–1871, when France suffered a humiliating defeat, followed in Paris by the horrors of the Commune. After these troubled times, Rodin moved to work in Brussels with Carrier-Belleuse. He also made a life-changing trip to Italy, where he saw the work of Donatello (Italian, ca. 1386–1466) and Michelangelo Buonarroti (Italian, 1475–1564) and proclaimed "It is Michelangelo who has freed me from academic sculpture."[iii] Michelangelo's work would influence Rodin throughout his career. For his first full-scale sculpture, *The Age of Bronze* (pl. 1), the raised arm of the Renaissance artist's *Dying Slave* (1513–1516, Musée du Louvre, Paris) informed the pose, although the treatment of the body was entirely Rodin's. The title *The Age of Bronze* refers to the third of the five Ages

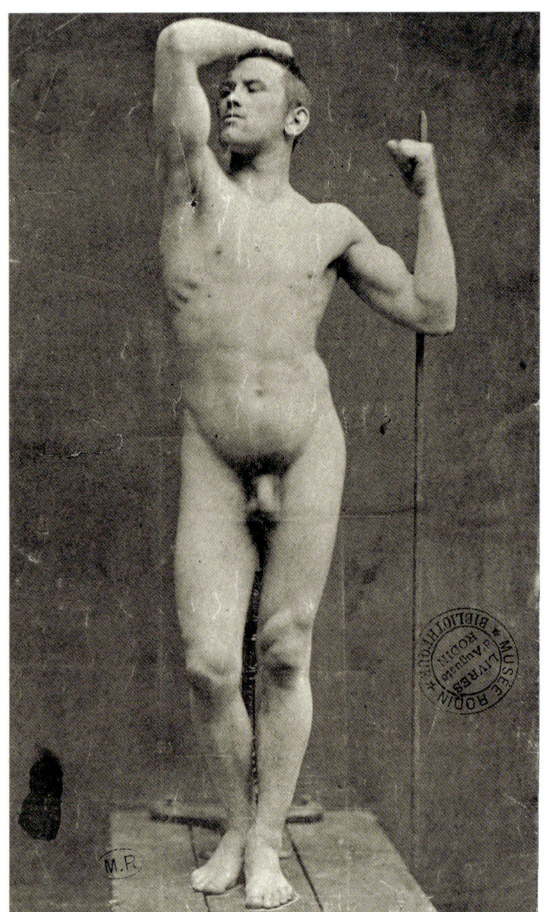

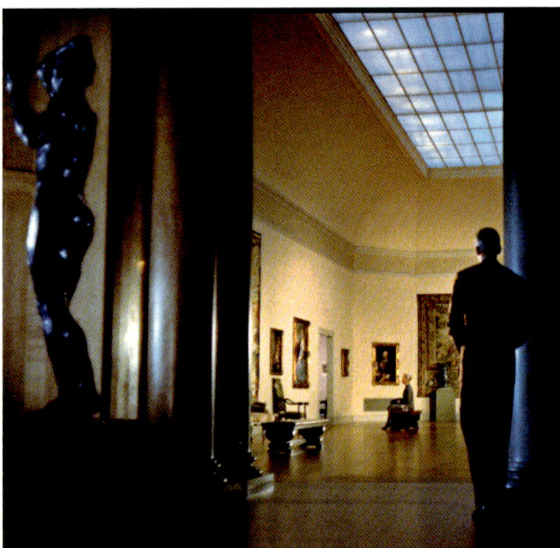

of Man articulated by the ancient Greek poet Hesiod, which is described as a declining era of war, violence, and destruction. In naming it, the sculptor also intended that *The Age of Bronze* be interpreted less as a defeated soldier associated with the recent war and more as a lifelike nude figure representing the human condition—a wider, more philosophical theme that Rodin would follow throughout his career. However, the figure's subtle modeling and naturalism led to the accusation that Rodin had taken casts directly from the model's body (fig. 11). This controversy had the paradoxical effect of pushing the sculptor even further into the limelight when the piece was exhibited at the Paris Salon in 1877. Since that time, *The Age of Bronze* has become recognized as one of Rodin's greatest works, with more than twenty-six casts made during the sculptor's lifetime. The Legion's cast was one of the first acquisitions made by its founder, Alma Spreckels, in 1915. Later it became a silent star in Alfred Hitchcock's cinematic masterpiece *Vertigo*, released in 1958; in the film, the actor James Stewart is shown repeatedly circling this sculpture in the Rotunda of the museum where it still stands today (fig. 12).

Another sculpture to have caused embroilment for Rodin is *The Call to Arms* (pl. 2), sometimes known as *La Défense*. Originally submitted by the sculptor to a public competition for a monument to the defense of Paris during the Franco-Prussian War, it did not even receive an honorable mention from the committee in 1879. The shrill gesturing of the winged Genius of Liberty surmounting the passive Michelangelesque figure [iv] of a wounded and dying soldier reflect the horrors of the war, but it was seen as too challenging for the committee's more stoic, neoclassical perception of monumental sculpture. Rodin admitted later that it must have "seemed too violent, too strident," but he was vindicated when *The Call to Arms*'s potent image of defiance and sacrifice was appropriated as a symbol for France's struggle during the First World War (1914–1918). Spreckels, indeed, acquired her cast in 1915 to raise funds for war-torn France, and then a greatly enlarged version was commissioned as a memorial to the defense of the French city of Verdun in 1917. [v]

Fig. 11 Gaudenzio Marconi, *Auguste Neyt, Model for* The Age of Bronze, 1877. Albumen print, 5 ⅛ x 4 ¼ in. (13 x 10.7 cm). Musée Rodin, Paris, Ph.270
Fig. 12 Film still from Alfred Hitchcock's film *Vertigo* showing James Stewart in the Legion's Rotunda with *The Age of Bronze* (pl. 1), 1958

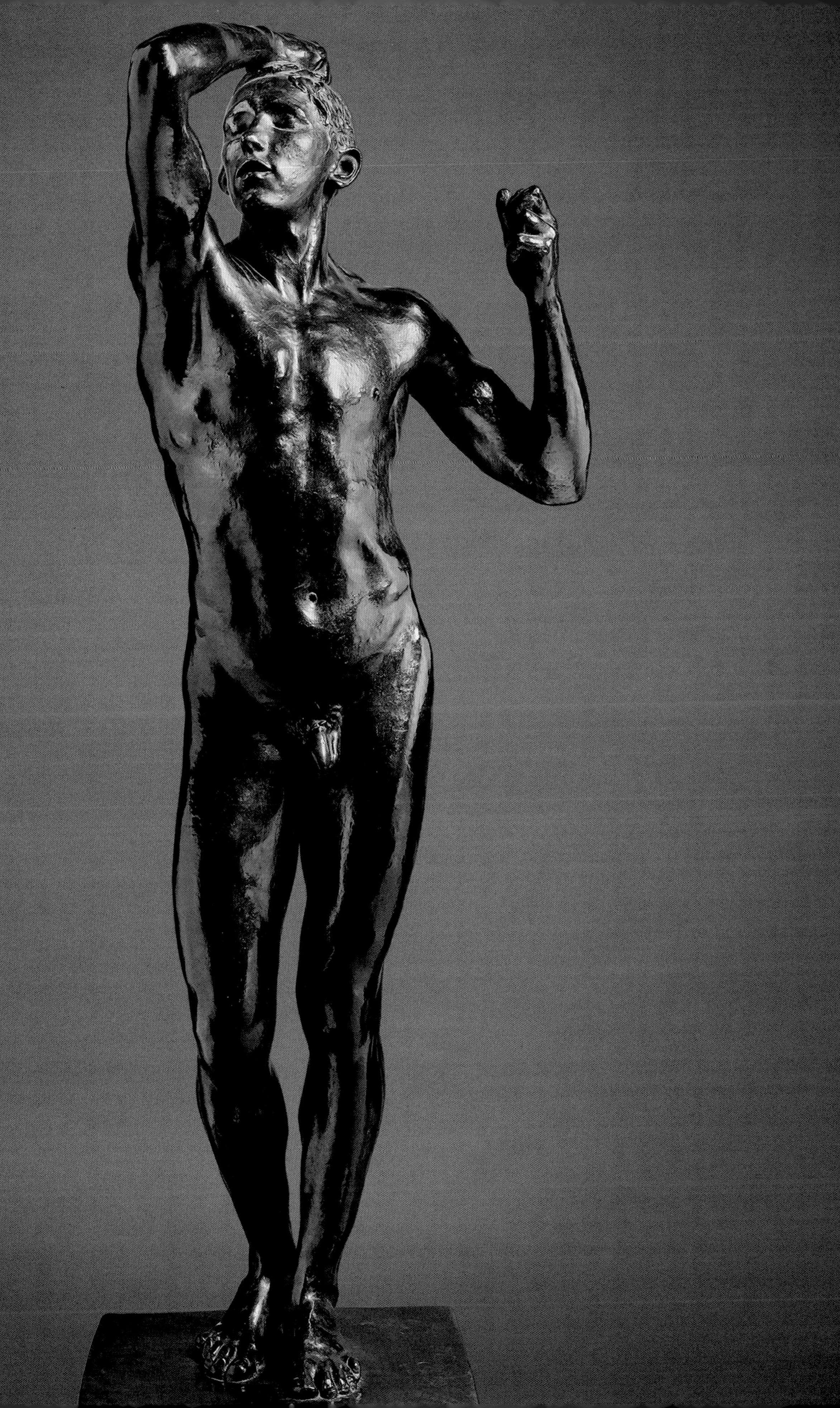

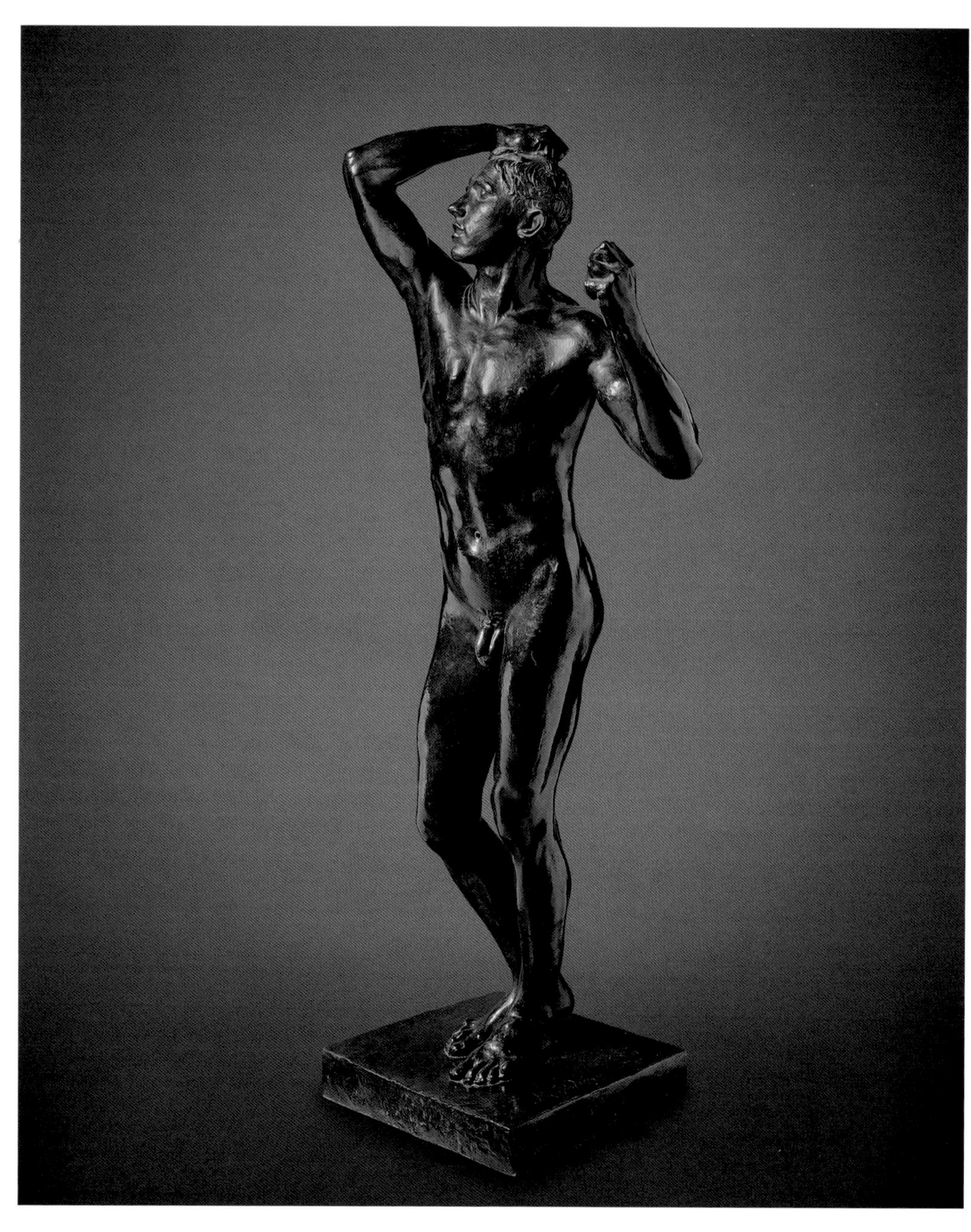

1. *The Age of Bronze,* 1877 (cast ca. 1914). Bronze, 71 ½ x 21 ¼ x 25 ½ in. (181.6 x 54 x 64.8 cm).
Inscribed: *Rodin* and *ALEXIS. RUDIER. / FONDEUR. PARIS.* Gift of Alma de Bretteville Spreckels, 1940.141

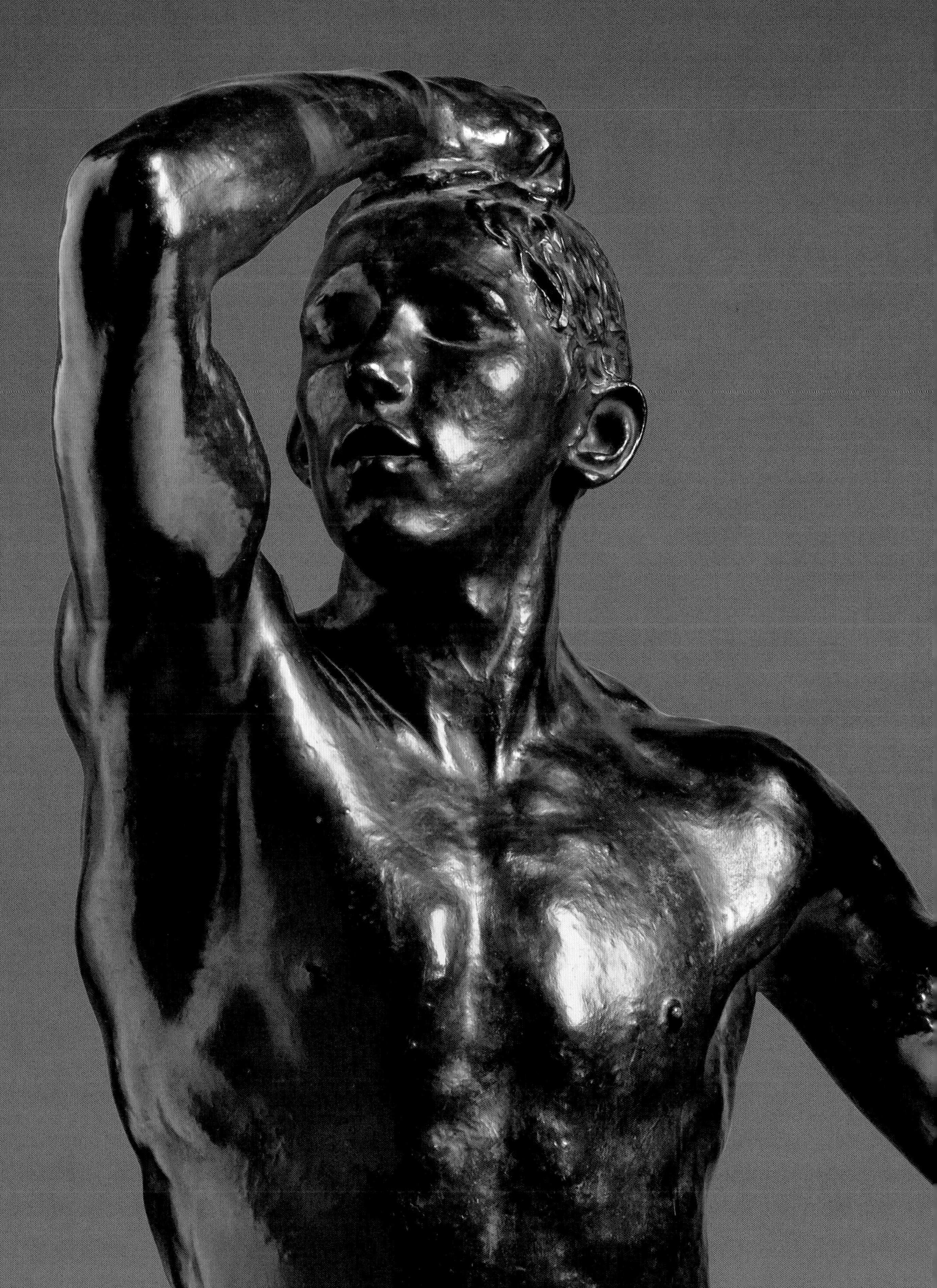

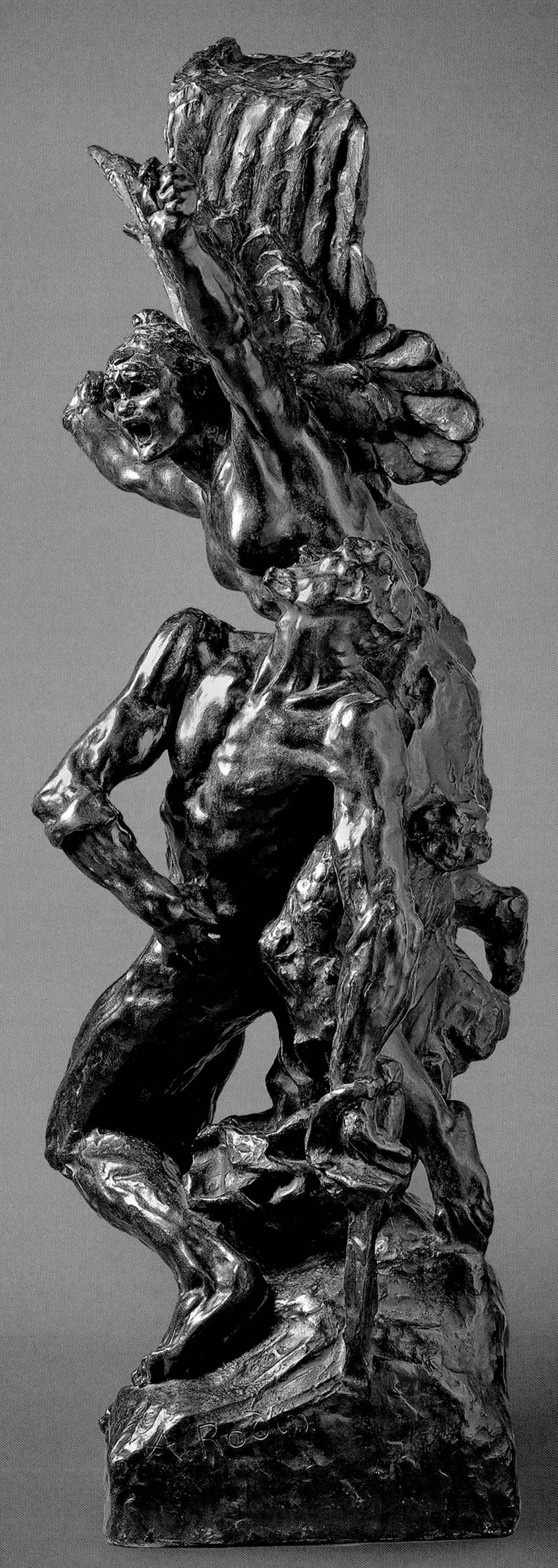

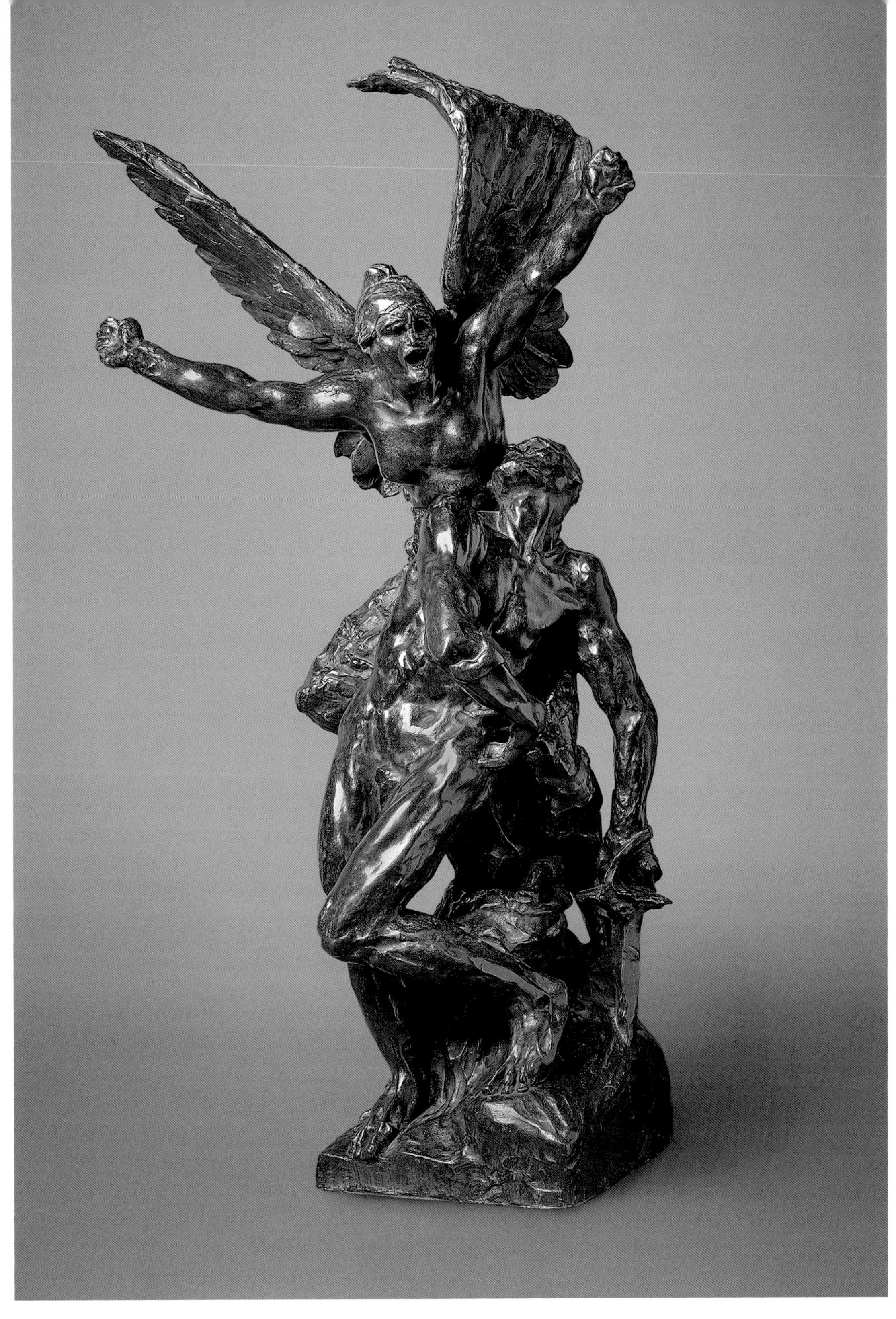

2. *The Call to Arms*, 1879 (cast 1915). Bronze, 44 ½ x 22 ¾ x 16 in. (113 x 57.8 x 40.5 cm).
Inscribed: *A. Rodin.* and *ALEXIS. RUDIER. / FONDEUR. PARIS.* Gift of Alma de Bretteville Spreckels, 1940.138

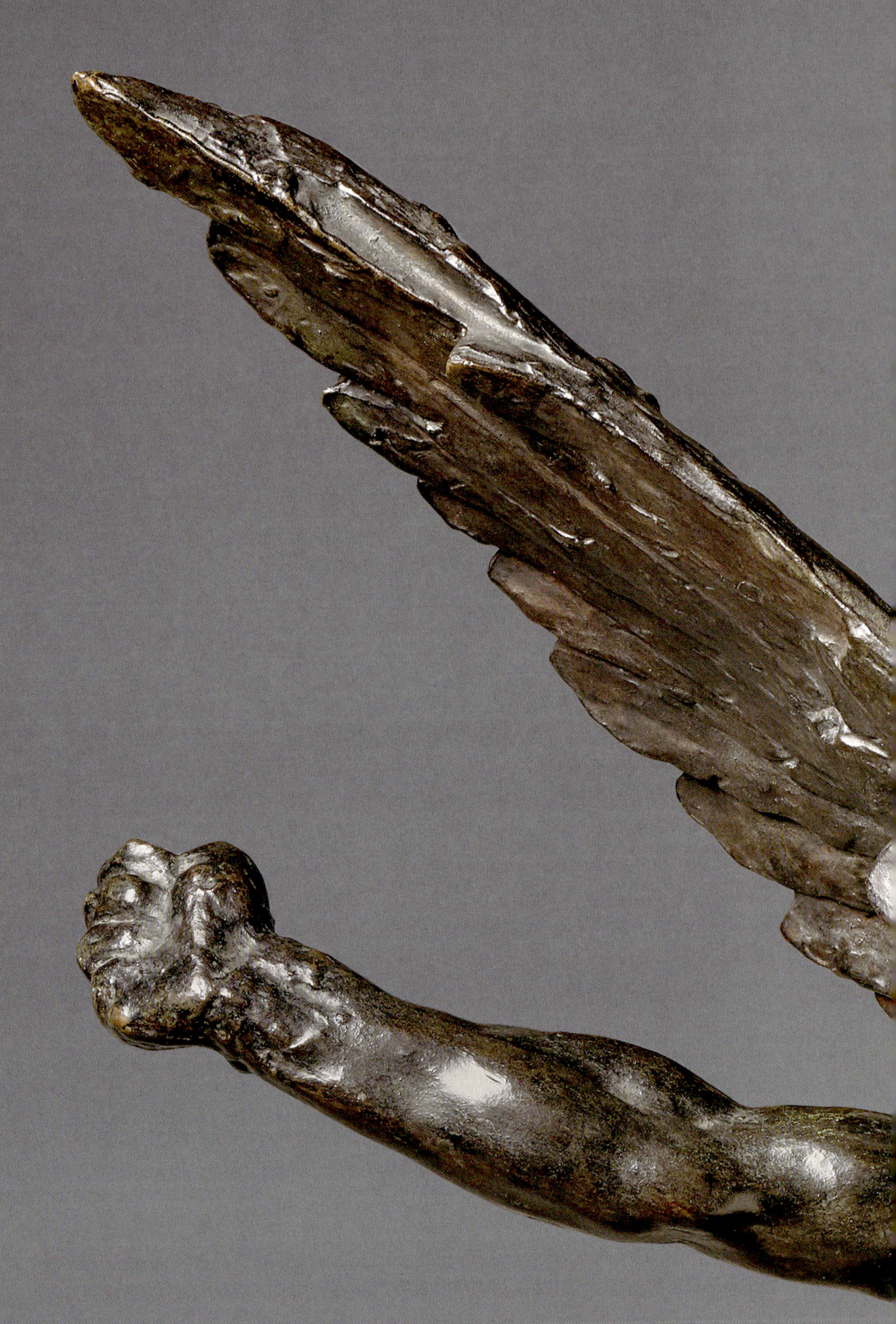

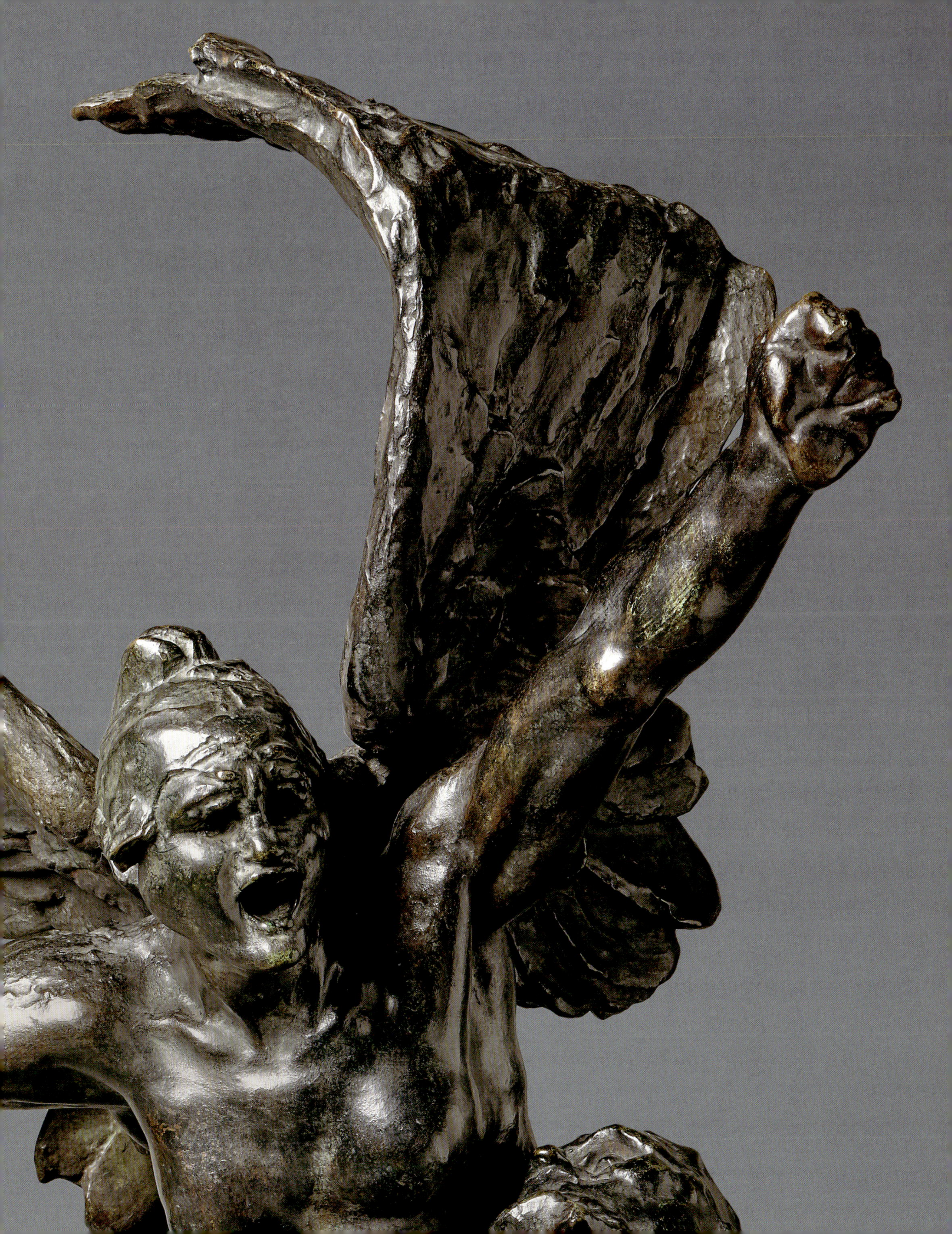

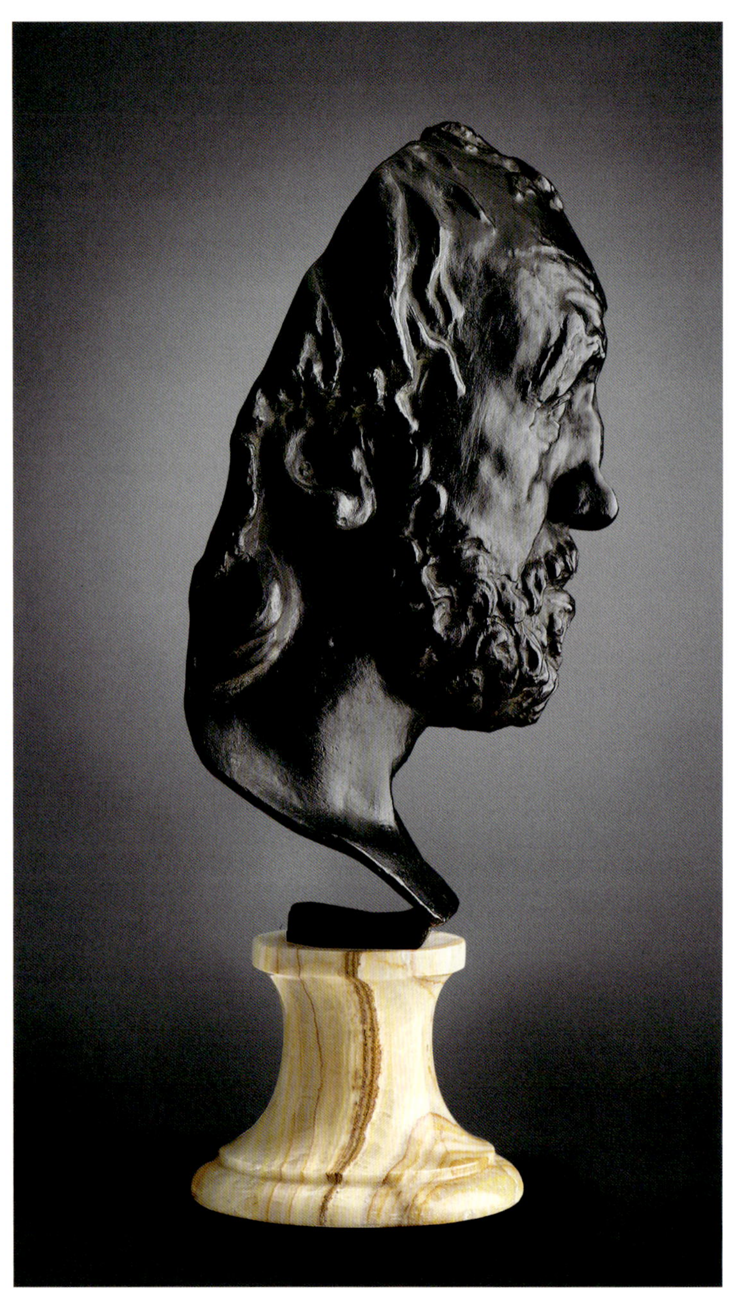

3. *Man with the Broken Nose*, 1864 (third model before 1885, cast ca. 1890s). Bronze, 12 ½ x 7 x 6 in. (31.8 x 17.8 x 15.2 cm).
Inscribed: *A. Rodin* and *ALEXIS RUDIER / FONDEUR. PARIS*. Gift of Alma de Bretteville Spreckels, 1941.34.10

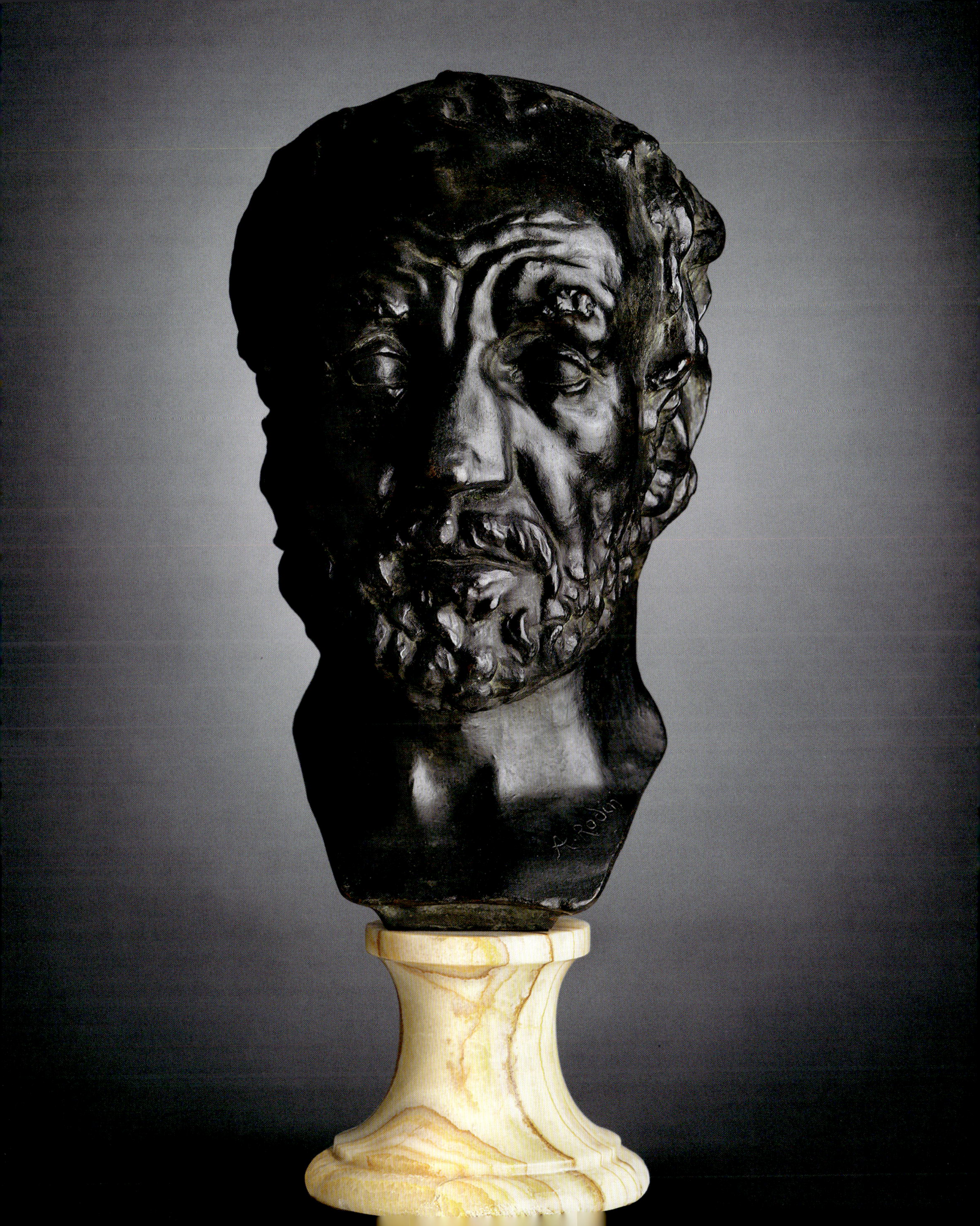

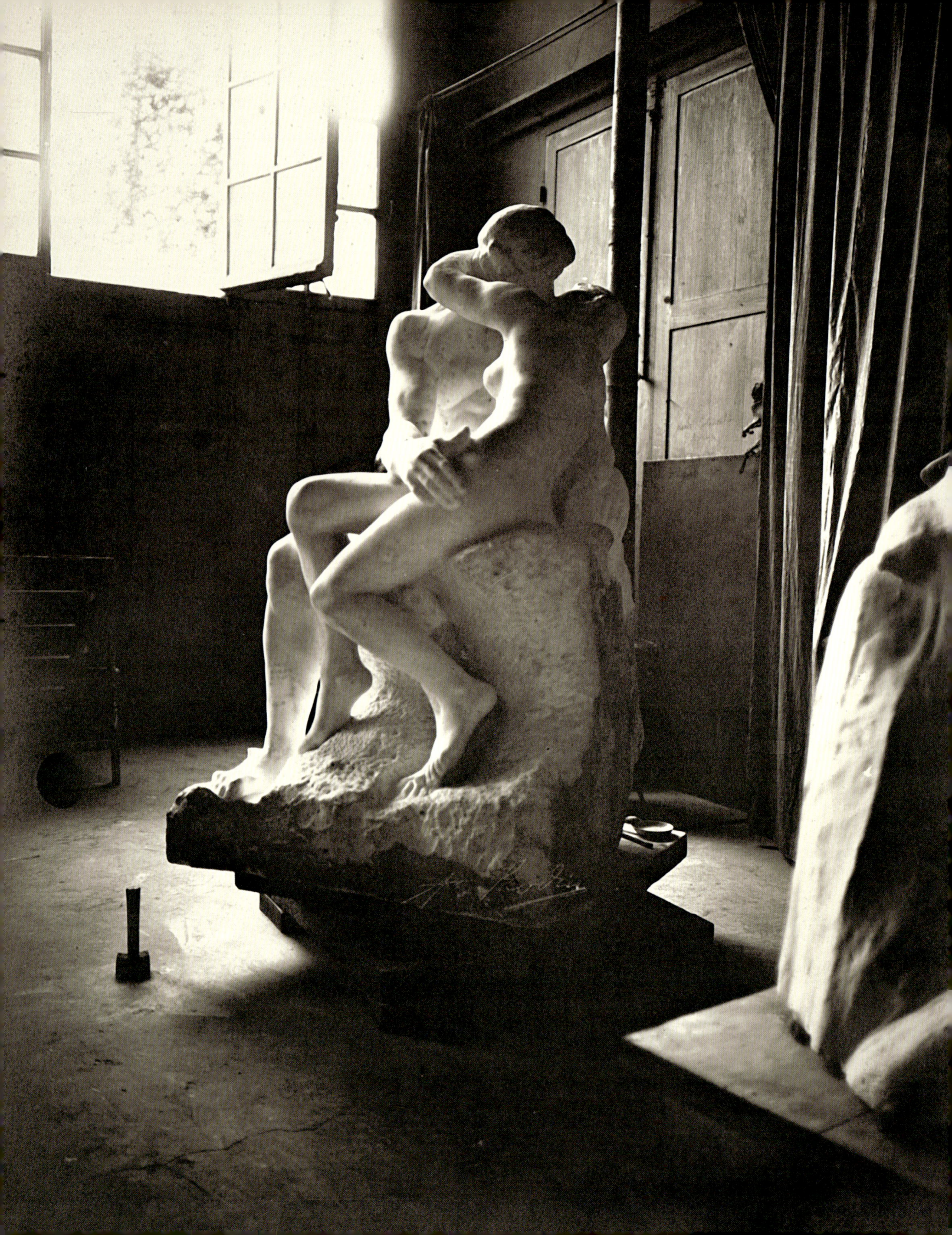

2

SUCCESS AND MATURITY
Acclaim and Public Commissions
(1880–1900)

By the 1880s, Rodin started to receive positive recognition from his contemporaries and gained public commissions, the latter of which were important components of a sculptor's career—and revenue—in the late nineteenth century. The reception of his *Saint John the Baptist Preaching* (pl. 4) represented his success. It was modeled at a larger-than-life scale to avoid the controversy of surmoulage (molding directly from an object or a model's body) surrounding *The Age of Bronze* (pl. 1). The new sculpture did not avoid contemporary criticism altogether, however, as the absence of the saint's usual attributes, including a hair shirt, cross, and scroll, created adverse responses. The roughness of the work's facial features and the hard, wiry quality of its musculature were further contrary to academic ideals of the time, even though these characteristics successfully conveyed the look of a man who lived in a desert. The most innovative aspect that broke this work from the academic tradition is its sense of movement—the saint appears to walk and speak simultaneously. In 1881, *Saint John* became the second of Rodin's sculptures to be acquired by the French government. It was also recognized as a masterpiece further afield in England, where Rodin had an enthusiastic following from the 1880s and where a bronze cast of *Saint John* was paid for by public subscription in 1902.[vi]

Rodin also made more personal works during these years, further pushing the boundaries of his artistic agenda. The intertwined figures of *The Sculptor and His Muse* (pl. 9) express not only an erotic relationship between a man and a woman, but also the creative connection between an artist and a model. Another sculpture of the 1890s with similarly writhing figures in sinuous forms is *The Fallen Angel* (pl. 7), composed of two female forms, one holding the other.[vii] As with *The Sculptor and His Muse*, there are sexual suggestions, as well as stylistic resonances with the contemporary aesthetic of Art Nouveau in the statue's swirling and rounded forms. A similar approach of connected and complex figures is also found in Rodin's large-scale work *Christ and the Magdalene* (pl. 45), one of his few religious compositions. In it, the two naked figures—Christ nailed to a rocky cross and Mary Magdalene clinging to his passive body—evoke an overtly sensuous overtone not traditionally chosen for this Crucifixion scene.

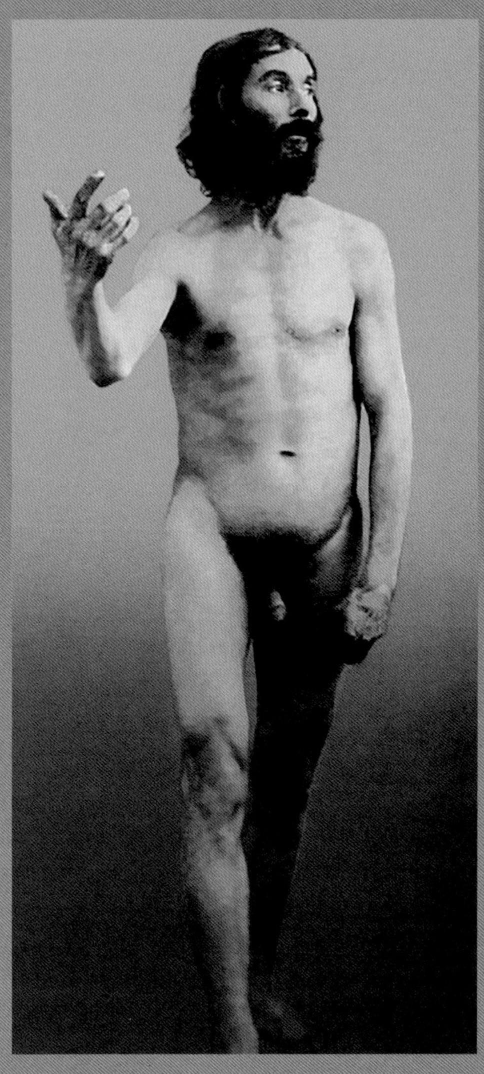

Rodin's Account of Modeling *Saint John the Baptist Preaching*:

"One morning, someone knocked at the studio door. In came an Italian, with one of his compatriots who had already posed for me. He was a peasant from Abruzzi, arrived the night before from his birthplace, and he had come to me to offer himself as a model. Seeing him, I was seized with admiration: that rough, hairy man, expressing in his bearing and physical strength all the violence, but also all the mystical character of his race.

I thought immediately of a St. John the Baptist; that is, a man of nature, a visionary, a believer, a forerunner come to announce one greater than himself."

"The peasant undressed, climbed onto the revolving stand as if he had never posed before; he planted himself firmly on his feet, head up, torso straight, at the same time putting his weight on both legs, open like a compass. The movement was so right, so straightforward and so true that I cried: 'But it's a man walking!' I immediately resolved to model what I had seen." [viii]

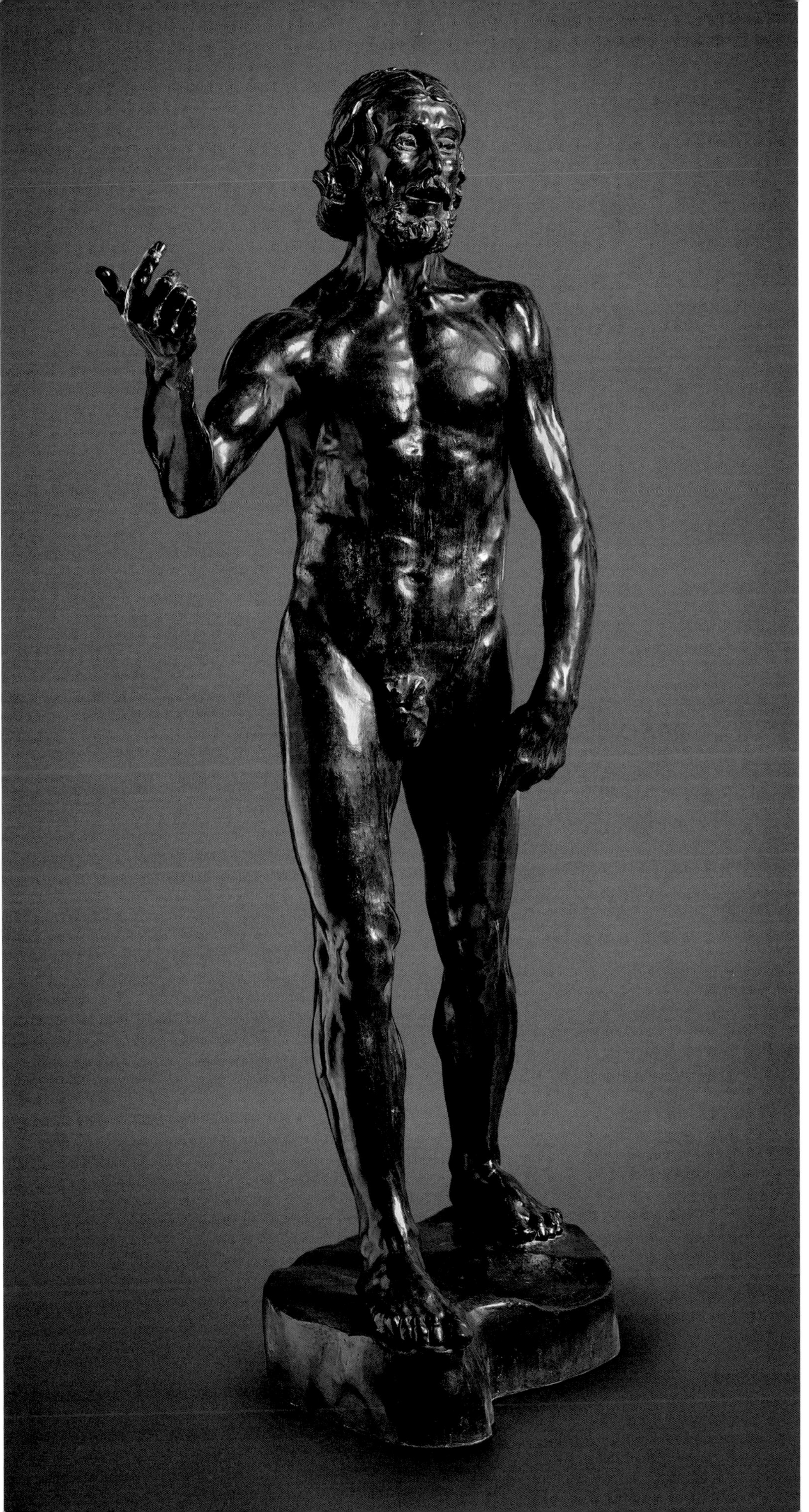

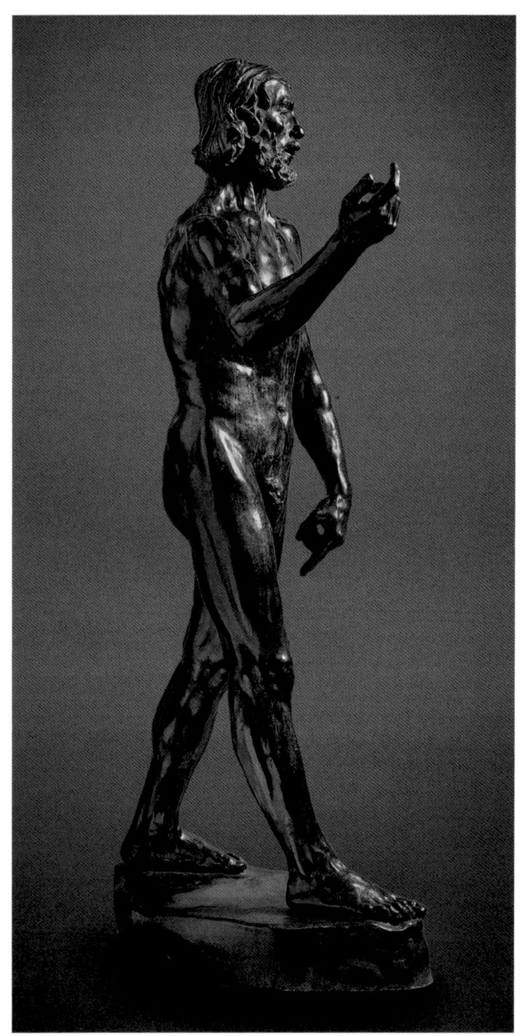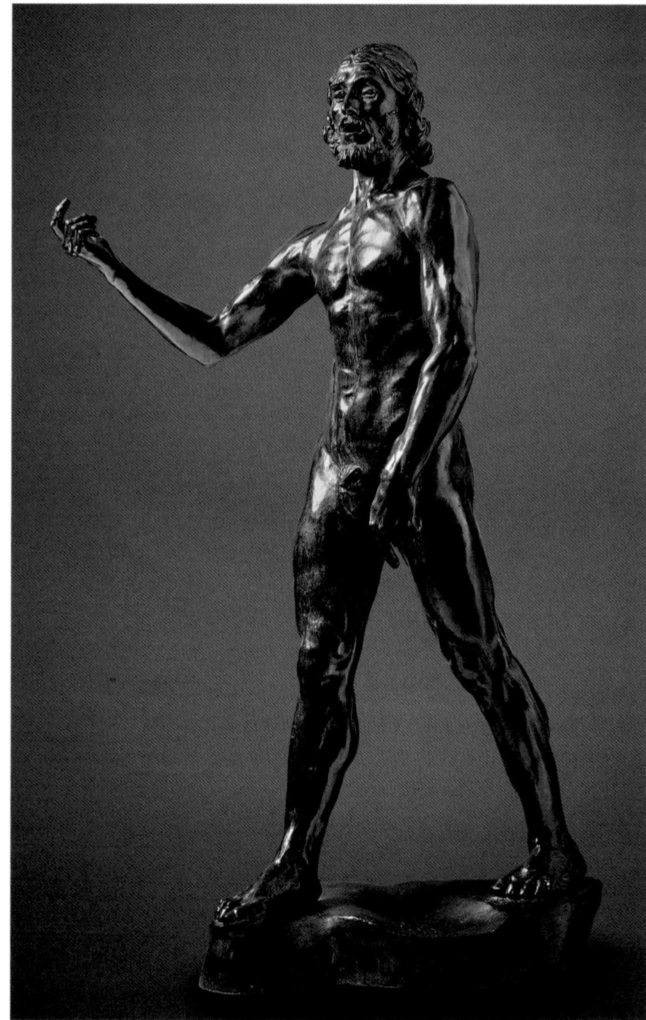

4. *Saint John the Baptist Preaching*, 1880 (cast ca. 1914). Bronze, 79 ½ x 51 ⅝ x 38 ⅝ in. (201.9 x 131.1 x 98.1 cm). Inscribed: *Rodin* and *A. RUDIER. FONDEUR. PARIS*. Gift of Alma de Bretteville Spreckels, 1940.140

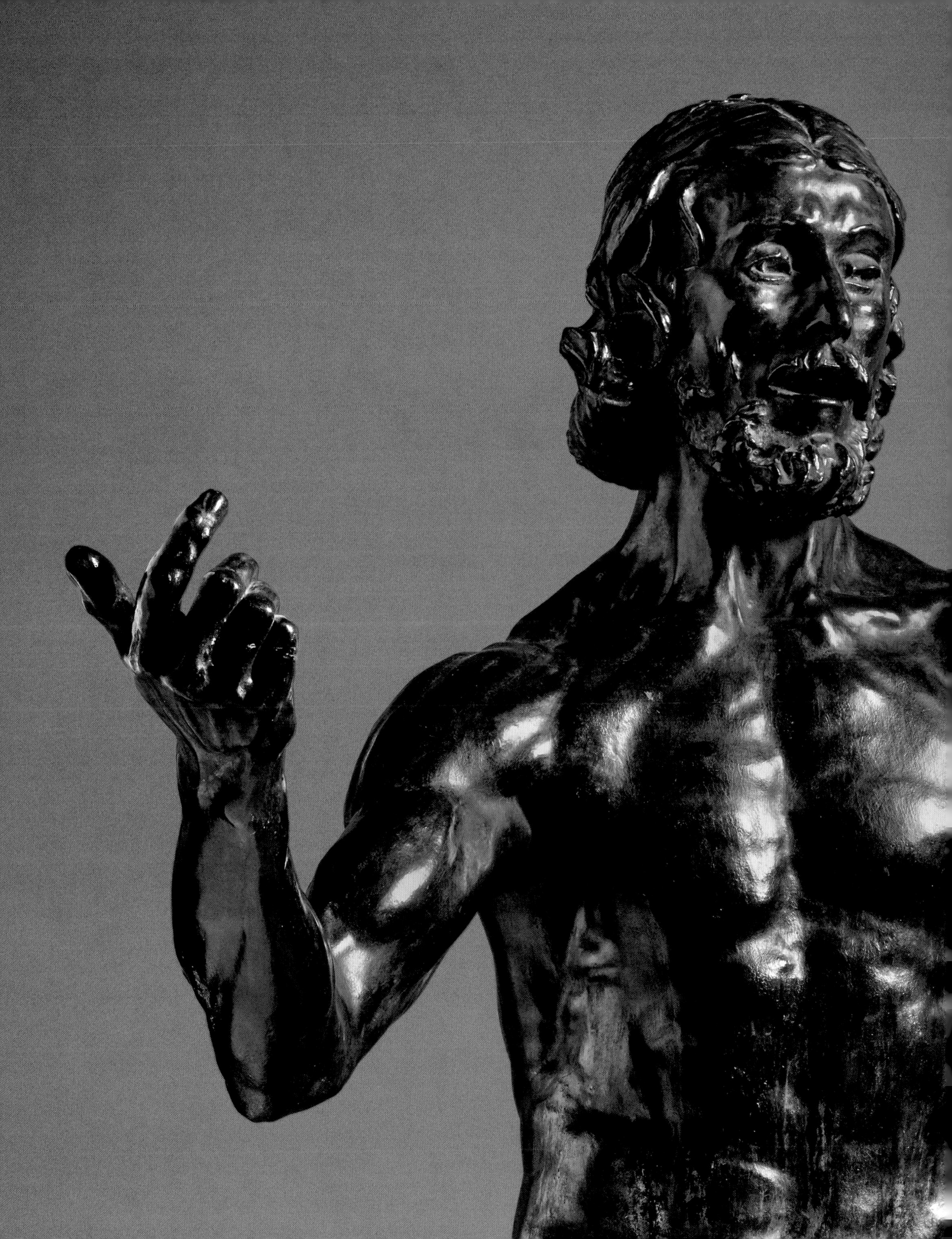

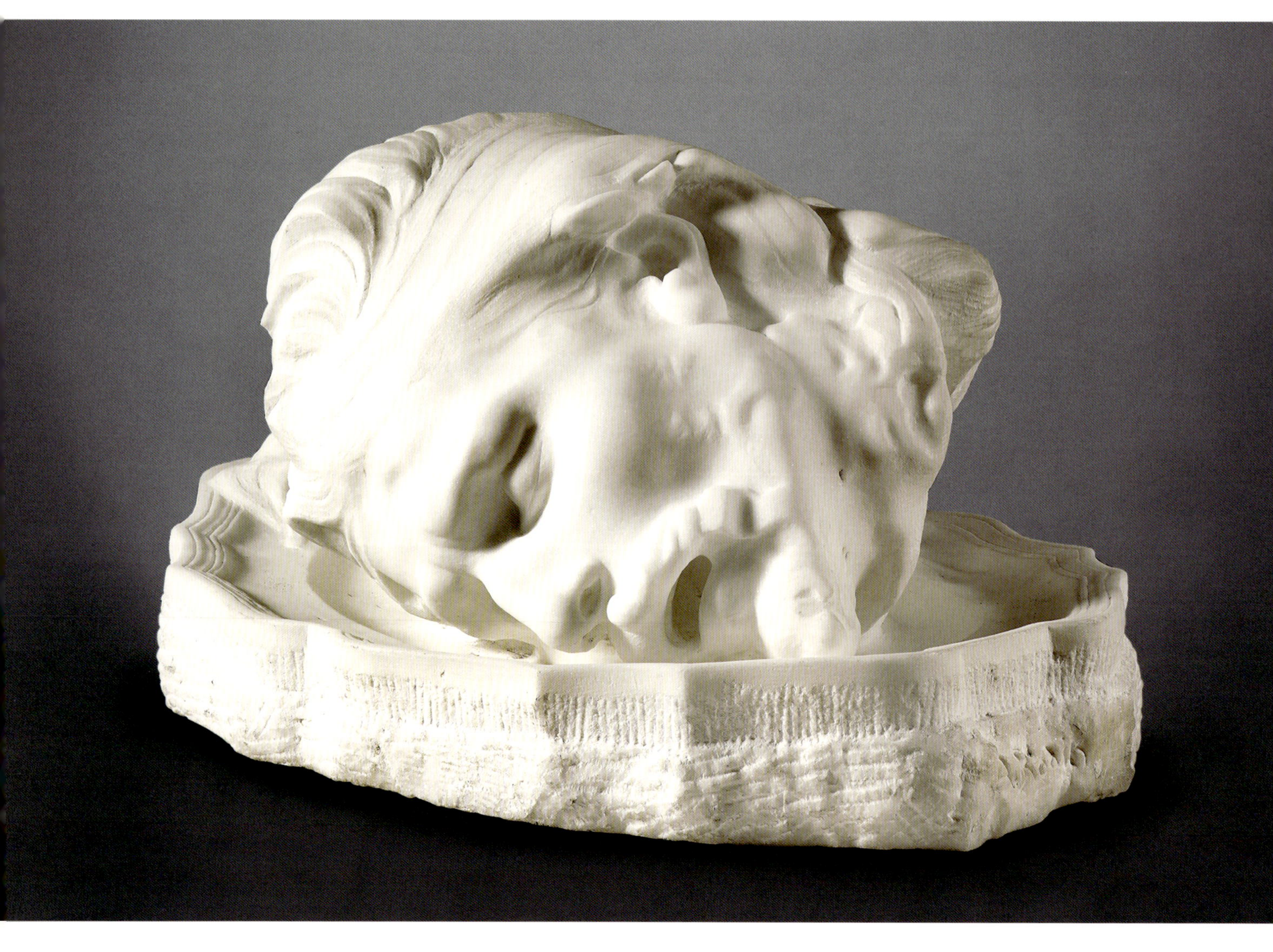

5. *Severed Head of Saint John the Baptist*, ca. 1887. Marble, 6 ¾ x 14 ½ x 14 in. (17.1 x 36.8 x 35.6 cm).
Inscribed: *A. Rodin*. Gift of Mr. and Mrs. Alfred S. Wilsey in honor of Ian McKibbin White, 1986.88

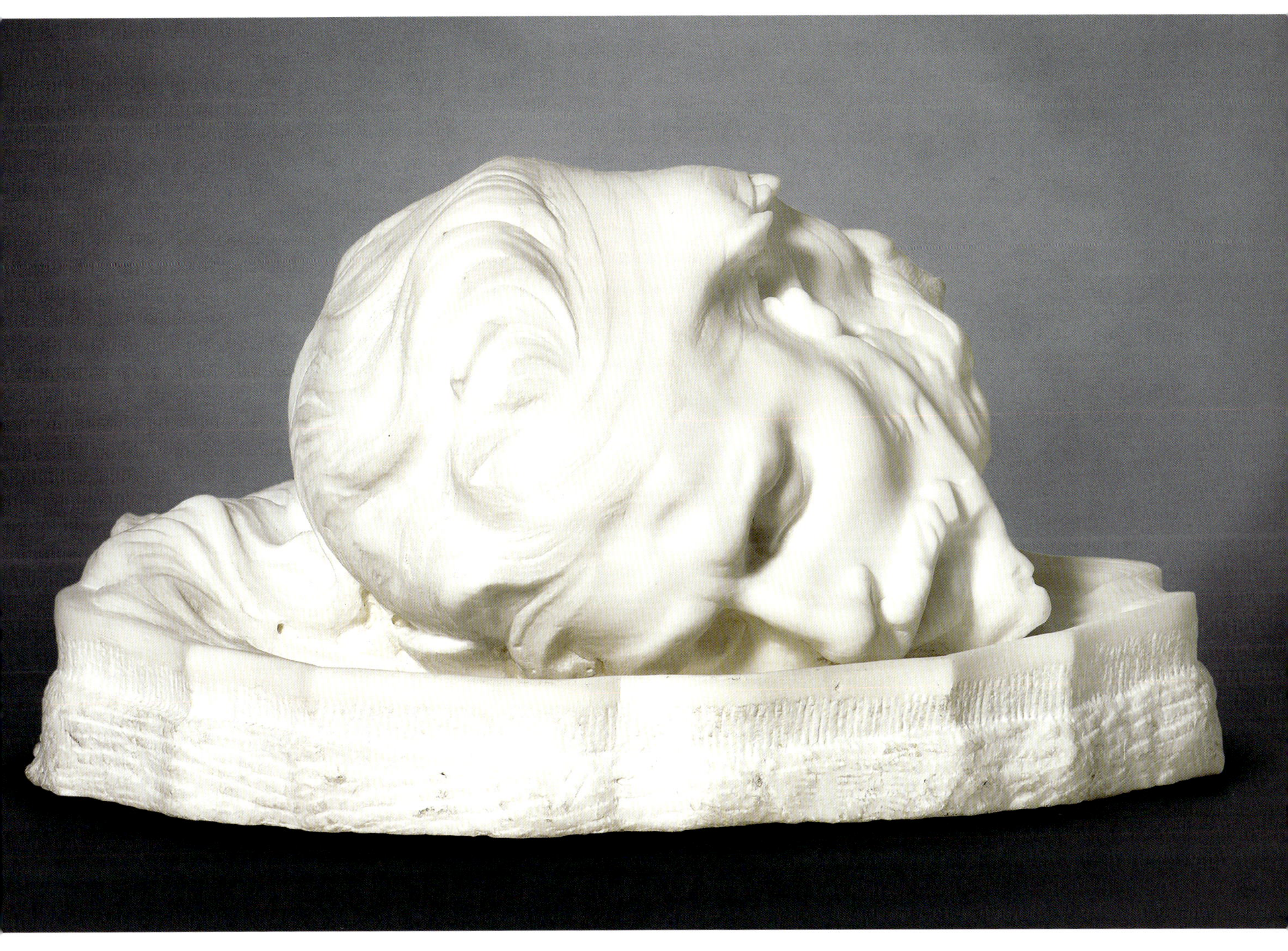

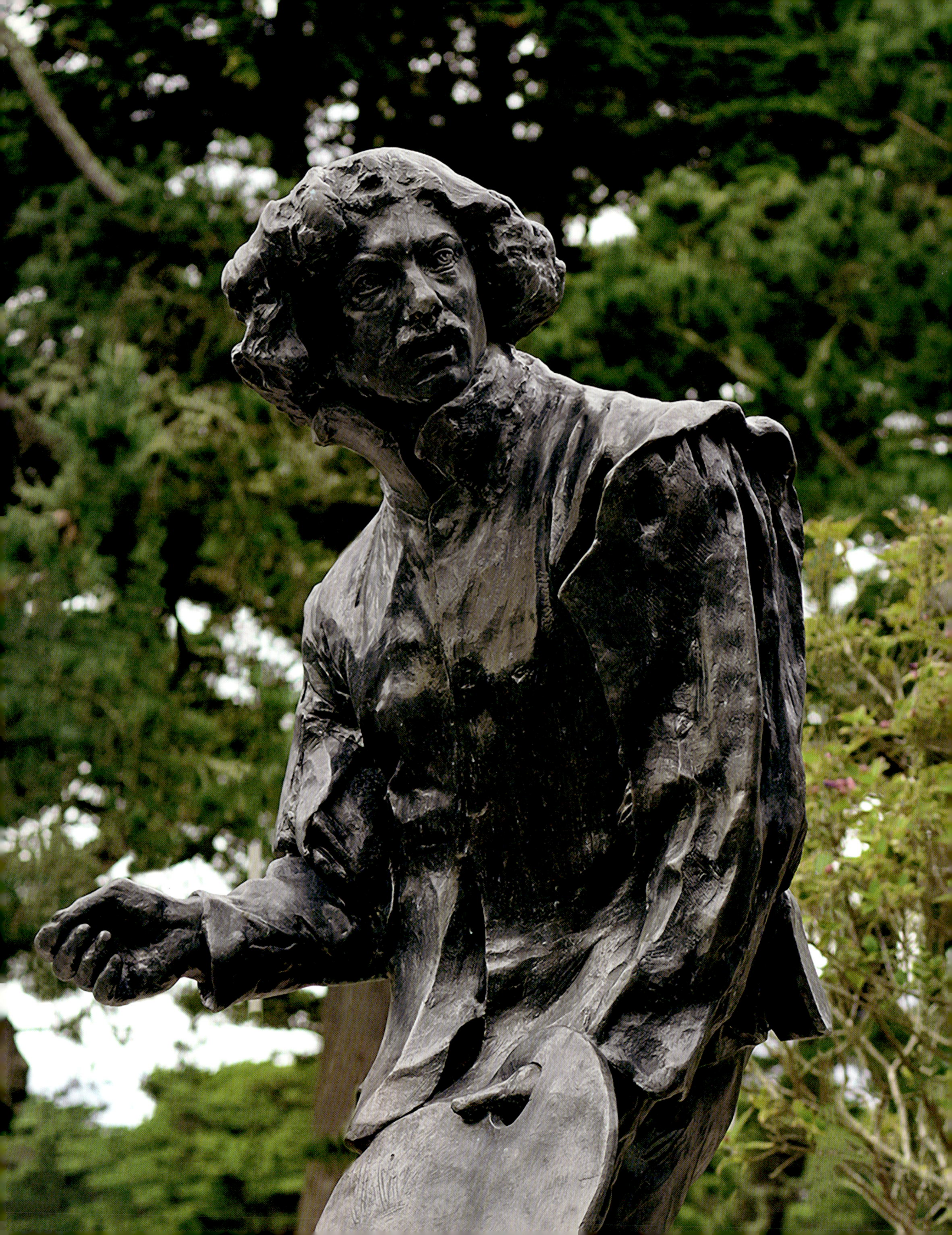

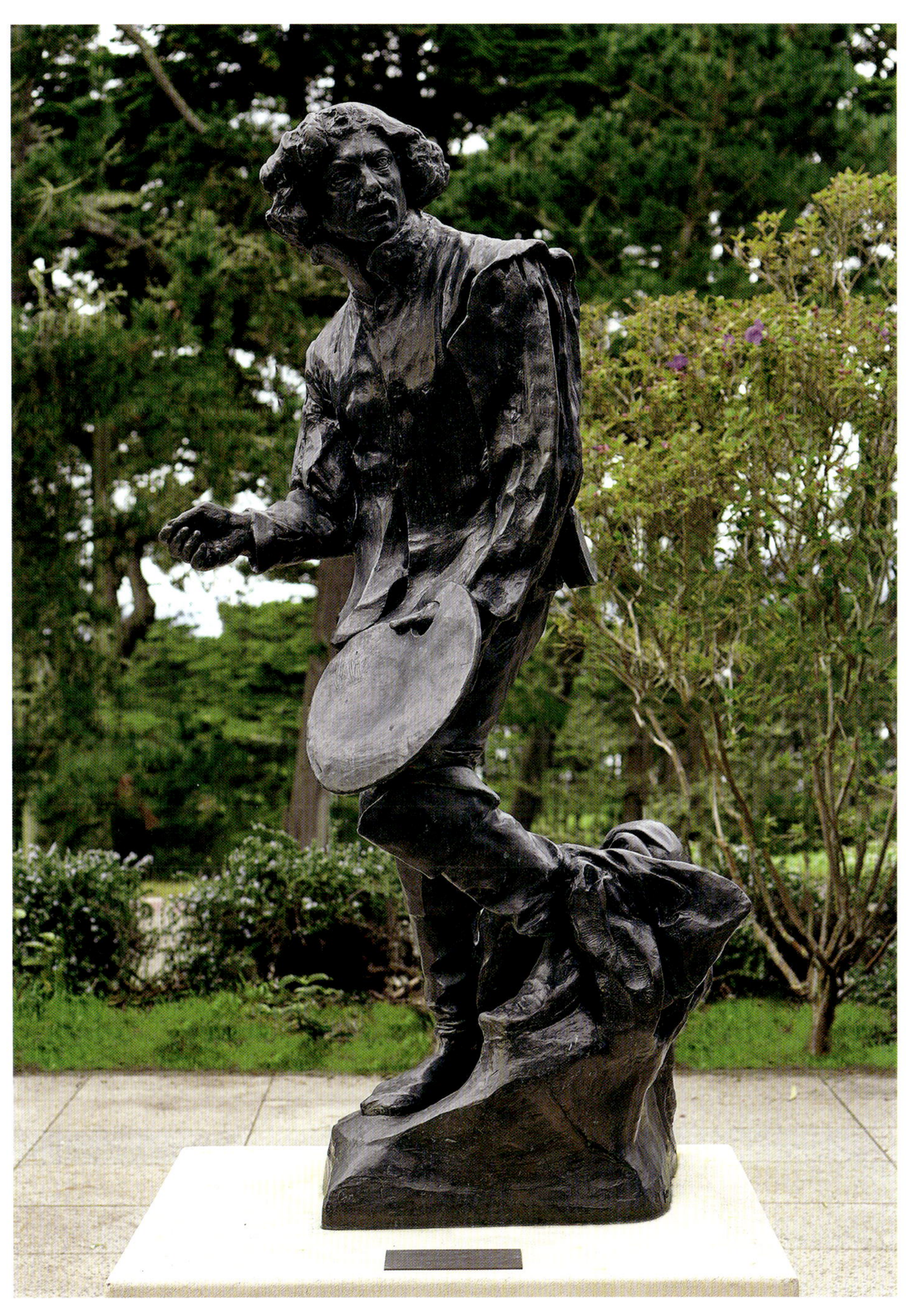

6. *Monument to Claude Lorrain*, 1892 (cast 1992). Bronze, 84 ½ x 42 ½ x 46 in. (214.6 x 108 x 116.8 cm).
Inscribed: *A. Rodin no III/IV. F ● C* [for Coubertin Foundry] © *By Musée Rodin 1992*.
Gift of the Iris and B. Gerald Cantor Foundation in honor of Lucy and John Buchanan, 2006.74

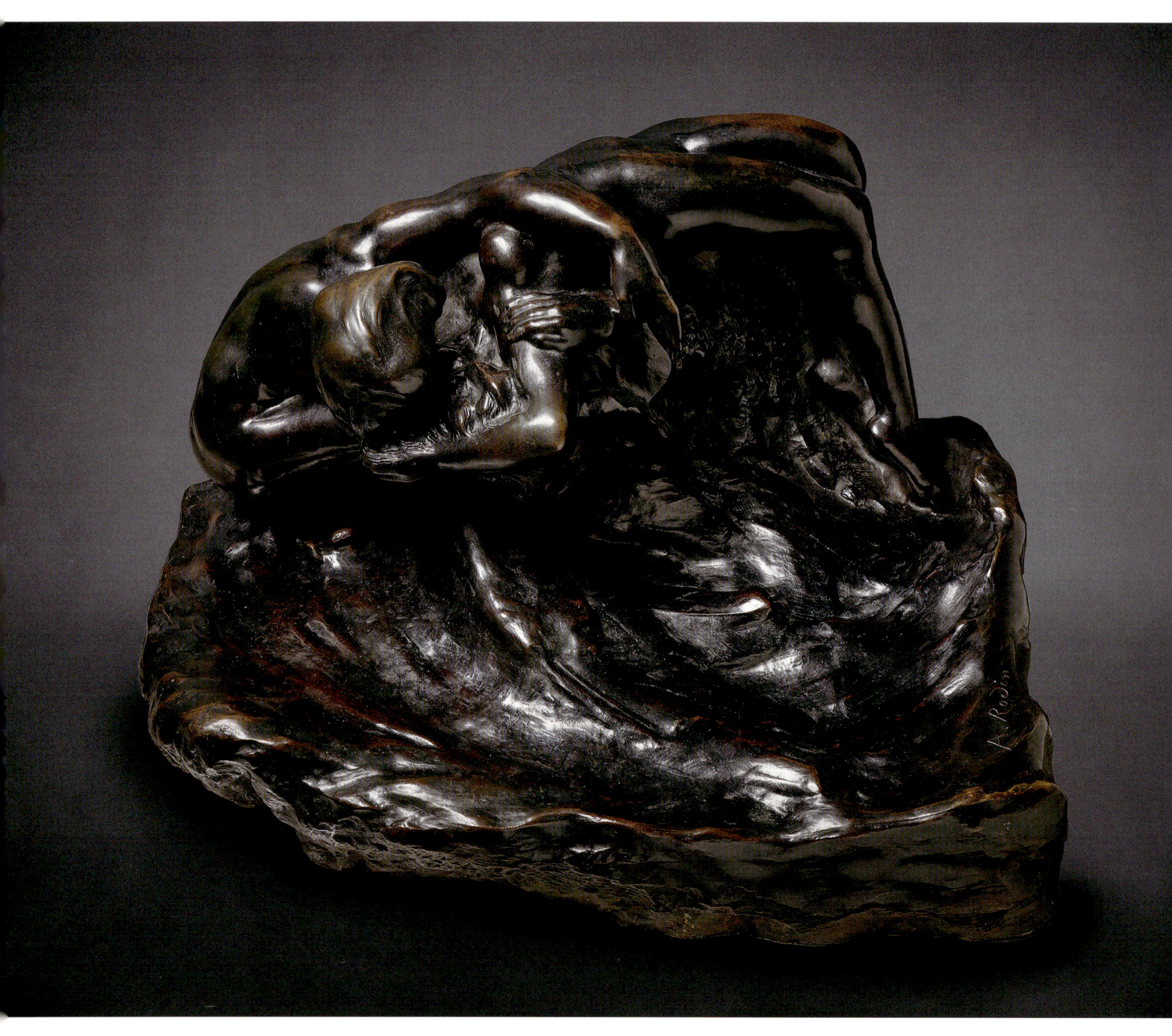

7. *The Fallen Angel*, ca. 1890 (cast before 1915). Bronze, 20⅛ x 21½ x 32 in. (51.1 x 54.6 x 81.3 cm).
Inscribed: *A. Rodin*. Gift of Alma de Bretteville Spreckels, 1940.139

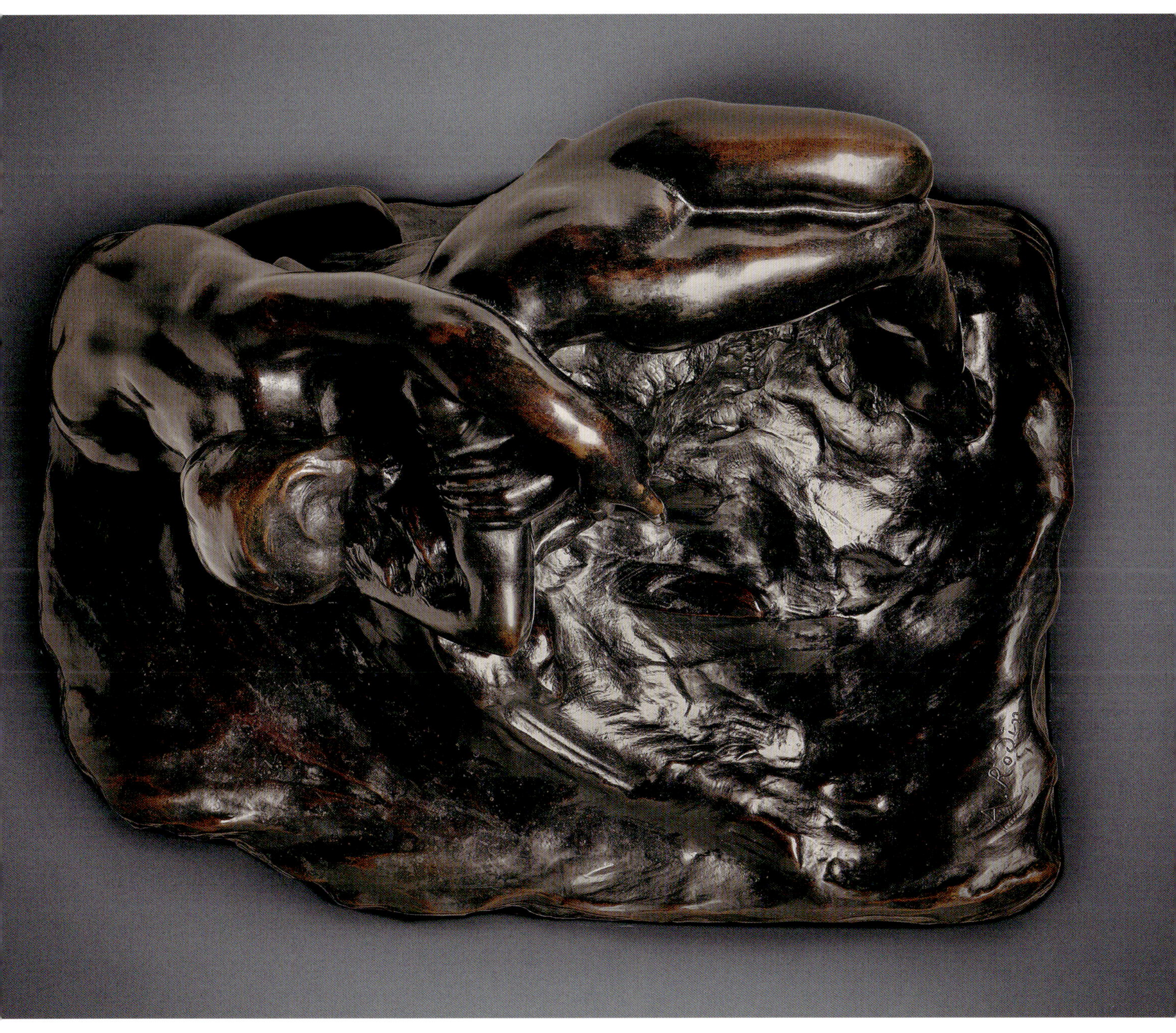

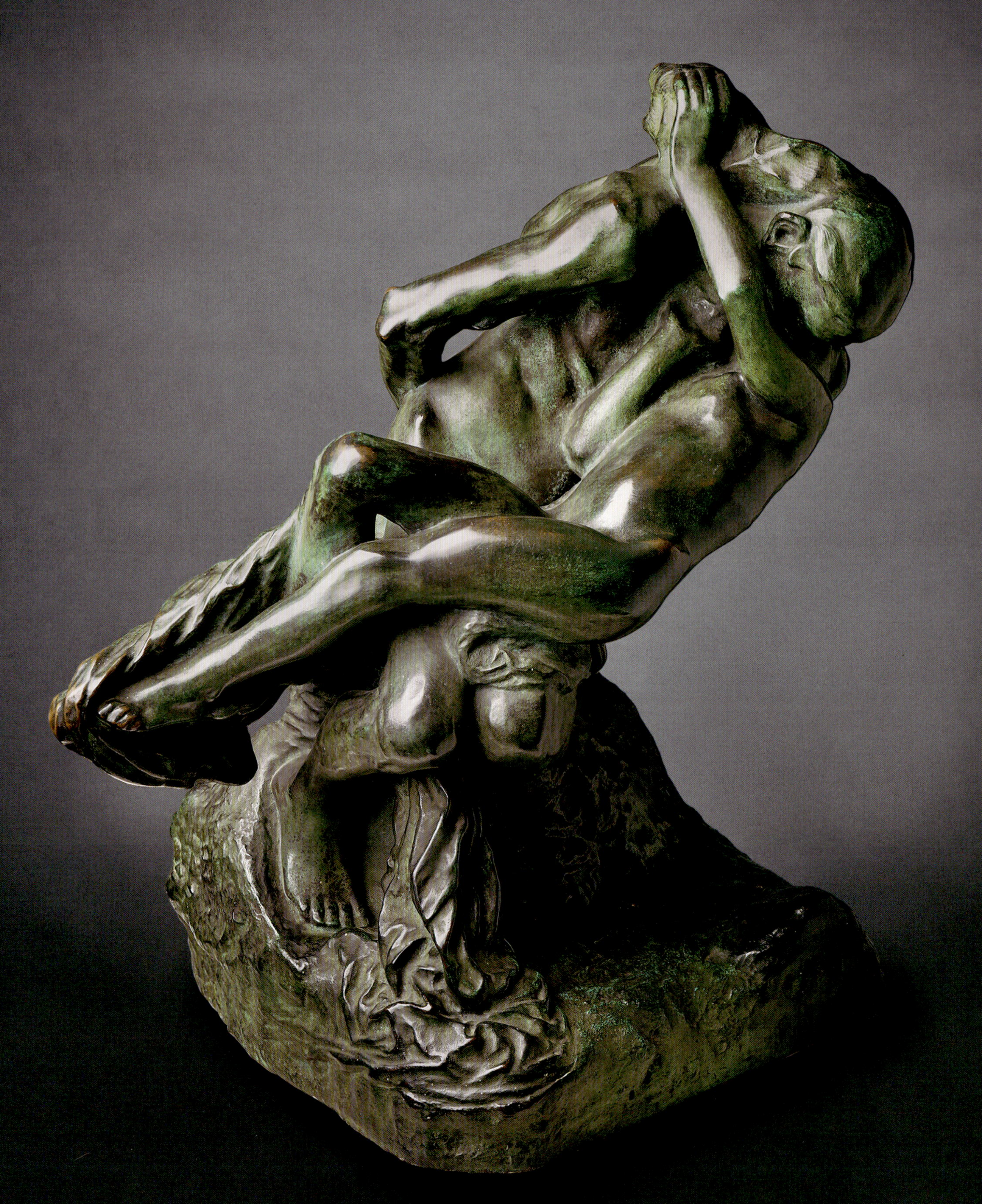

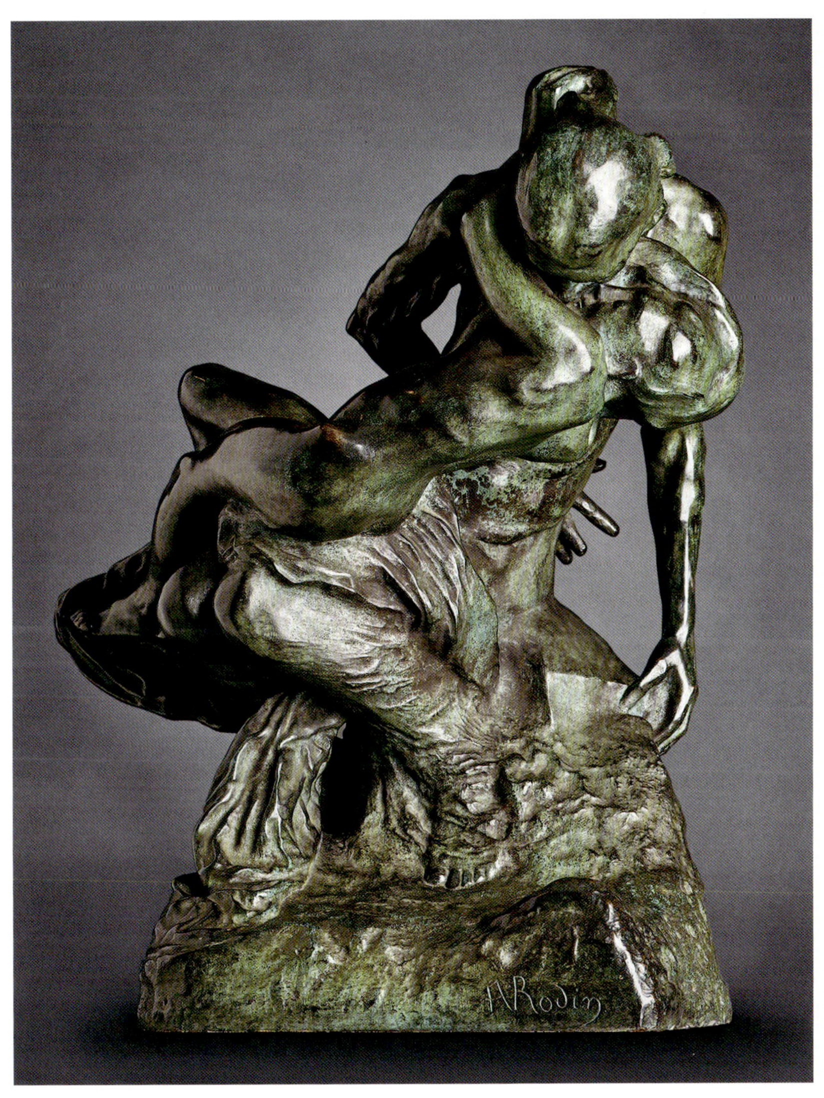

8. *Youth and Old Age* or *Triumphant Youth*, 1898 (cast before 1915). Bronze, 20 ½ x 18 x 13 ⅜ in. (52.1 x 45.7 x 34 cm).
Inscribed: *A. Rodin*. Gift of Alma de Bretteville Spreckels, 1941.34.3

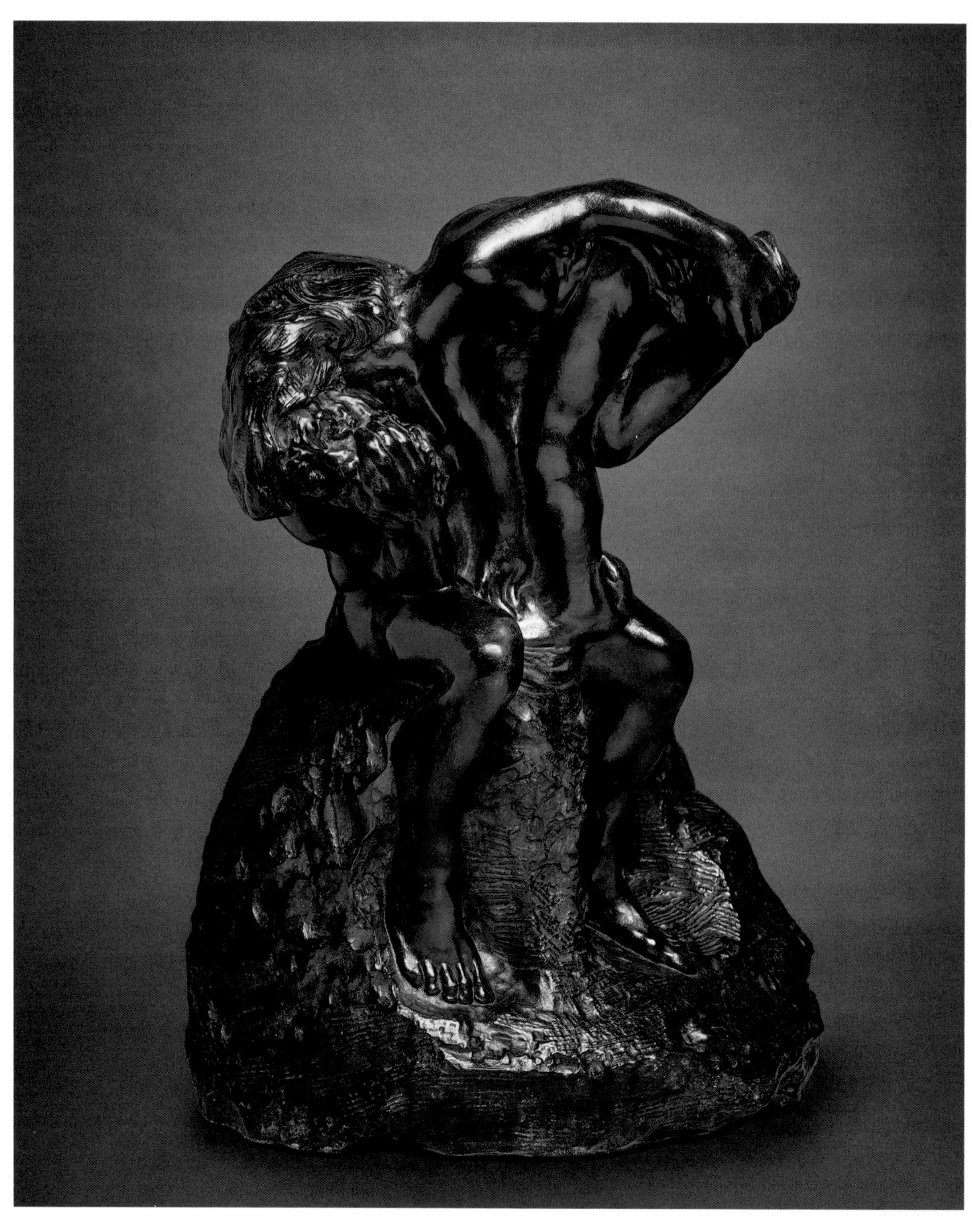

9. *The Sculptor and His Muse*, 1890s (cast ca. 1908–1917). Bronze, 26 x 18 ⅞ x 19 ⅞ in. (65.9 x 47.8 x 50.6 cm).
Inscribed: *A. Rodin* and *ALEXIS.RUDIER. / FONDEUR.PARIS.* Gift of Alma de Bretteville Spreckels, 1941.34.2

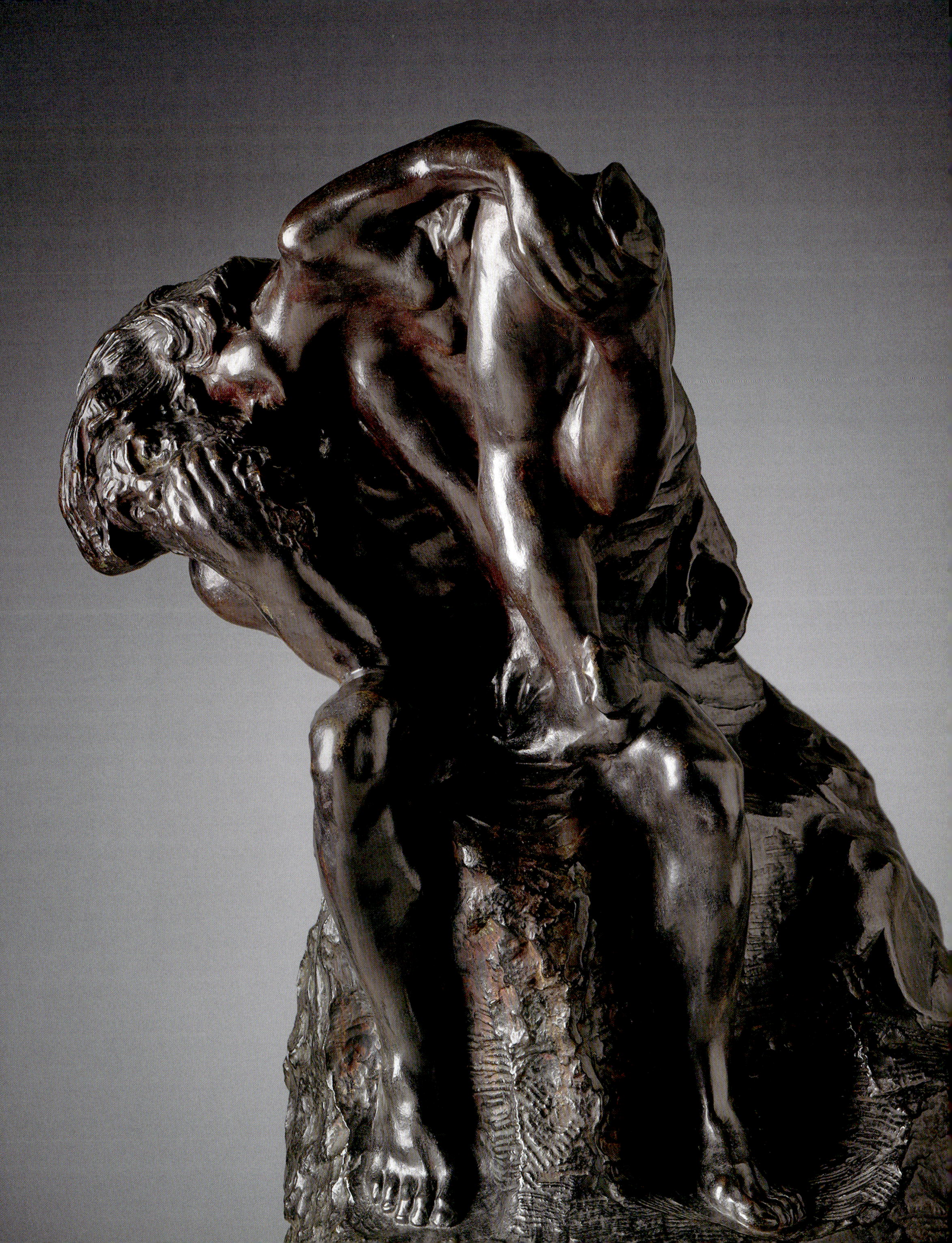

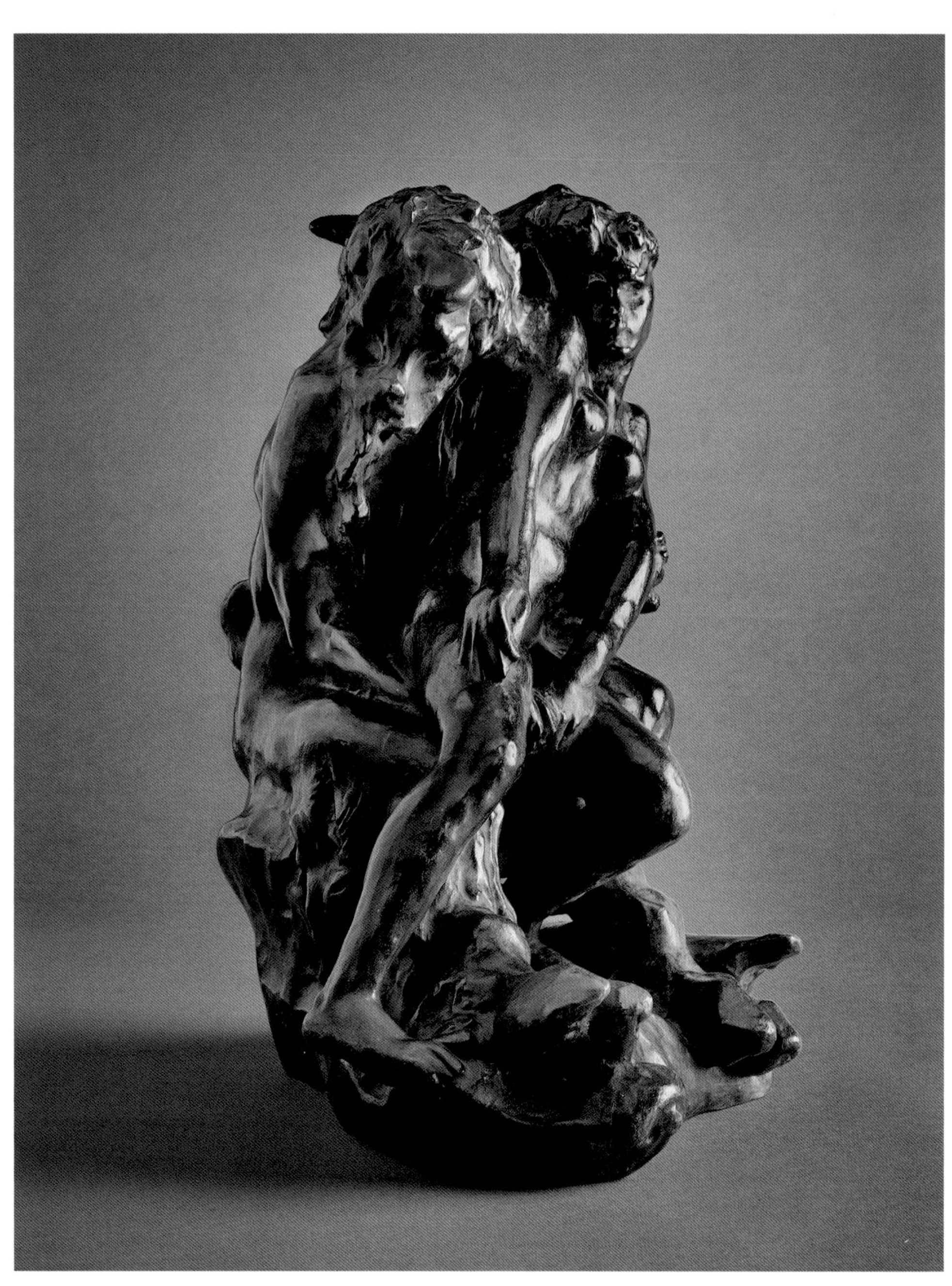

10. *Faun and Nymph* or *The Minotaur*, ca. 1886 (cast 1917). Bronze, 12 ⅞ x 8 ½ x 11 ¾ in. (32.7 x 21.6 x 29.7 cm).
Inscribed: *A. Rodin* and *ALEXIS RUDIER / Fondeur PARIS*. Gift of Alma de Bretteville Spreckels, 1942.42

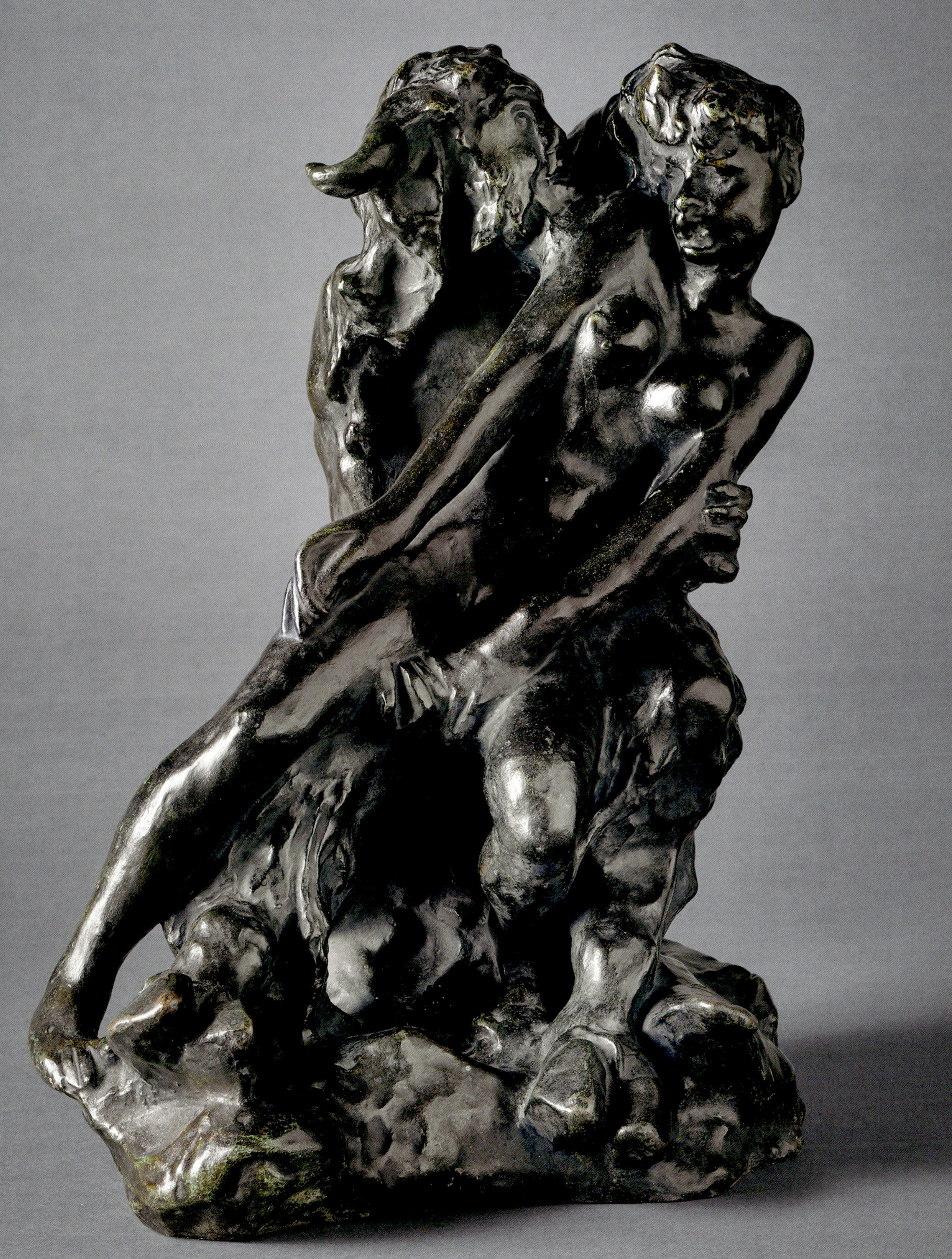

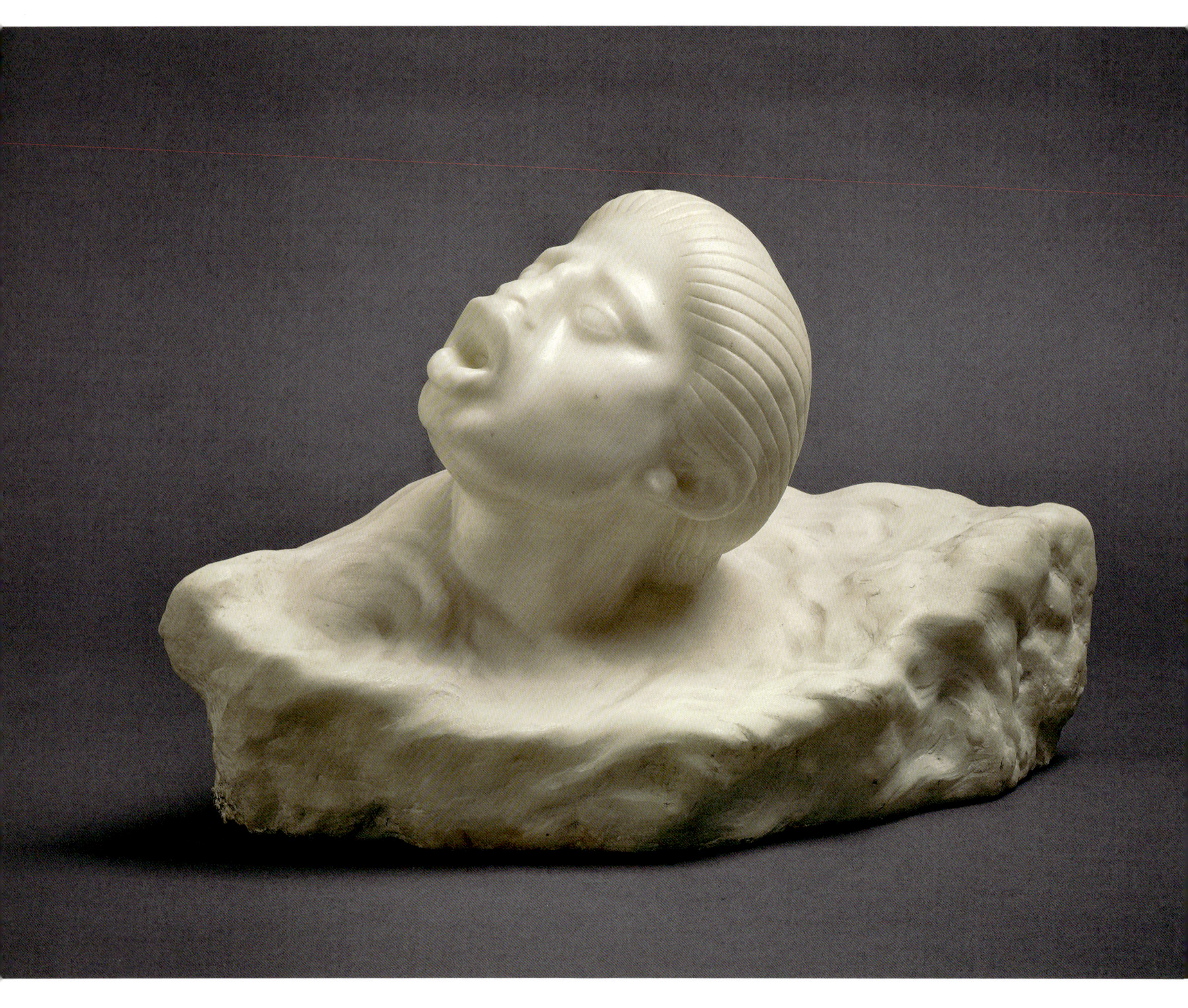

11. *The Siren of the Sea*, ca. 1906. Marble, 10 ¼ x 11 ½ x 18 ¼ in. (25.9 x 29.2 x 46.5 cm).
Inscribed: *A. Rodin*. Gift of Alma de Bretteville Spreckels, 1941.34.16

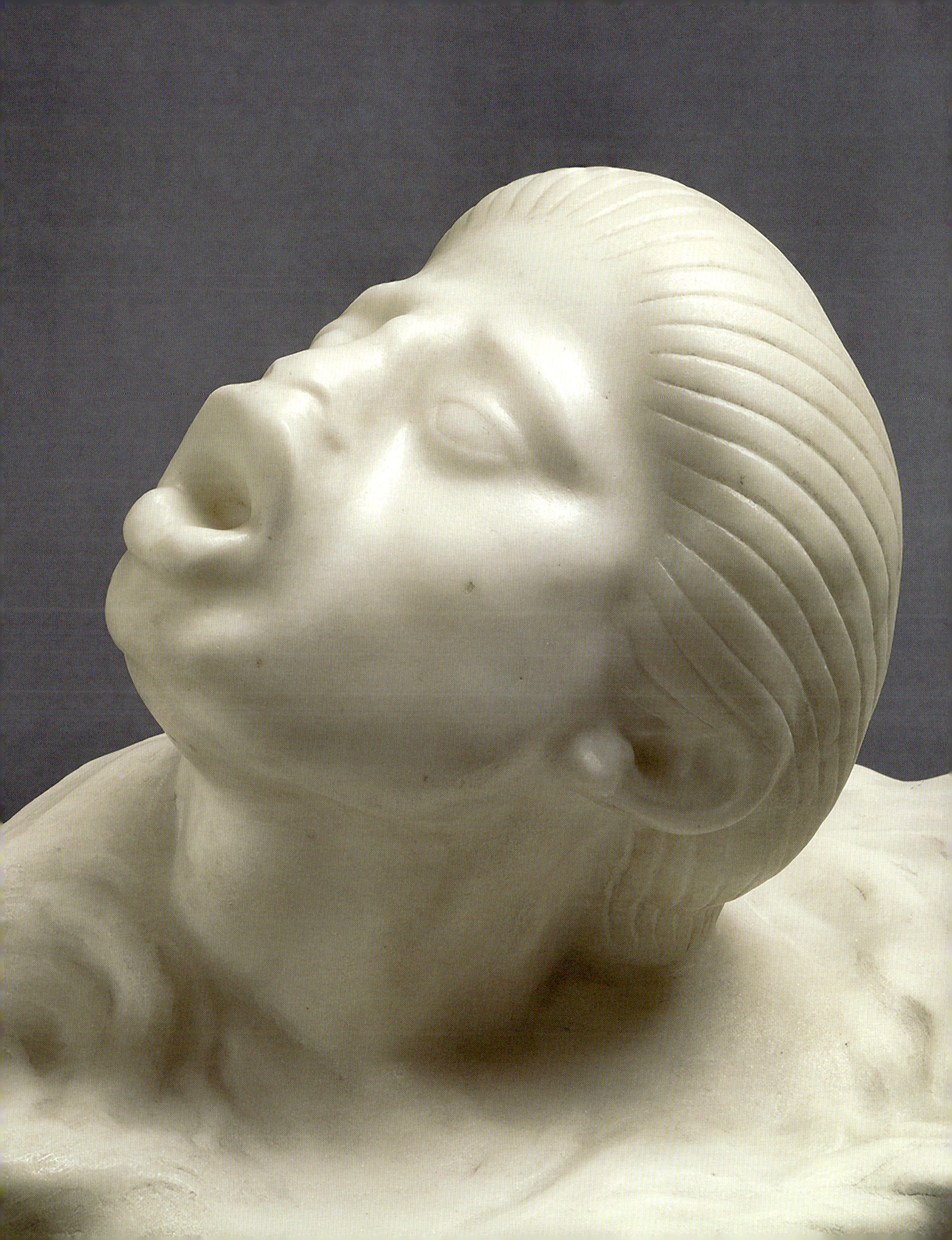

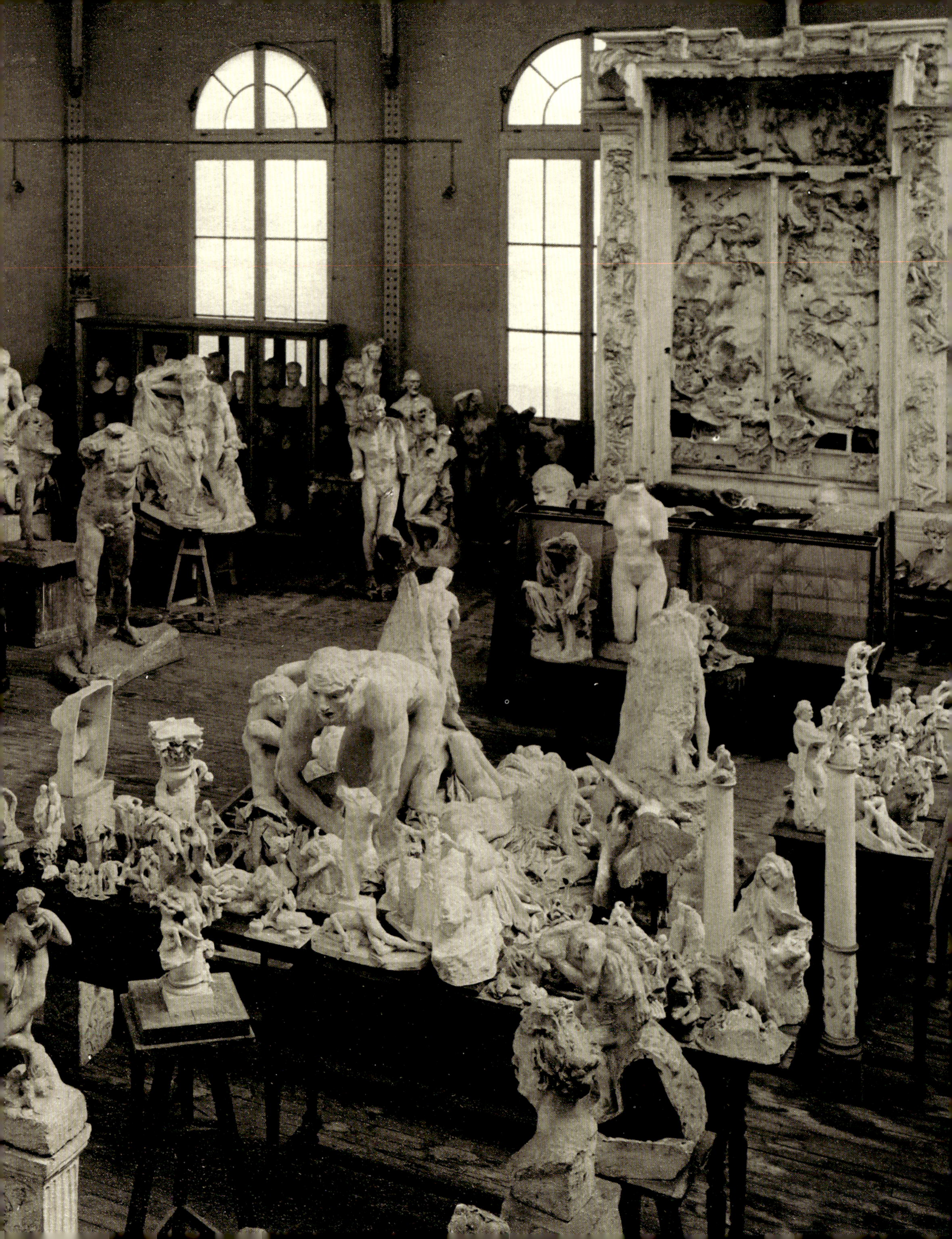

3

GATES OF HELL
Rodin's Incomplete Masterpiece
(1 8 8 0 – 1 9 0 0)

In 1880, Rodin was commissioned to make a portal for a future museum of decorative arts in Paris. Although the building was never realized, the artist continued to work assiduously on aspects of the project until 1900 and then in part for the rest of his life. His ambitious idea was to create a great doorway more than twenty feet high in the manner of the famous bronze doors by Lorenzo Ghiberti (Italian, 1378–1455) for the Florence Baptistery known as the *Gates of Paradise* (1425–1452), but with themes from the *Inferno* (ca. 1308–1320) by Dante Alighieri (Italian, ca. 1265–1321). For twenty years Rodin toiled on a plaster model, creating complex and fluid sculptures that would burst out of the architectural framework of the vast doors. The writhing, densely modeled figures tumble down the structure, creating an impression of terror, confusion, chaos, and torment (figs. 14 and 15).

Through to the end of the nineteenth century, Rodin labored on many of the figures originally intended for the *Gates of Hell*, changing and adapting them to fit into the doorway that existed only as a plaster model during his lifetime.[ix] As time went by, he further transformed many of these pieces into independent sculptures that now comprise some of the sculptor's most famous works—several of which are represented in the Legion's collection. *The Thinker* (pl. 12), seen in the museum's Court of Honor, was originally meant to be placed, in a much smaller version, above the doors of the *Gates*, surveying the action. It was first known as *The Poet*, alluding to Dante himself. Rodin may have adopted the pose from Michelangelo Buonarroti's tomb figure of Lorenzo de' Medici (1524–1531) in San Lorenzo, Florence (fig. 16).[x] He also could have been influenced by the more contemporary sculpture *Ugolino and His Sons* (1865–1867, Metropolitan Museum of Art, New York) by Jean-Baptiste Carpeaux (French, 1827–1875), a plaster study for which is in the Legion's collection (fig. 17). However, like so many of Rodin's sculptures, *The Thinker* grew to represent something even more universal—the struggle for inspiration.

The Thinker was first exhibited as an autonomous sculpture in 1888 in Copenhagen[xi] though it had earlier been cast in bronze for an English collector in 1884.[xii] A greatly enlarged version of it was first cast in 1904, with eight lifetime casts created for Rodin. The model proved to be so popular that it is today synonymous with Rodin's work, with many examples of it featured in museums and institutions throughout the world.[xiii] This monumental version—suggested by the English collector Ernest Beckett—was given to the French state in 1906 to be installed outside the Panthéon (the secular

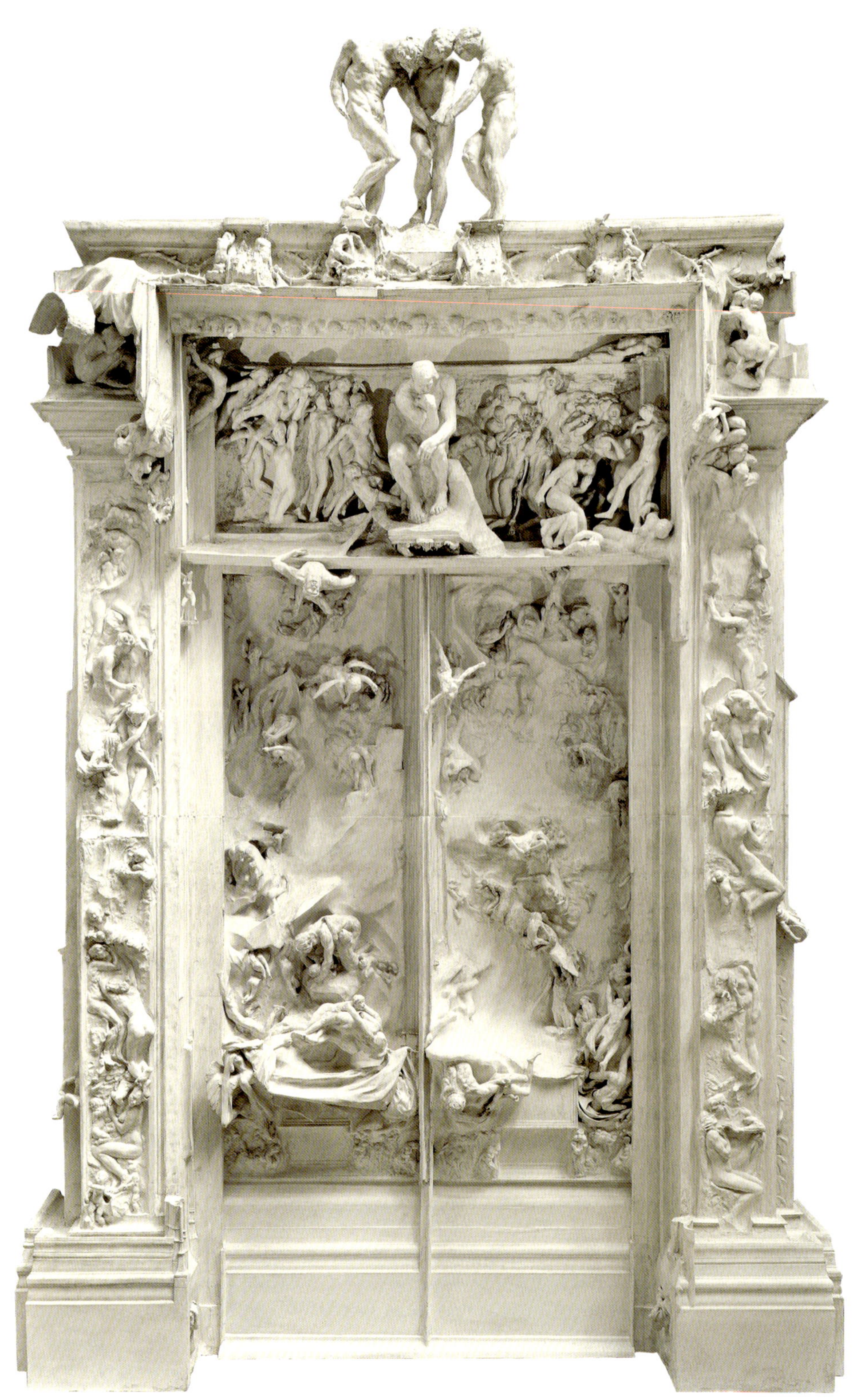

Fig. 14 *Gates of Hell*, 1880–1888. Plaster, 217 ⅜ x 157 ½ x 37 in. (552 x 400 x 94 cm). Musée d'Orsay, Paris, DO 1986 4, S 2450

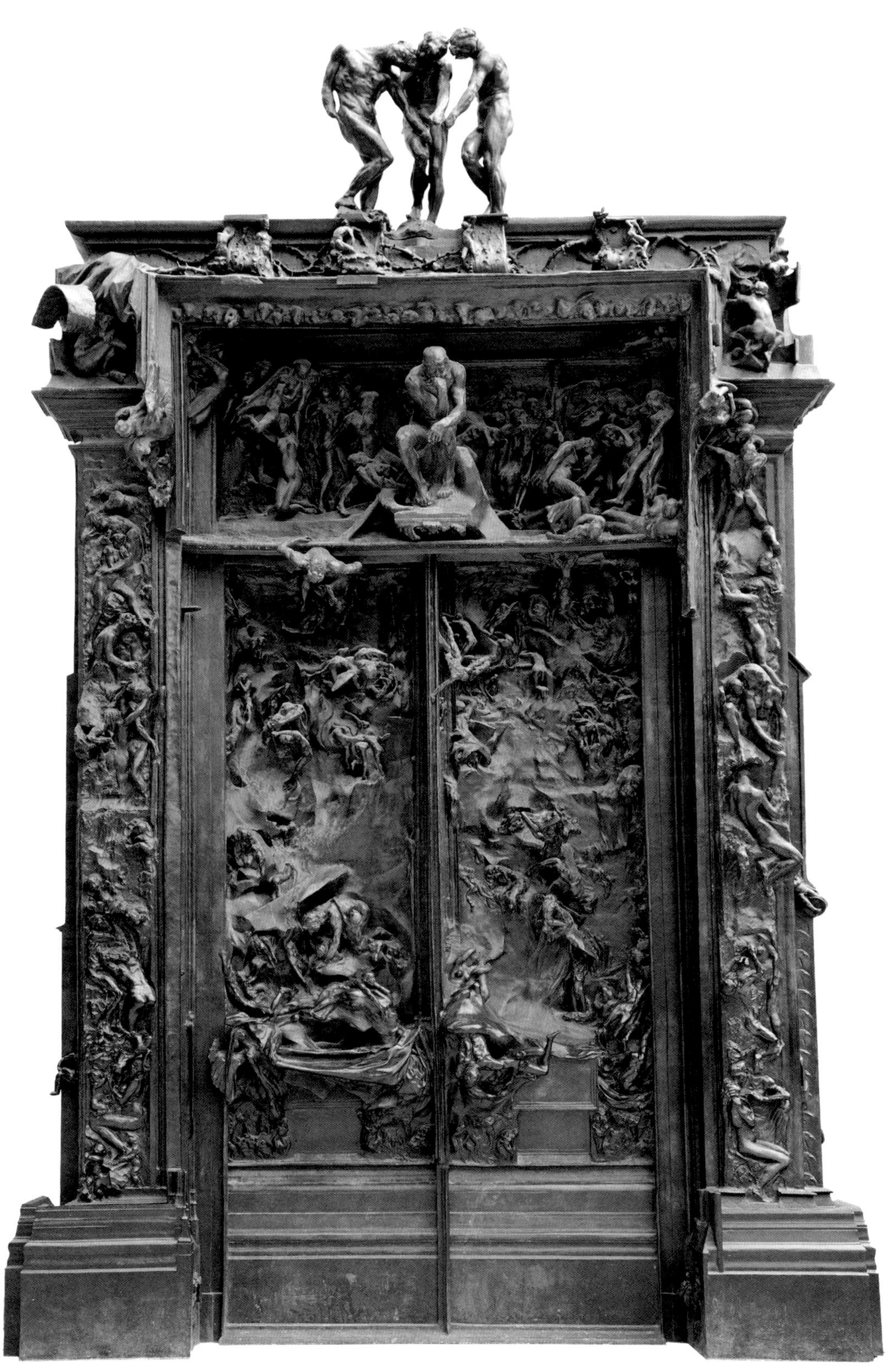

Fig. 15 *Gates of Hell*, 1880–1890 (cast 1928). Bronze, 236 ⅜ x 157 ¼ x 39 ⅝ in. (600.5 x 399.3 x 100.6 cm). Musée Rodin, Paris

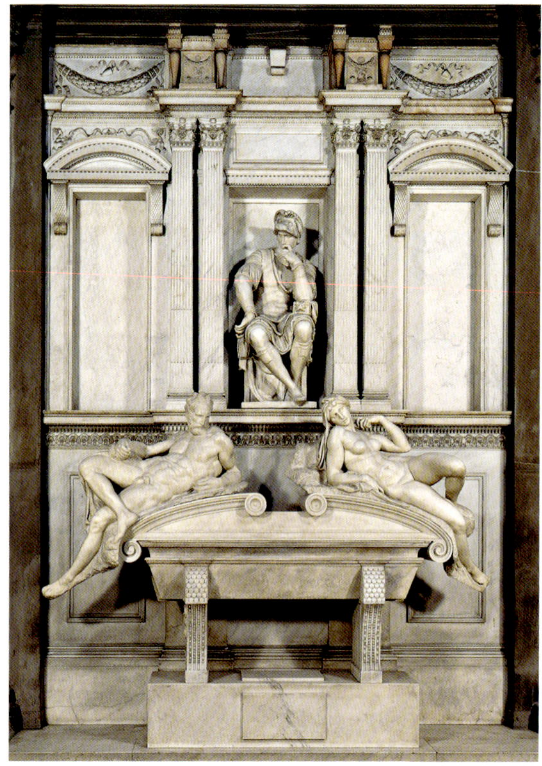

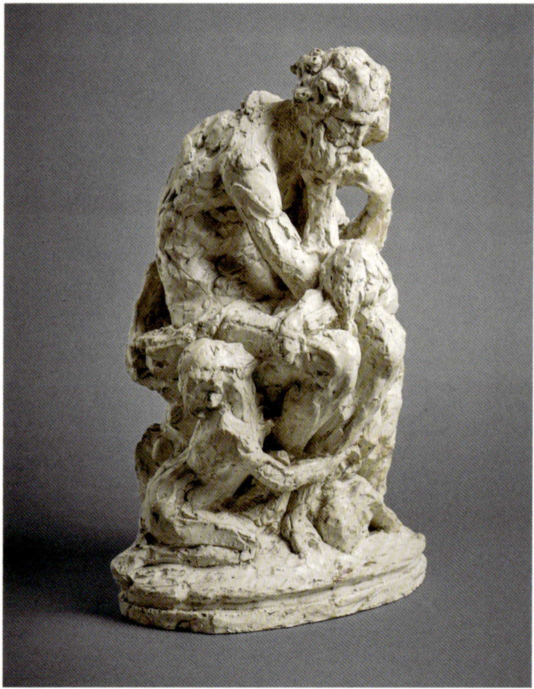

resting place of distinguished French citizens) in Paris (fig. 19).[xiv] The Legion's cast at this size was made around 1914, shortly before it was sent to the Panama-Pacific International Exposition under the auspices of Loïe Fuller.[xv] It was purchased by Alma and Adolph Spreckels, and placed in the Legion's entry court when the museum opened in 1924. It has remained there ever since, serving as a signature piece for the institution.

The Three Shades (pl. 17) planned for the top of the *Gates* was originally conceived with the statues pointing down to an engraving of Dante's famous words "Abandon hope all ye who enter here." Although the work appears to feature three different figures, Rodin used just one model thrice repeated and set at various angles to form a complex composition. Records show that Rodin increased the size of the Legion's version by 1905.[xvi] *The Kiss* (pl. 13) was titled *Paolo and Francesca* when it was first exhibited in 1887, but shortly after that presentation Rodin removed the statue from the *Gates of Hell* because he felt it no longer befitted the narrative. Scandalous to its initial audiences because Rodin portrayed Dante's lovers naked, once stripped of its literary associations, *The Kiss* became one of the sculptor's most famous and best-loved works.

Also intended for the *Gates* is the figure of *Eve* (pl. 14), which was modeled to flank the doors with its counterpart *Adam* (ca. 1881), but both were eventually eliminated from Rodin's more evolved design and the artist changed them into autonomous sculptures. *The Prodigal Son* (pl. 20) was conceived as a tiny figure struggling to rise hopelessly from the bottom right of the doors in the complete *Gates*. As reflected in the Legion's version, it was later enlarged as a separate sculpture. *Three Faunesses* (pl. 16) was also originally intended as a single figure that would appear in different parts of the *Gates*. Similar to *The Three Shades*, Rodin combined three versions of the same figure to make a completely different composition that suggests dancing and movement. A record of the *Gates* project in the Legion's holdings is a reduction of the lower portion of the left pilaster of the doorway (pl. 22). This plaster work shows piles of writhing women interspersed with babies that float upward, suggesting that the composition represents the first cycle of hell from the *Inferno*.

Fig. 16 Michelangelo Buonarroti, *Tomb of Lorenzo de' Medici*, 1520–1534. Marble, height: 72 ⅞ in. (185 cm). Medici Chapels, Sagrestia Nuova, San Lorenzo, Florence

Fig. 17 Jean-Baptiste Carpeaux, Study for *Ugolino and His Sons*, ca. 1858. Plaster, 20 ⅞ x 13 ⅜ x 9 ⅝ in. (53 x 34 x 24.4 cm). Fine Arts Museums of San Francisco, Museum purchase, Donald McLeod Lewis Bequest fund, 1993.44

Fig. 18 Ferdinand Paillet, *Caricature of Rodin*, 1884. Watercolor. Sèvres – Cité de la Céramique, France

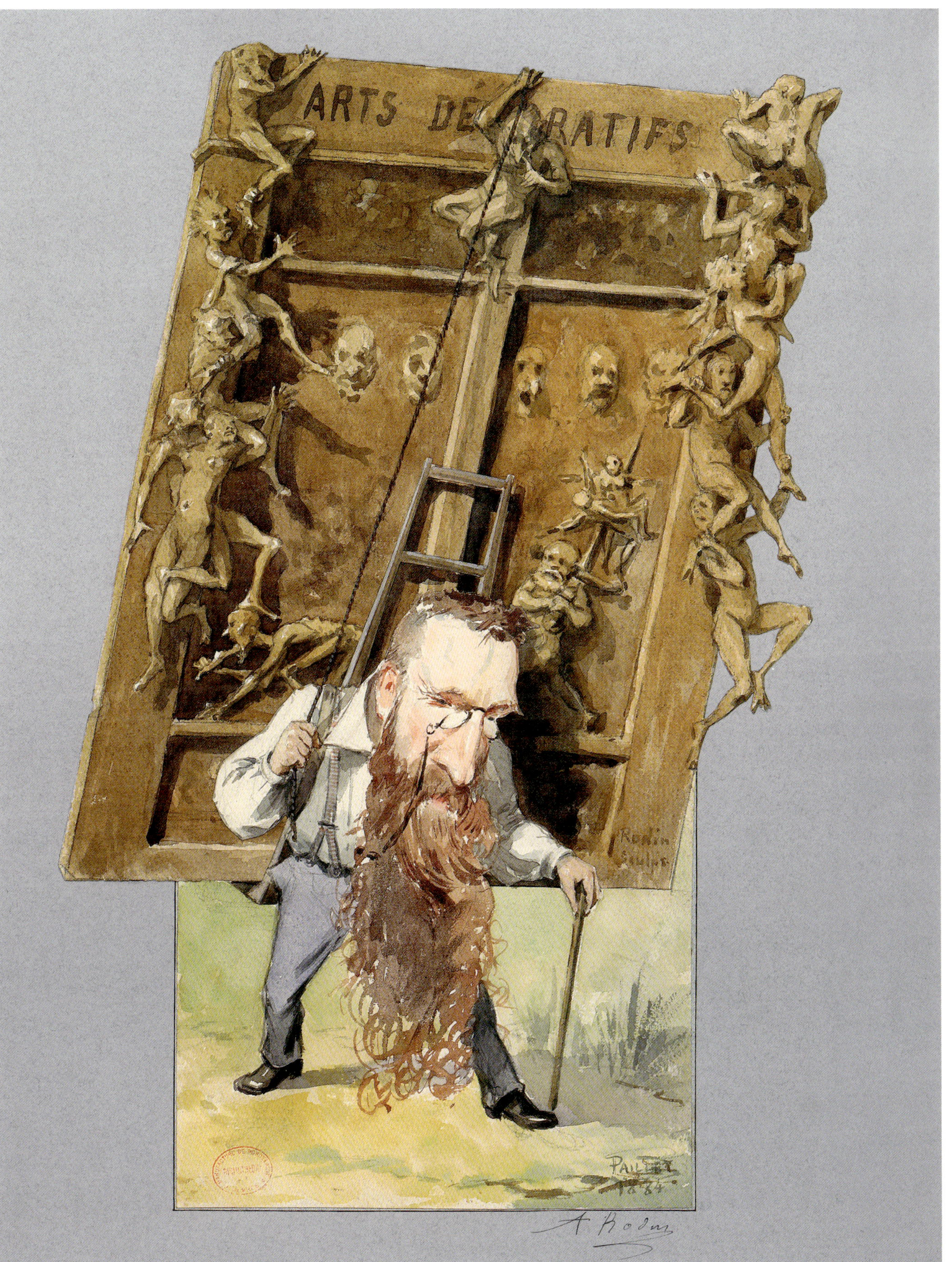

ARTS DÉCORATIFS
PAILLET
1884
A. Rodin

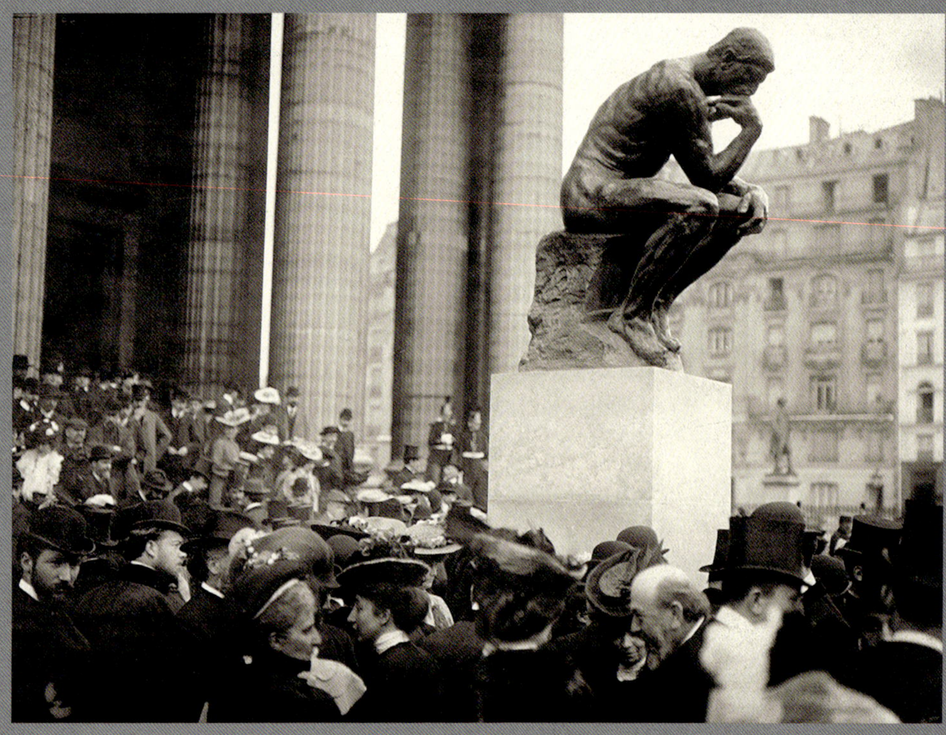

"What makes my Thinker think is that he thinks not only with his brain, with his knitted brow, his distended nostrils, and compressed lips but with every muscle of his arms, back, and legs, and with his clenched fist and gripping toes." —Auguste Rodin[xvii]

Rodin also described the history of *The Thinker* thus: "*The Thinker* has a story. In the days long gone by, I conceived the idea of 'The Gates of Hell.' Before the door, seated on a rock, Dante, thinking of the plan of his poem. Behind him, Ugolino, Francesca, Paolo, all the characters of *The Divine Comedy*. This project was not realized. Thin, ascetic, Dante separated from the whole world would have been without meaning. Guided by my first inspiration I conceived another thinker, a naked man seated on a rock, his feet drawn under him, his fist against his teeth, he dreams. The fertile thought slowly elaborates itself within his brain. He is no longer a dreamer, he is creator."[xviii]

———

Fig. 19 Marcel Hutin, Unveiling *The Thinker* in front of the Panthéon, Paris, 1906. Aristotype, 4 ⅝ x 6 ½ in. (11.8 x 16.6 cm). Musée Rodin, Paris, Ph.754

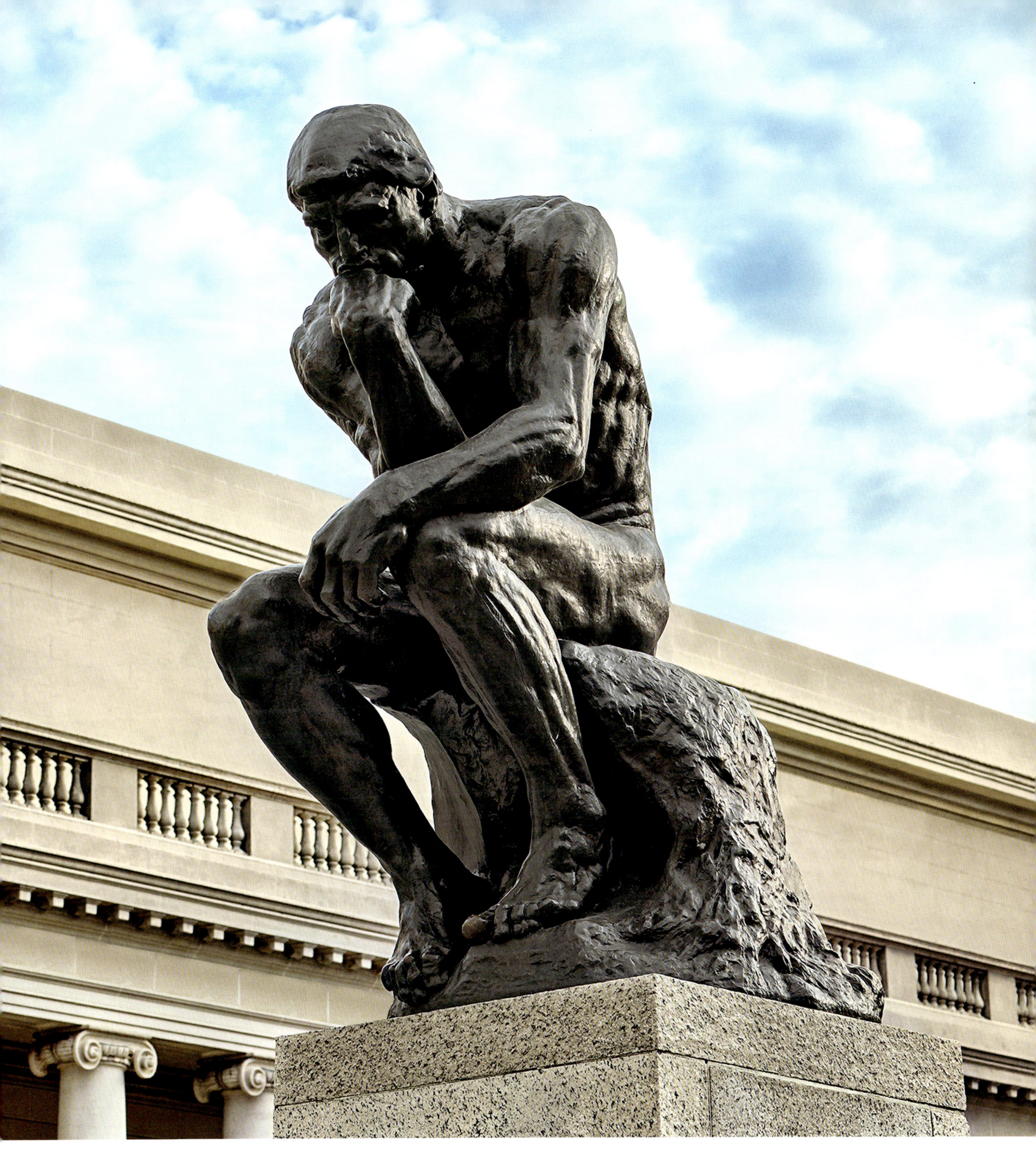

12. *The Thinker*, 1888 (enlarged 1902–1903, cast ca. 1914). Bronze, 74 ⅜ x 38 ⅝ x 55 ⅛ in. (189 x 98 x 140 cm). Inscribed: *A. Rodin* and *A. Rudier / Fondeur. Paris.* Gift of Alma de Bretteville Spreckels, 1924.18.1

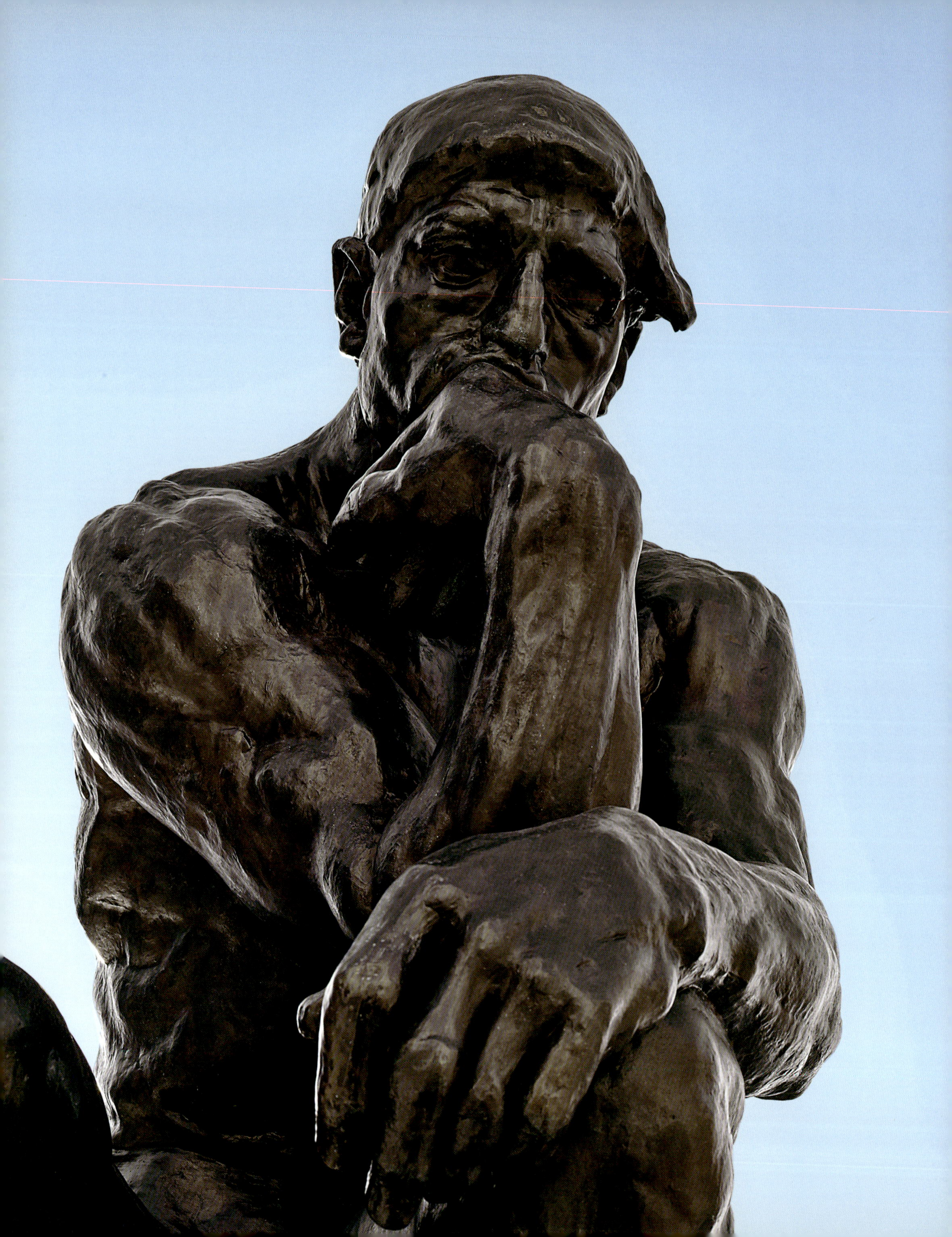

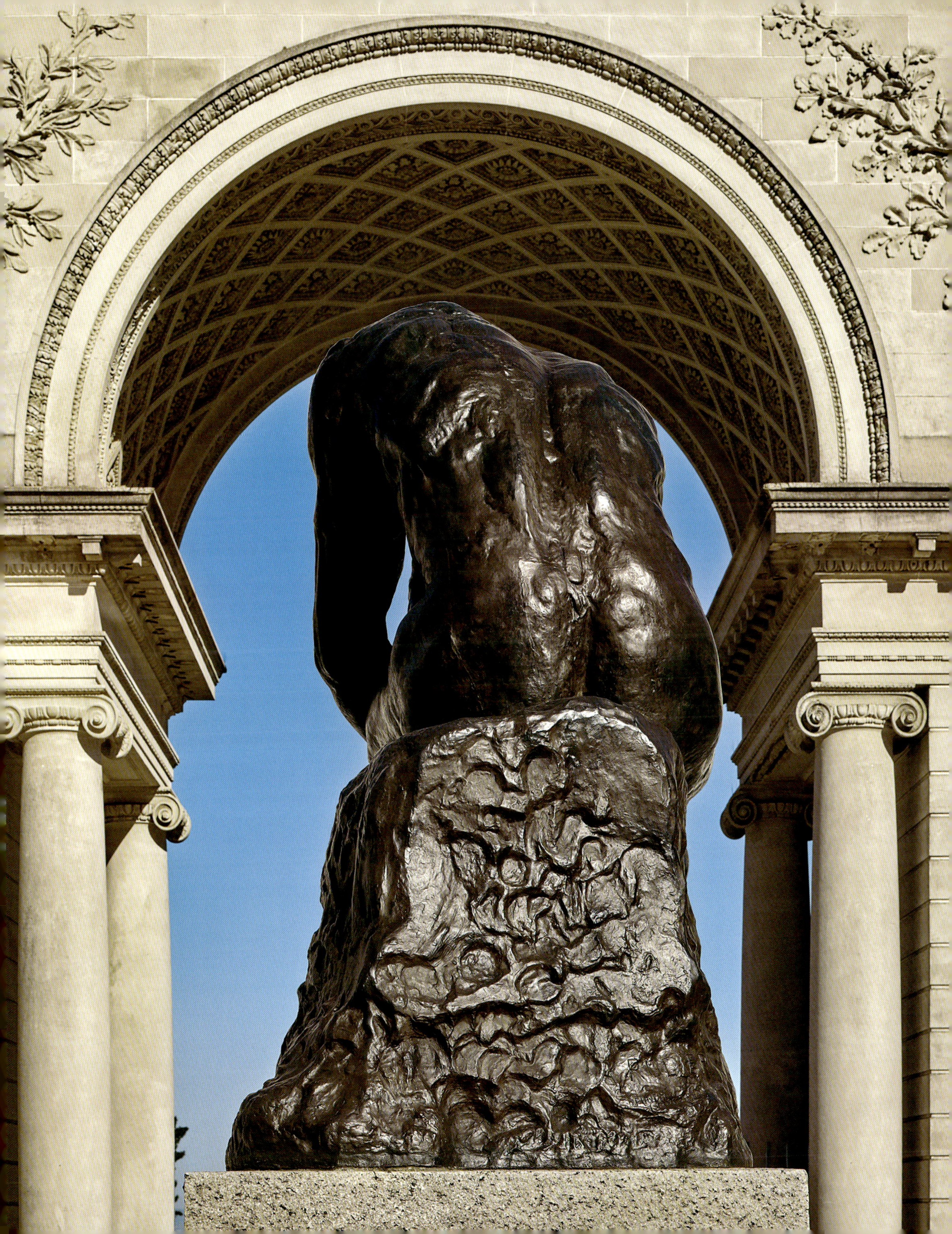

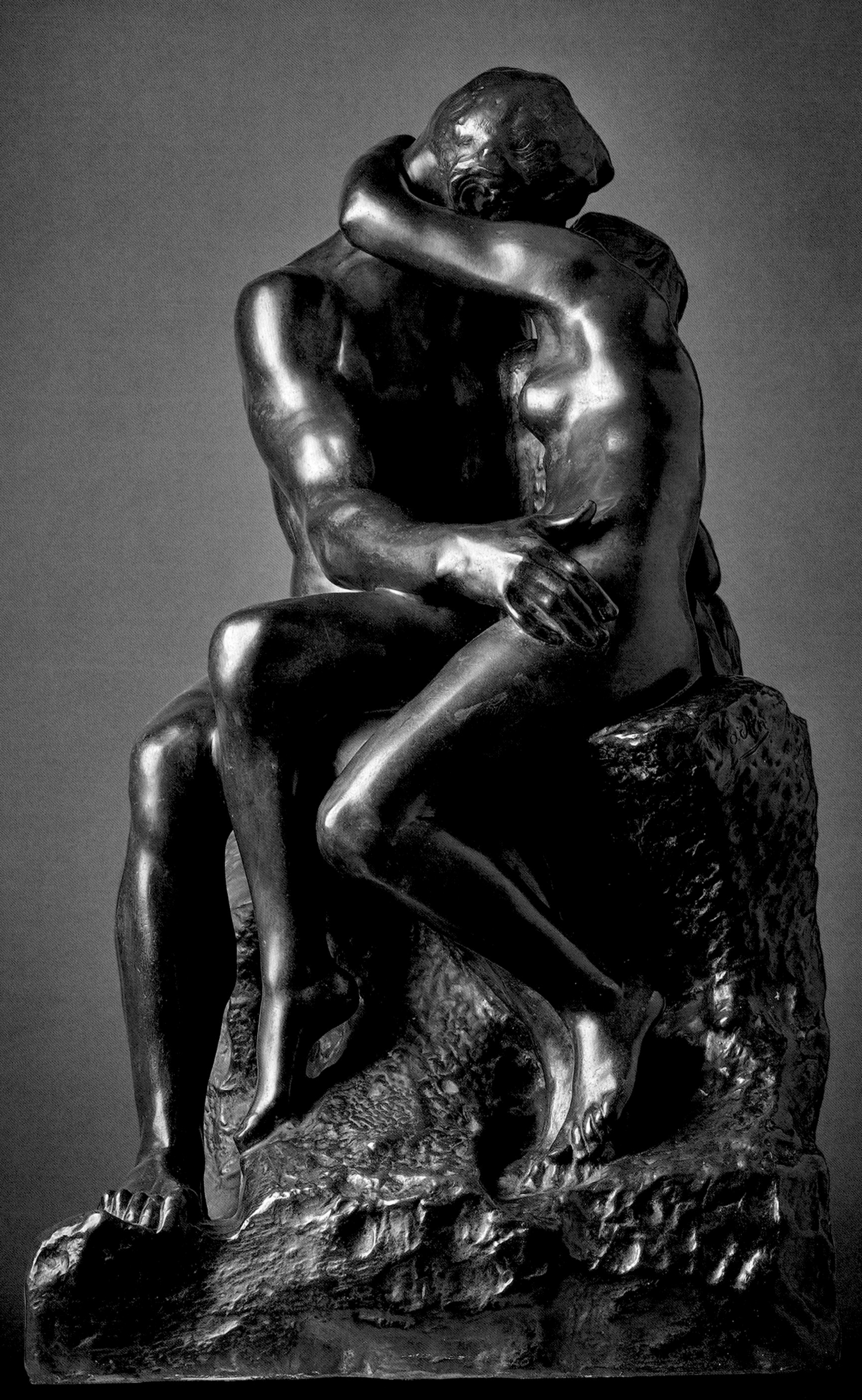

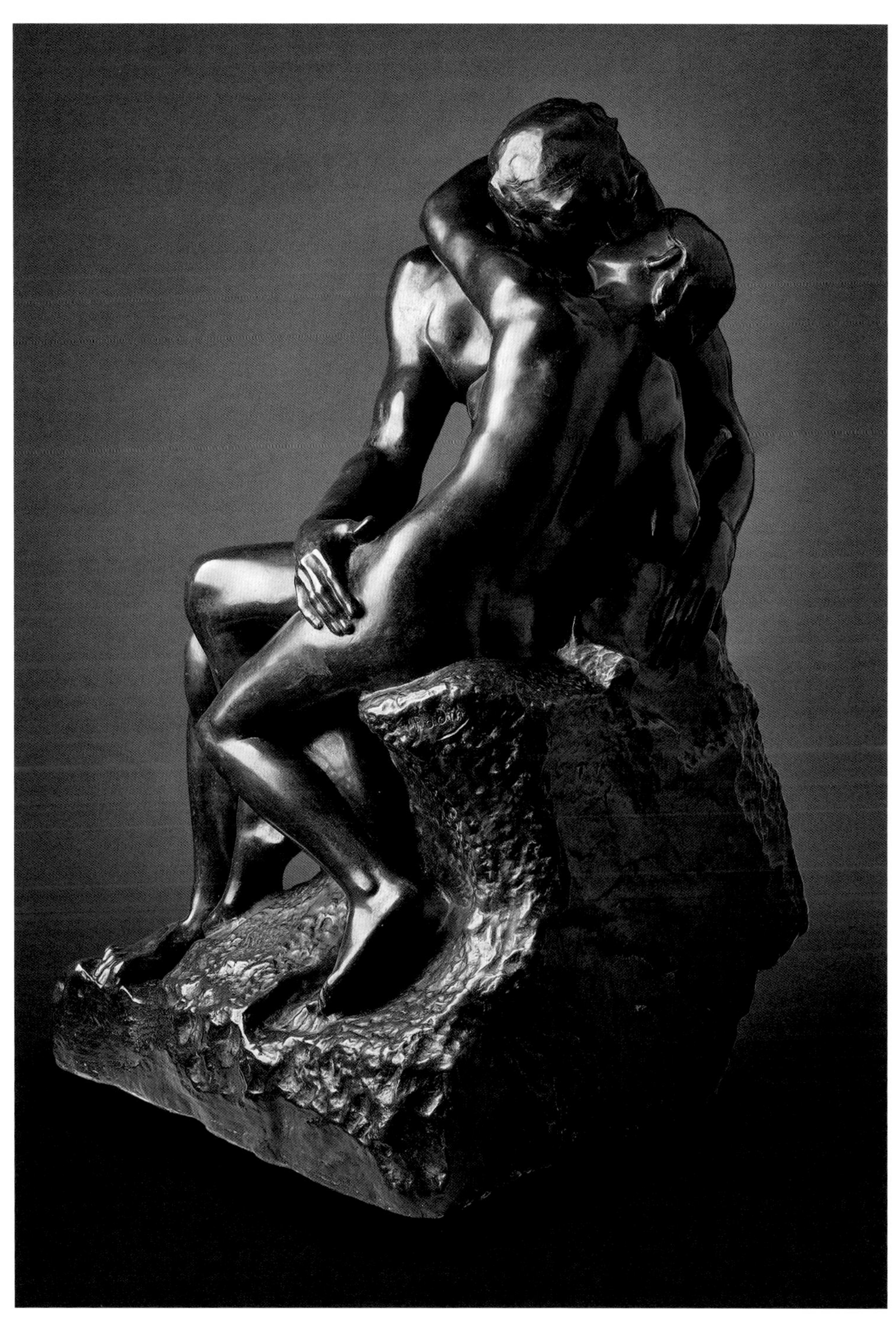

13. *The Kiss*, 1881–1882 (reduced 1904 [no. 4], cast ca. 1914). Bronze, 23¼ x 14¼ x 14⅞ in. (59.1 x 36.2 x 37.9 cm).
Inscribed: *Rodin*. Gift of Alma de Bretteville Spreckels, 1941.34.8

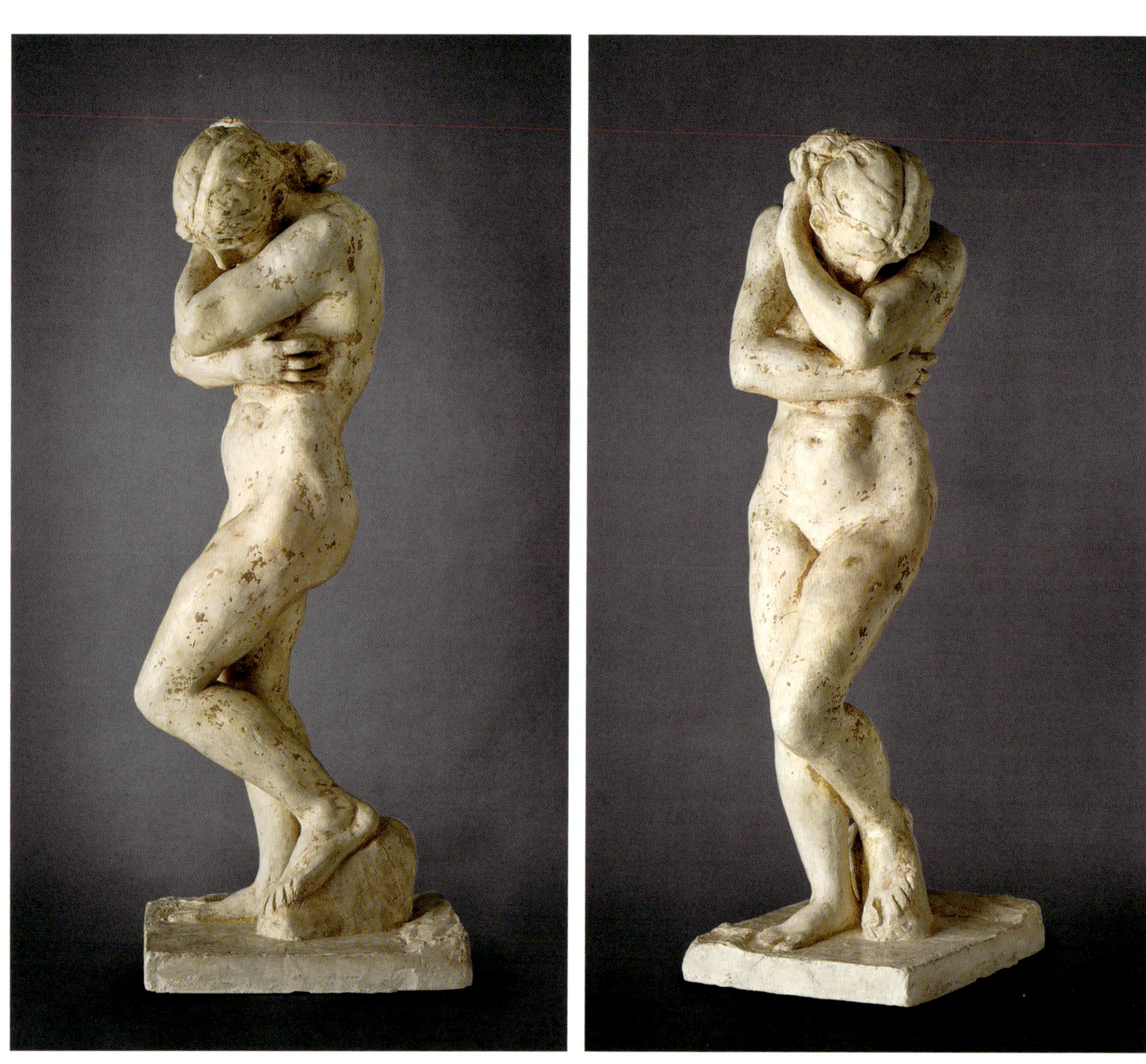

14. *Eve*, 1881 (reduced ca. 1883). Plaster, 30 x 11 ⅜ x 9 ¼ in. (76.2 x 28.9 x 23.5 cm).
Inscribed: *Modèle pour le bronze* and *Eve* and *Rodin*. Gift of Alma de Bretteville Spreckels, 1949.15

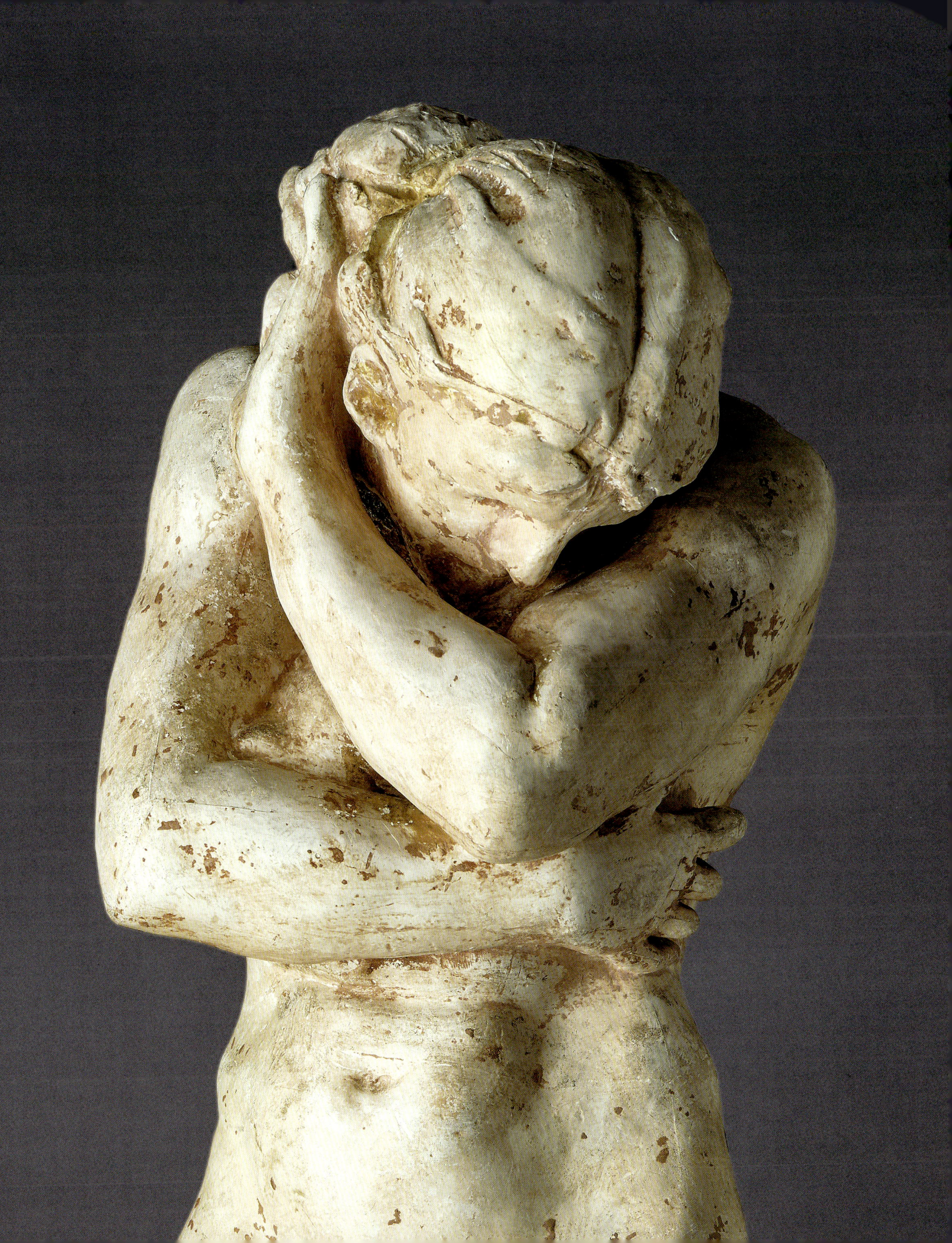

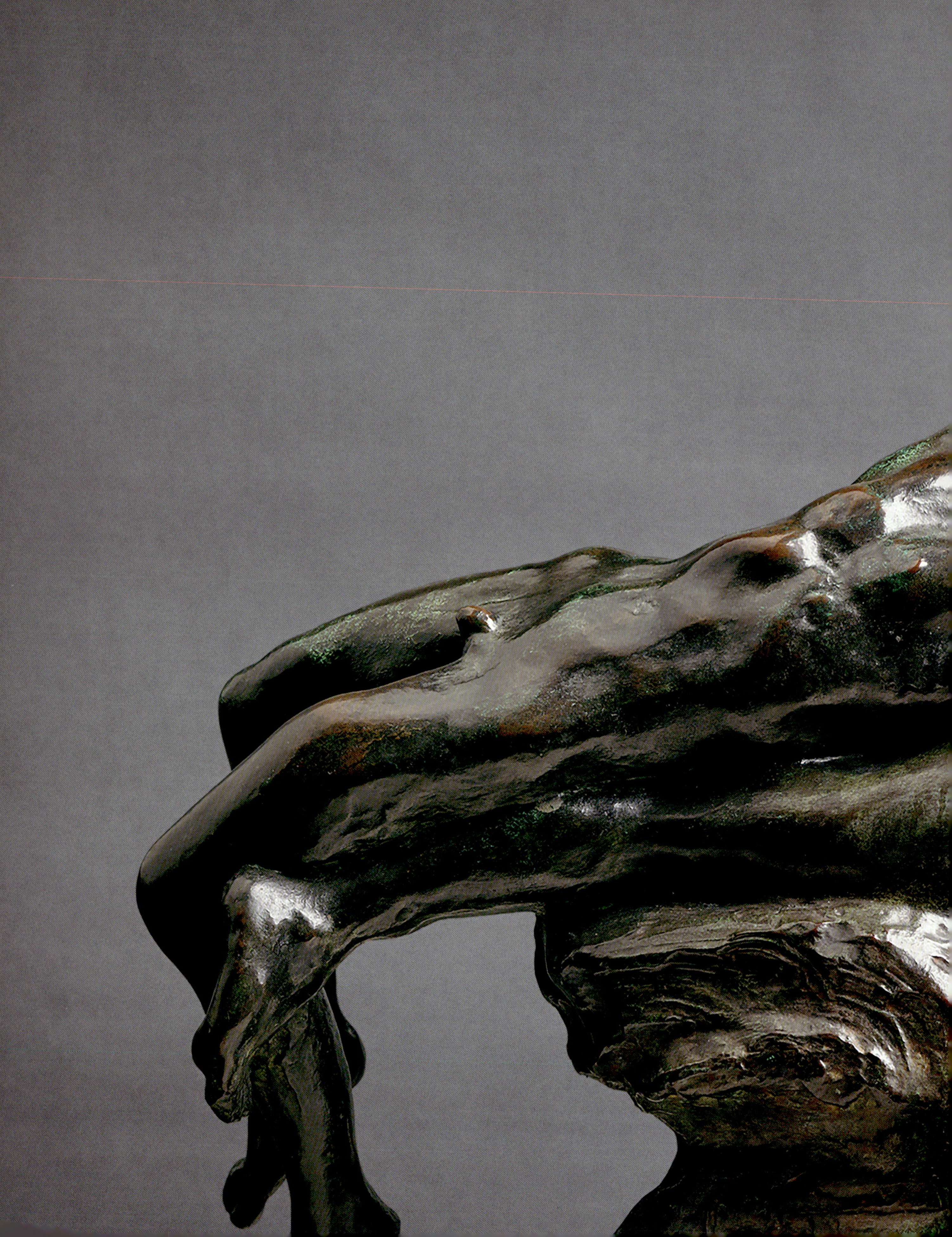

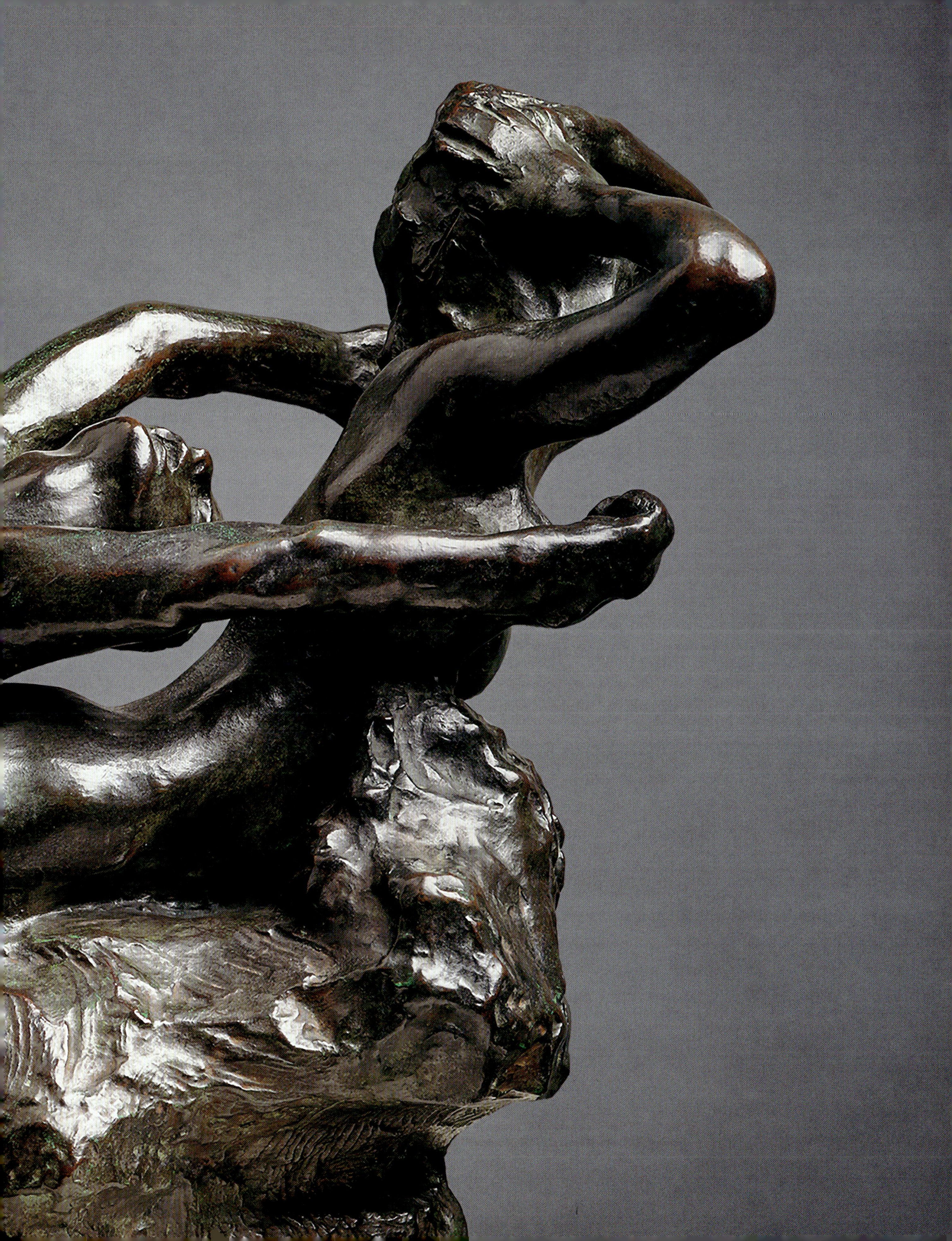

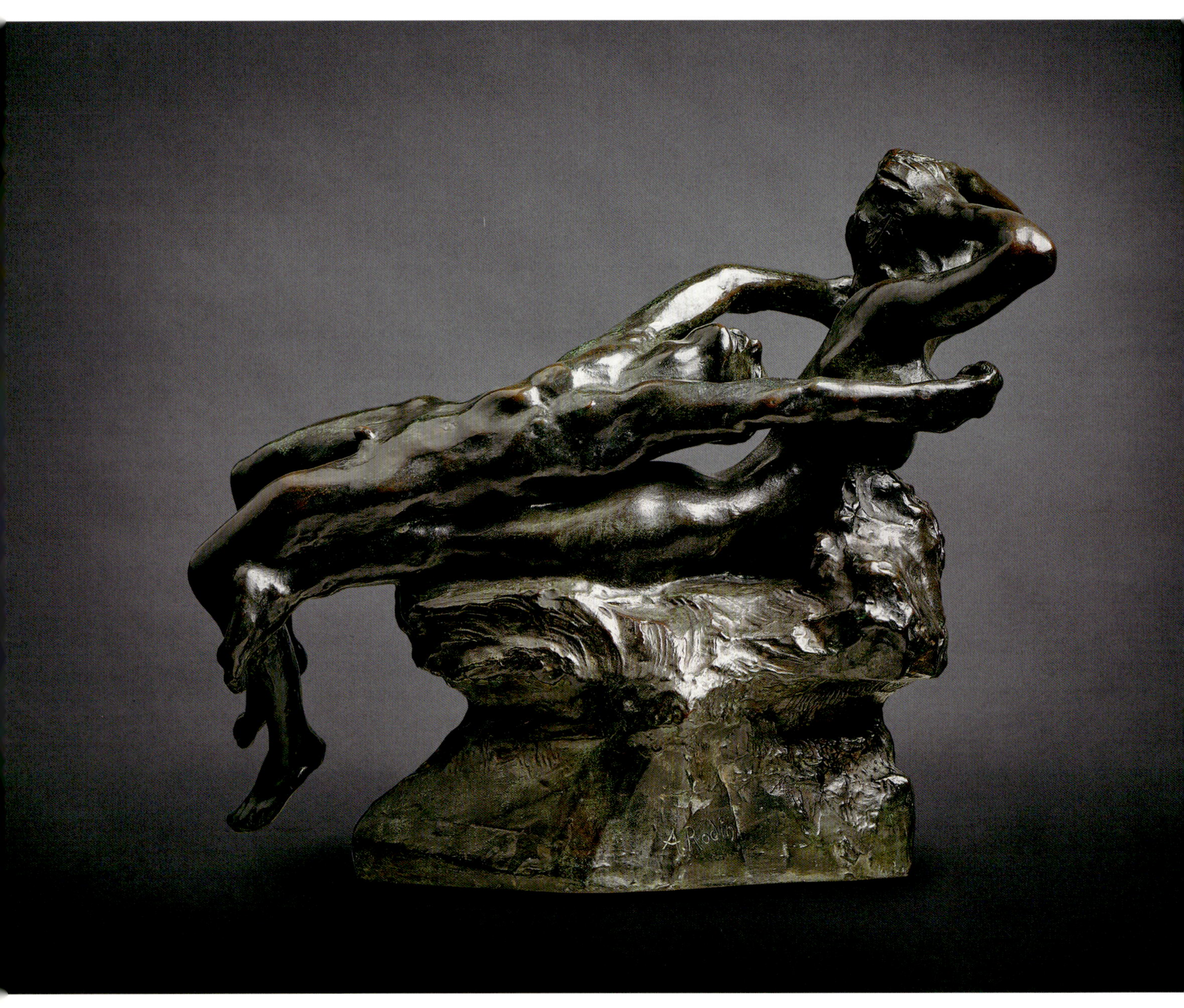

15. *Fugit Amor*, before 1887. Bronze, 14 ½ x 7 ⅝ x 17 ½ in. (36.8 x 19.4 x 44.5 cm).
Inscribed: *A. Rodin* and *Alexis RUDIER. / Fondeur.PARIS*. Gift of Alma de Bretteville Spreckels, 1942.41

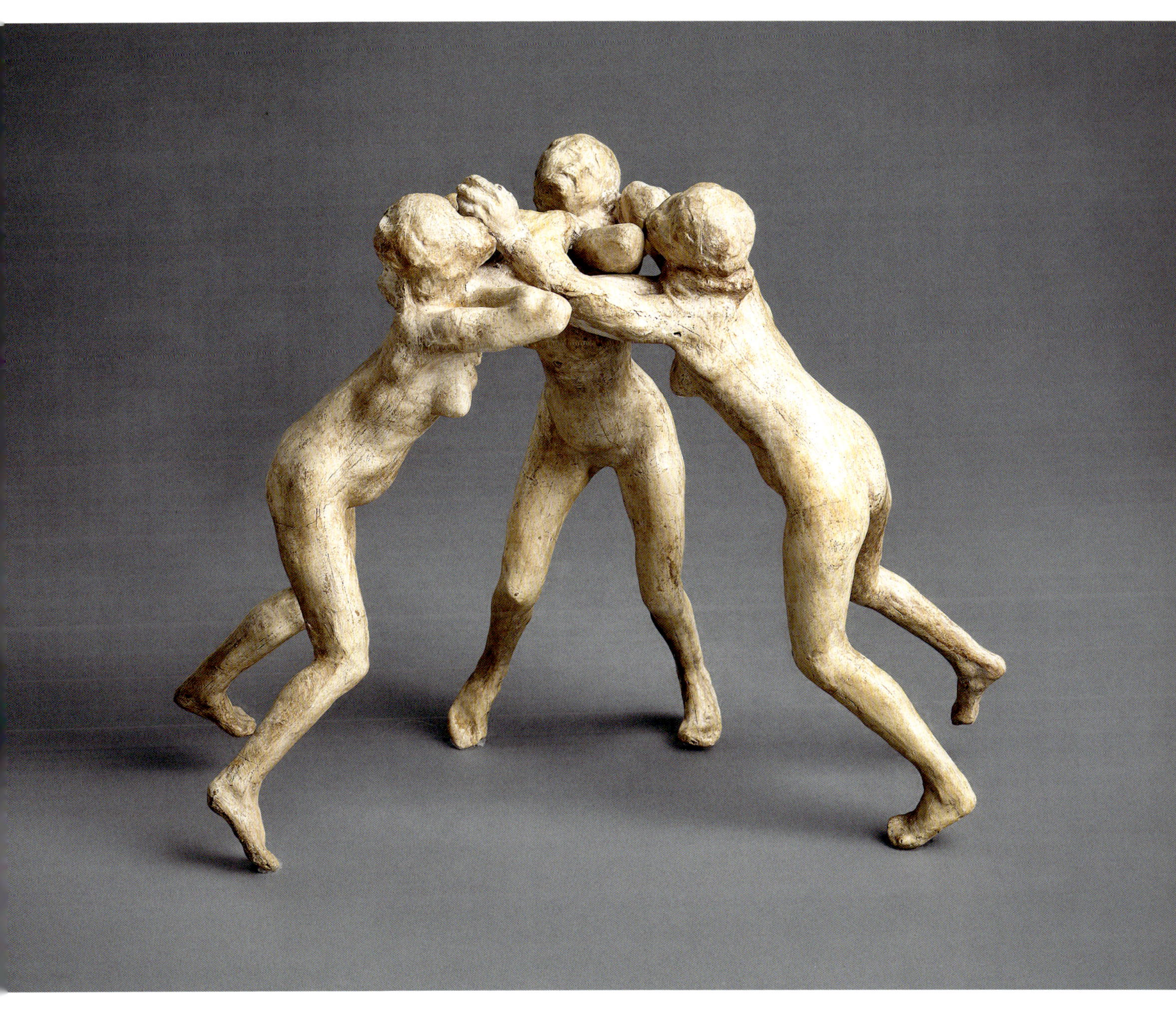

16. *Three Faunesses*, before 1896. Plaster, 9 ⅜ x 13 x 6 ½ in. (23.9 x 32.9 x 16.5 cm). Gift of Adolph B. Spreckels, Jr., 1933.12.5

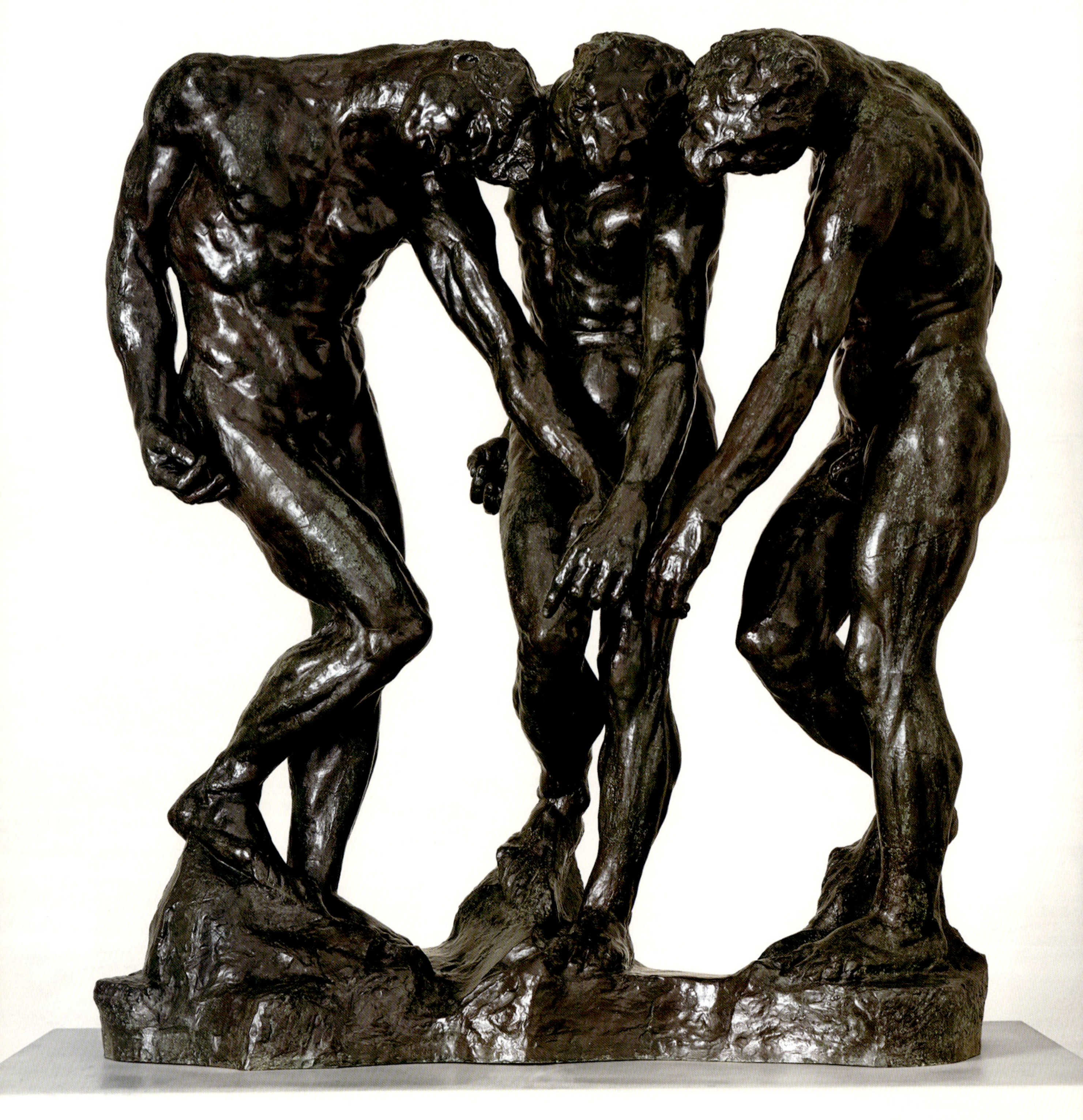

17. *The Three Shades*, 1898 (enlarged 1902–1904, cast ca. 1923). Bronze, 75 ½ x 73 ½ x 41 ½ in. (191.8 x 186.7 x 105.4 cm).
Inscribed: *A. Rodin* and *ALEXIS RUDIER / Fondeur. PARIS*.
Collection of the City and County of San Francisco, Gift of the Raphael Weill Memorial Committee, L95.74

ADOLPH B. AND ALMA DE BRETTEVILLE SPRECKELS GALLERY

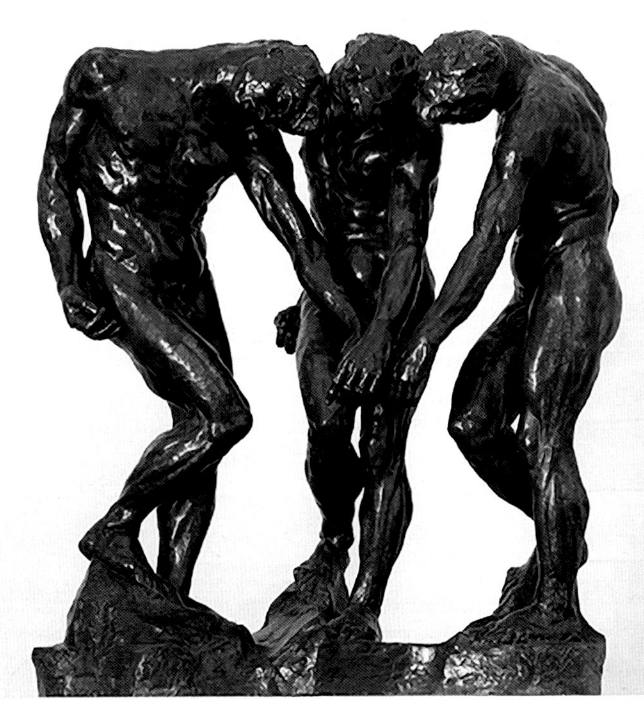

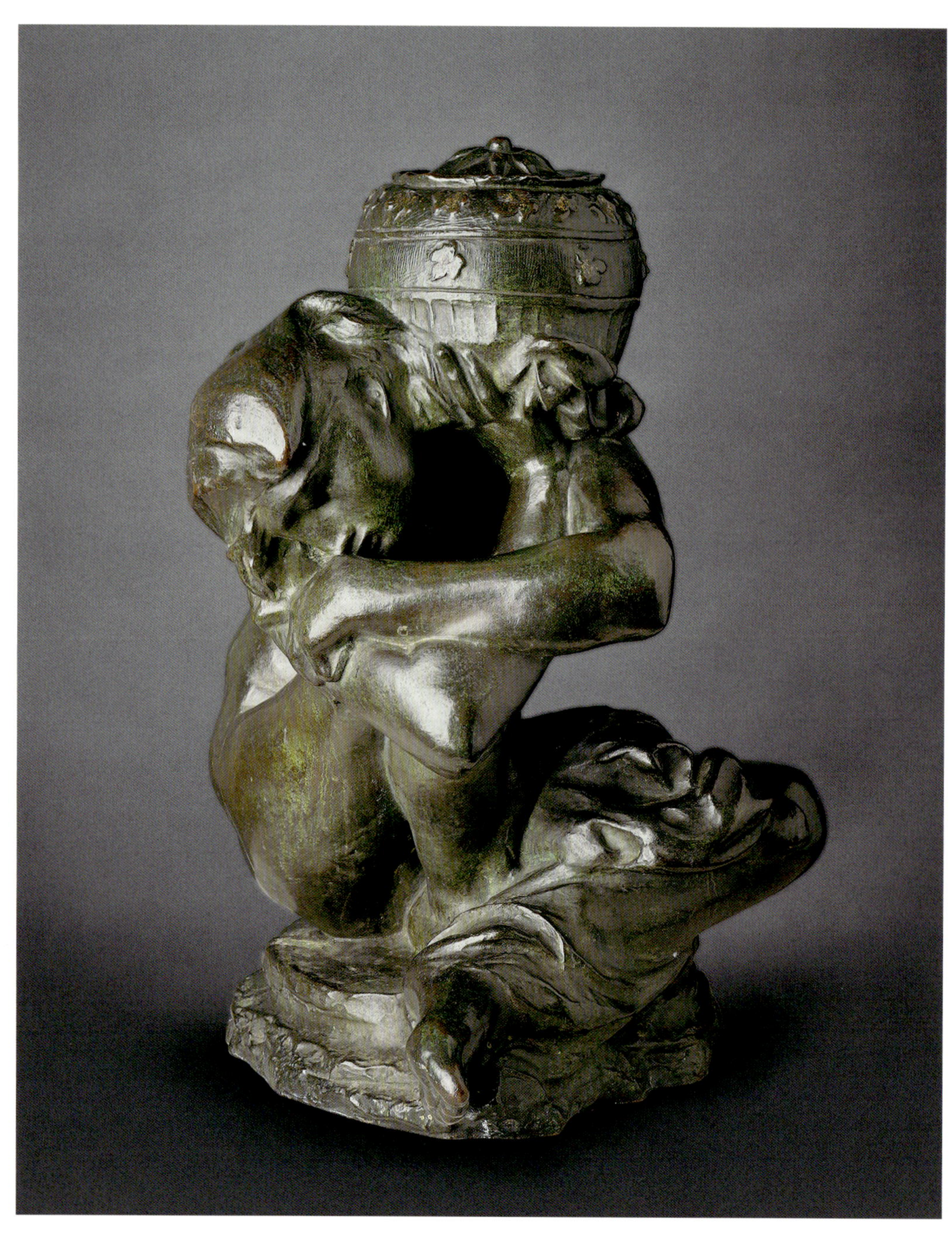

18. *Fallen Caryatid Carrying an Urn*, after 1900 (cast 1927). Bronze, 16 x 10 ⅞ x 9 ⅝ in. (40.6 x 27.6 x 24.4 cm).
Inscribed: *A. Rodin No. 2* and *Alexis. Rudier. / Fondeur. PARIS.* Gift of Alma de Bretteville Spreckels, 1950.60

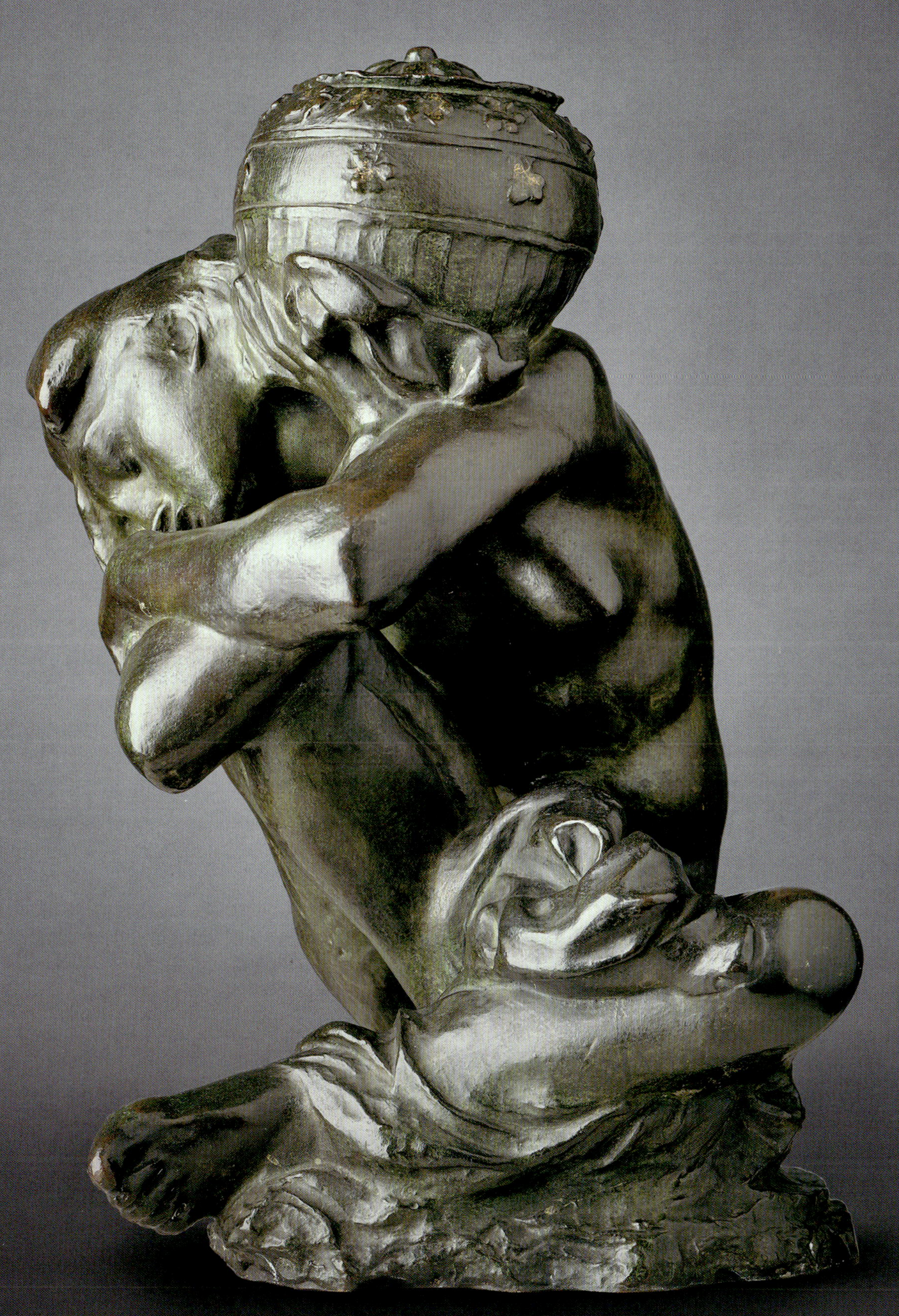

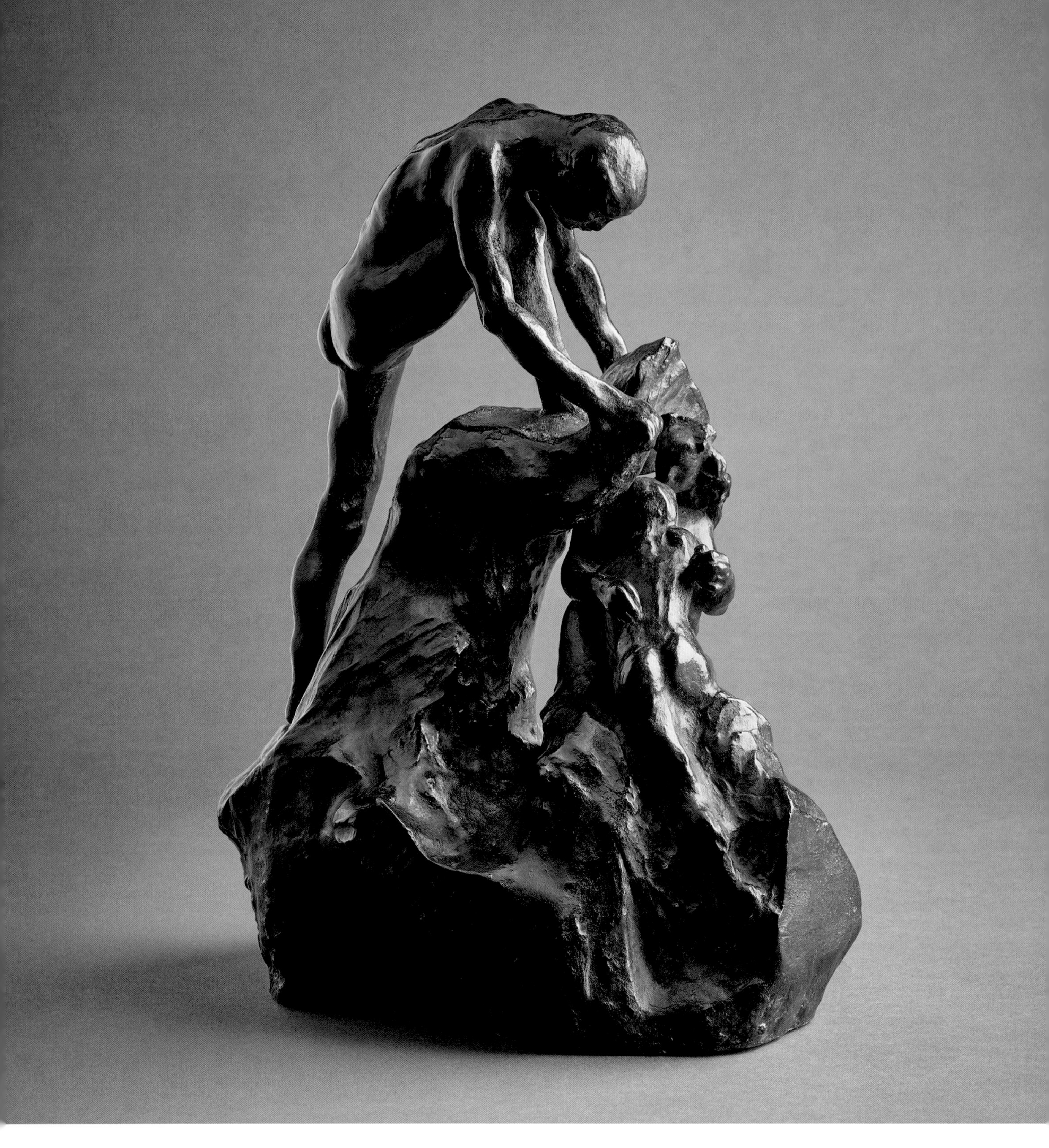

19. *Polyphemus and Acis*, 1888 (cast 1929). Bronze, 11 ⅛ x 5 ⅞ x 8 ⅞ in. (28.2 x 14.9 x 22.5 cm). Inscribed: *A. Rodin* and *Alexis Rudier / Fondeur. PARIS.* Gift of Alma de Bretteville Spreckels, 1950.58

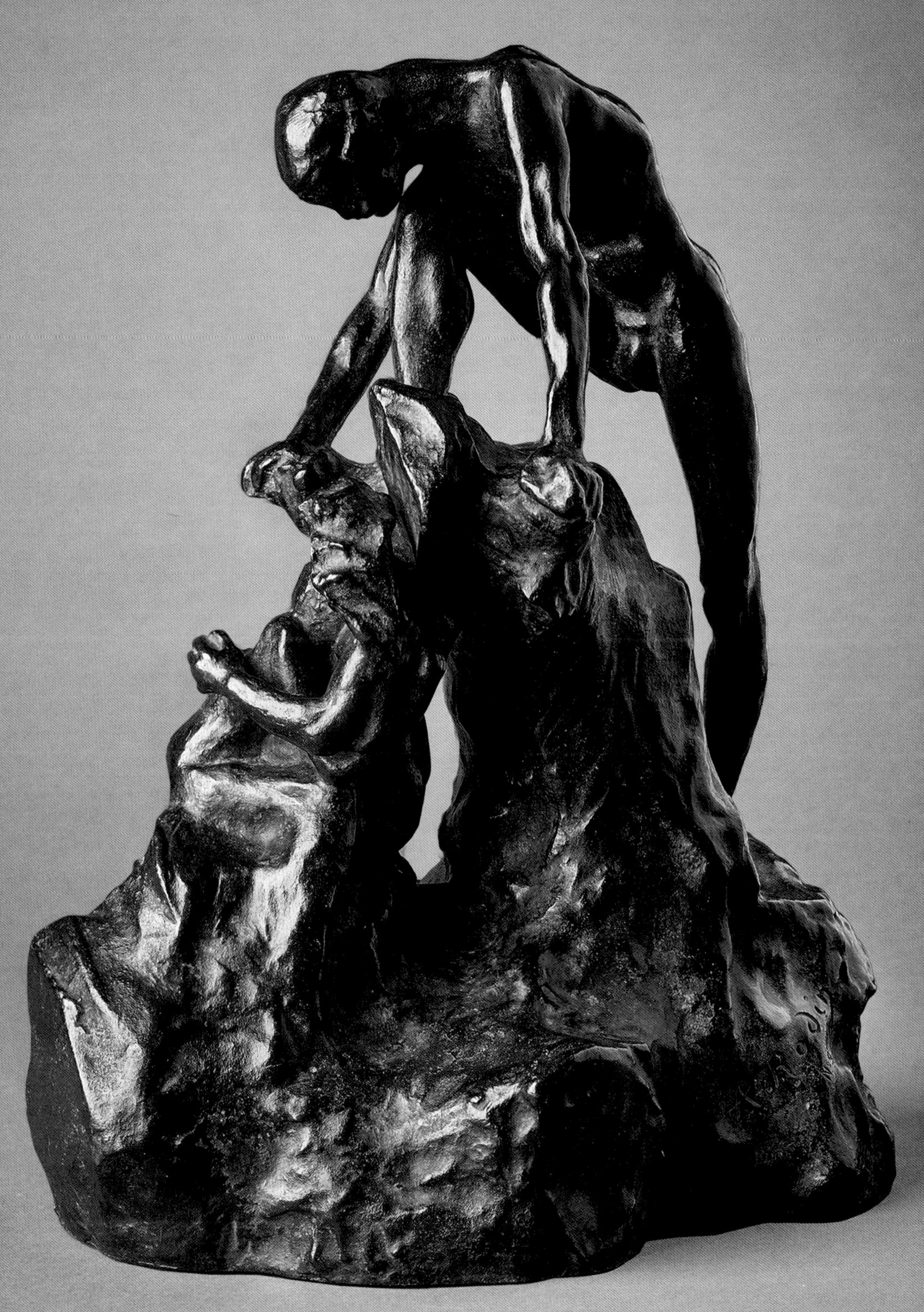

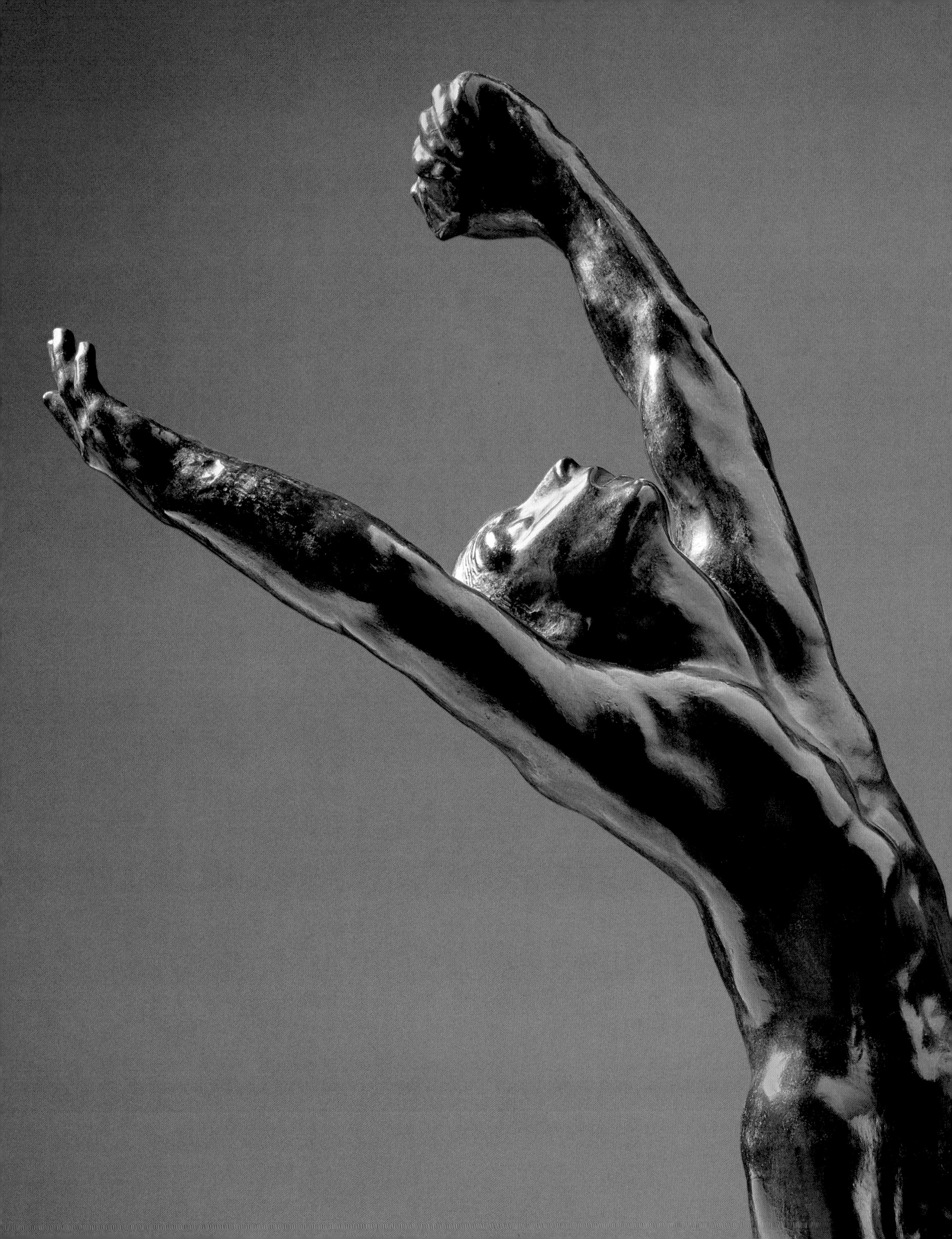

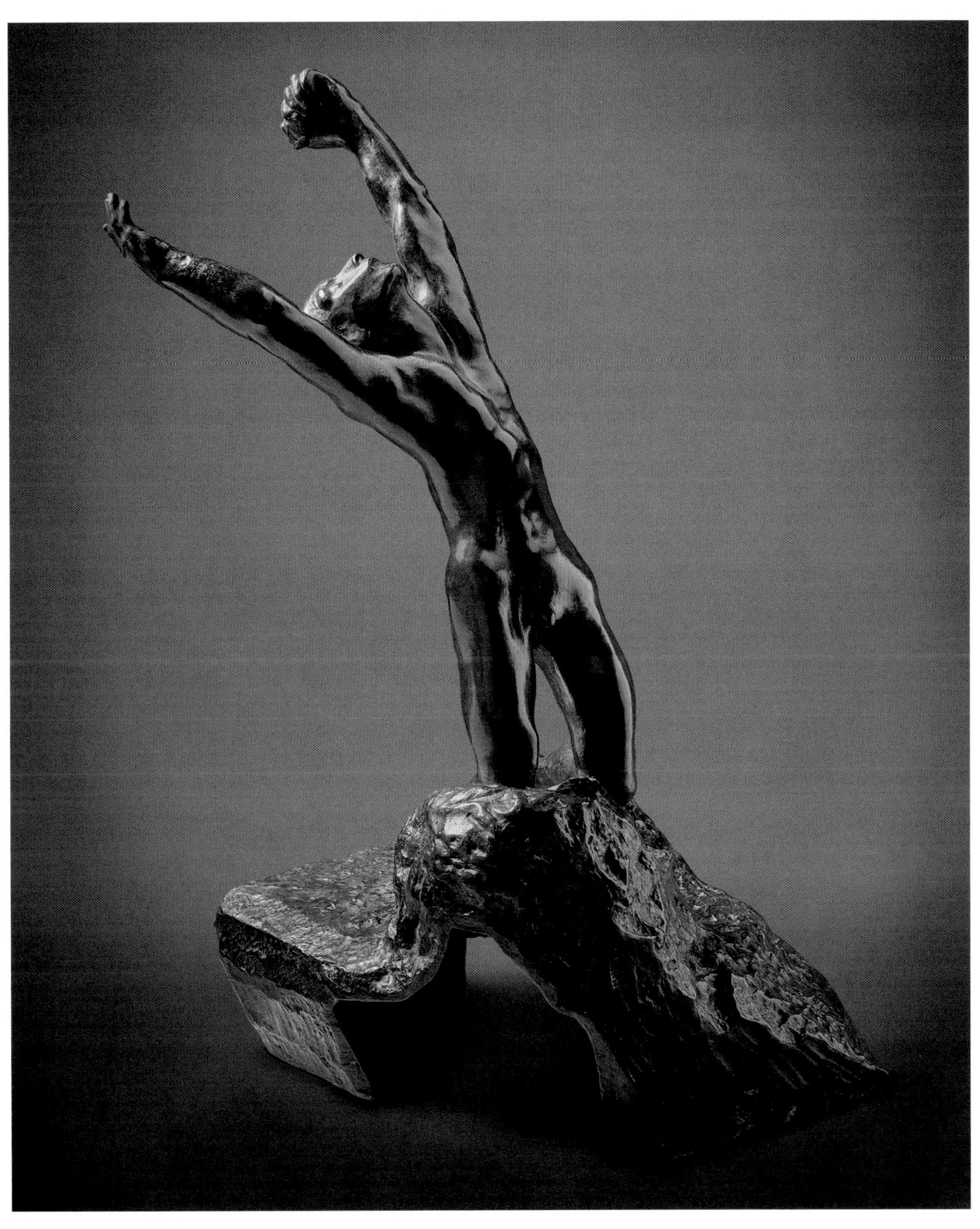

20. *The Prodigal Son*, 1886–1893 (enlarged 1905, cast ca. 1914). Bronze, 64 x 28 x 34½ in. (162.6 x 71.1 x 87.6 cm). Inscribed: *A. Rodin* and *Ais RUDIER. Fondeur. PARIS*. Gift of Alma de Bretteville Spreckels, 1940.137

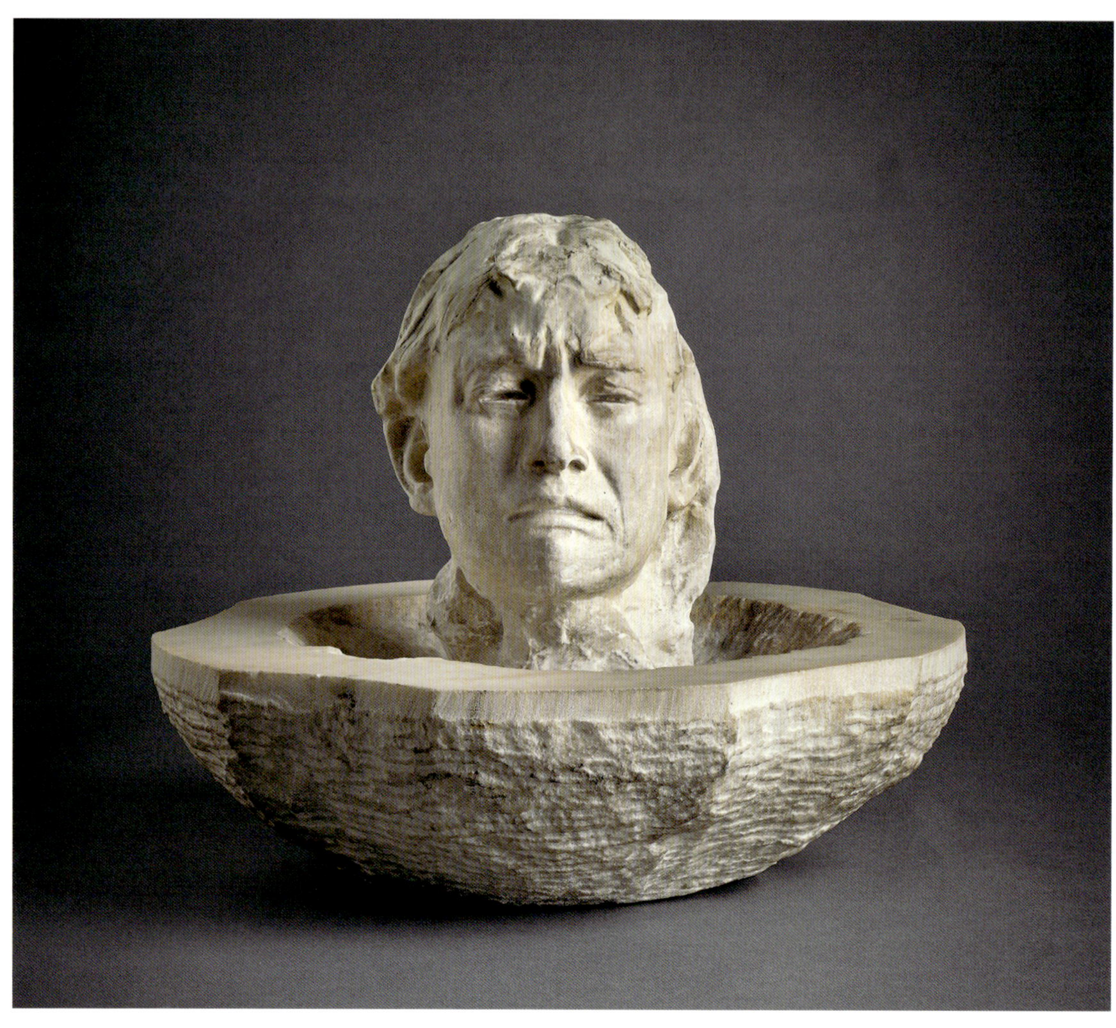

21. *Crying Girl Disheveled*, before 1885 (reworked after 1900). Plaster in marble basin, 8½ x 6⅛ x 5⅞ in. (21.6 x 15.6 x 14.9 cm).
Inscribed: *Rodin*. Gift of Alma de Bretteville Spreckels, 1949.17

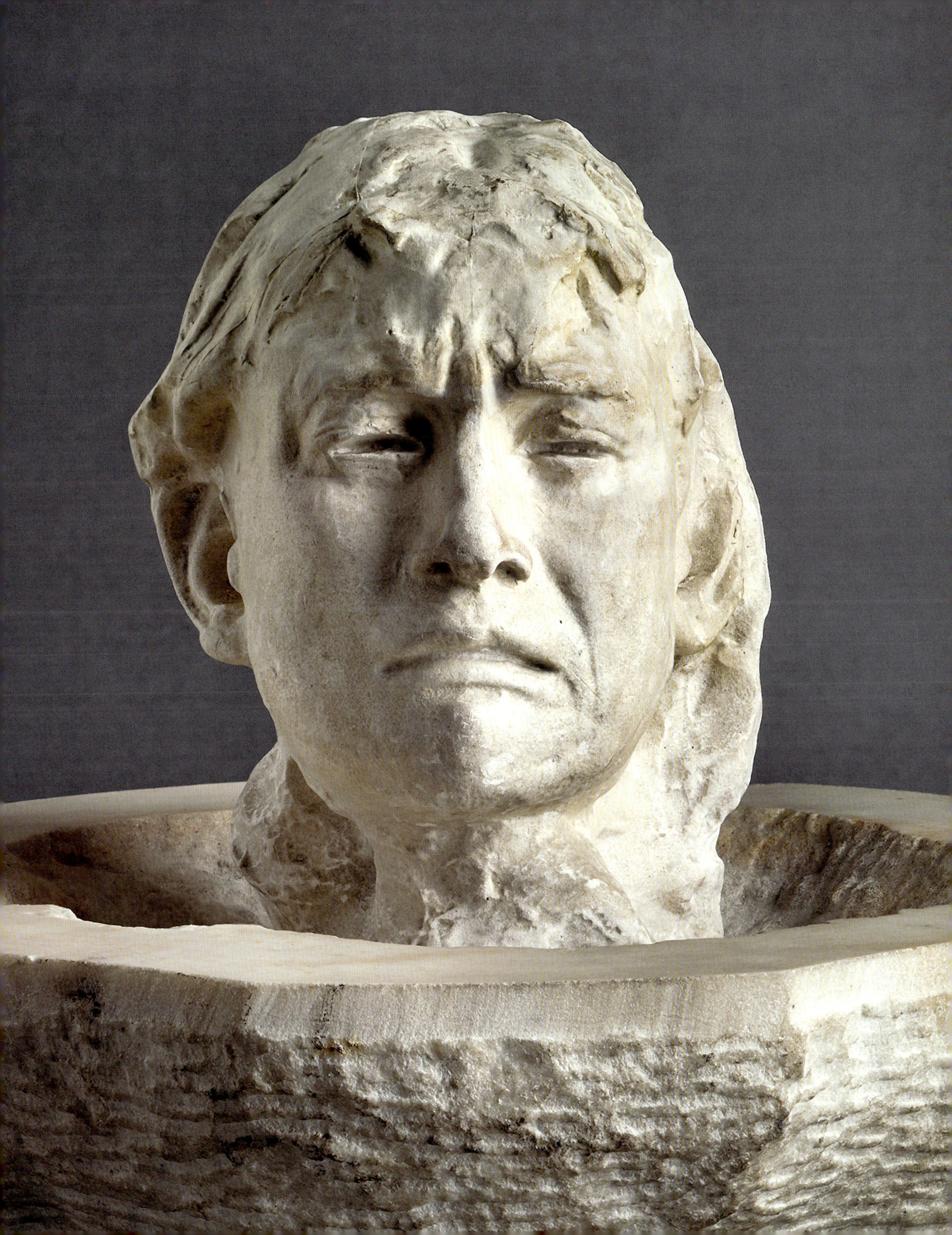

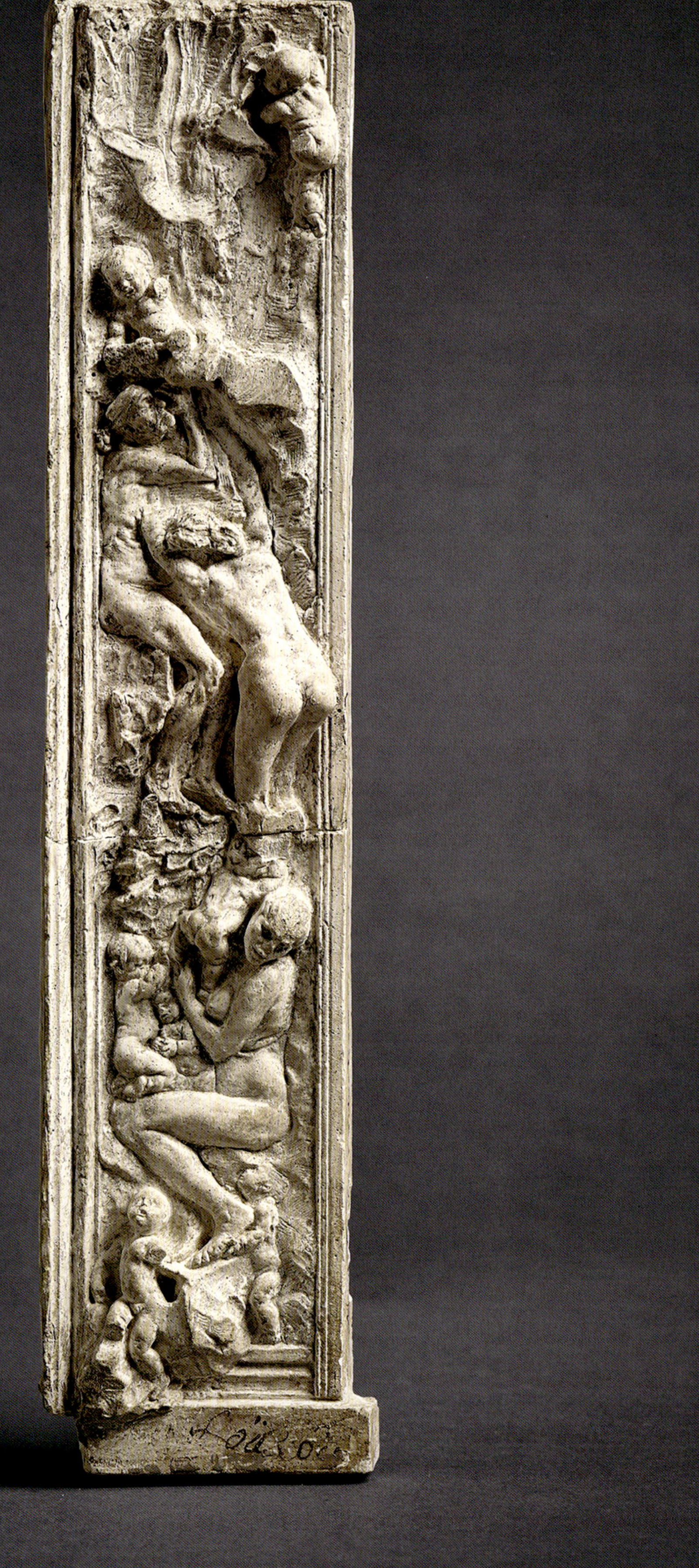

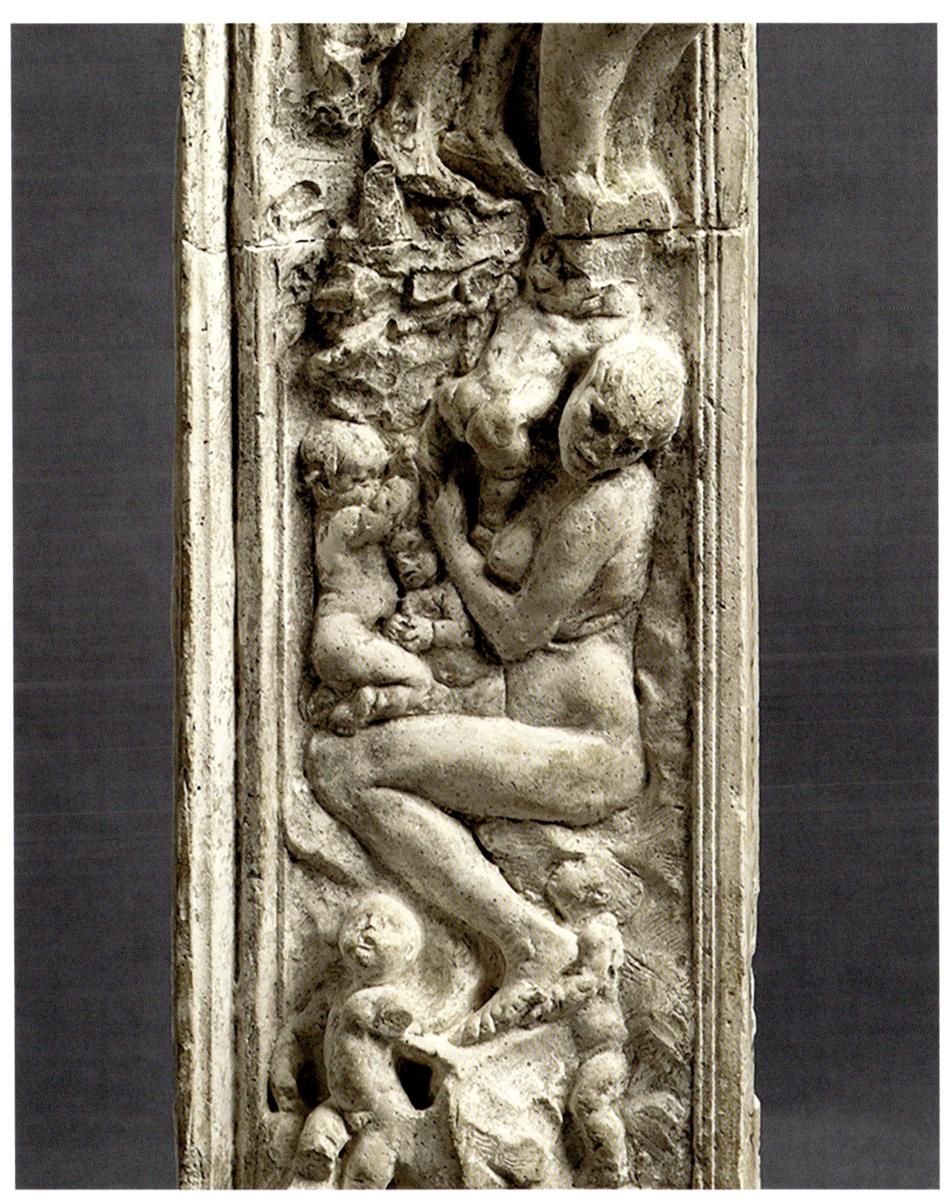

22. *Fragment Showing the* Gates of Hell, ca. 1886 (reduced ca. 1900). Plaster, 11 ⅛ x 2 ½ x 1 in. (28.2 x 6.4 x 2.5 cm).
Inscribed in ink: (*Original*) *Modéle* [*sic*] *d'après la reduction* [*sic*] *Guiochè* [*sic*] *mouleur* and *Modèle en réduction exécuté par*
Mon Père Henri Le Bossé R. Le. Bossé and *L'aurore*. Gift of Adolph B. Spreckels, Jr., 1933.12.21

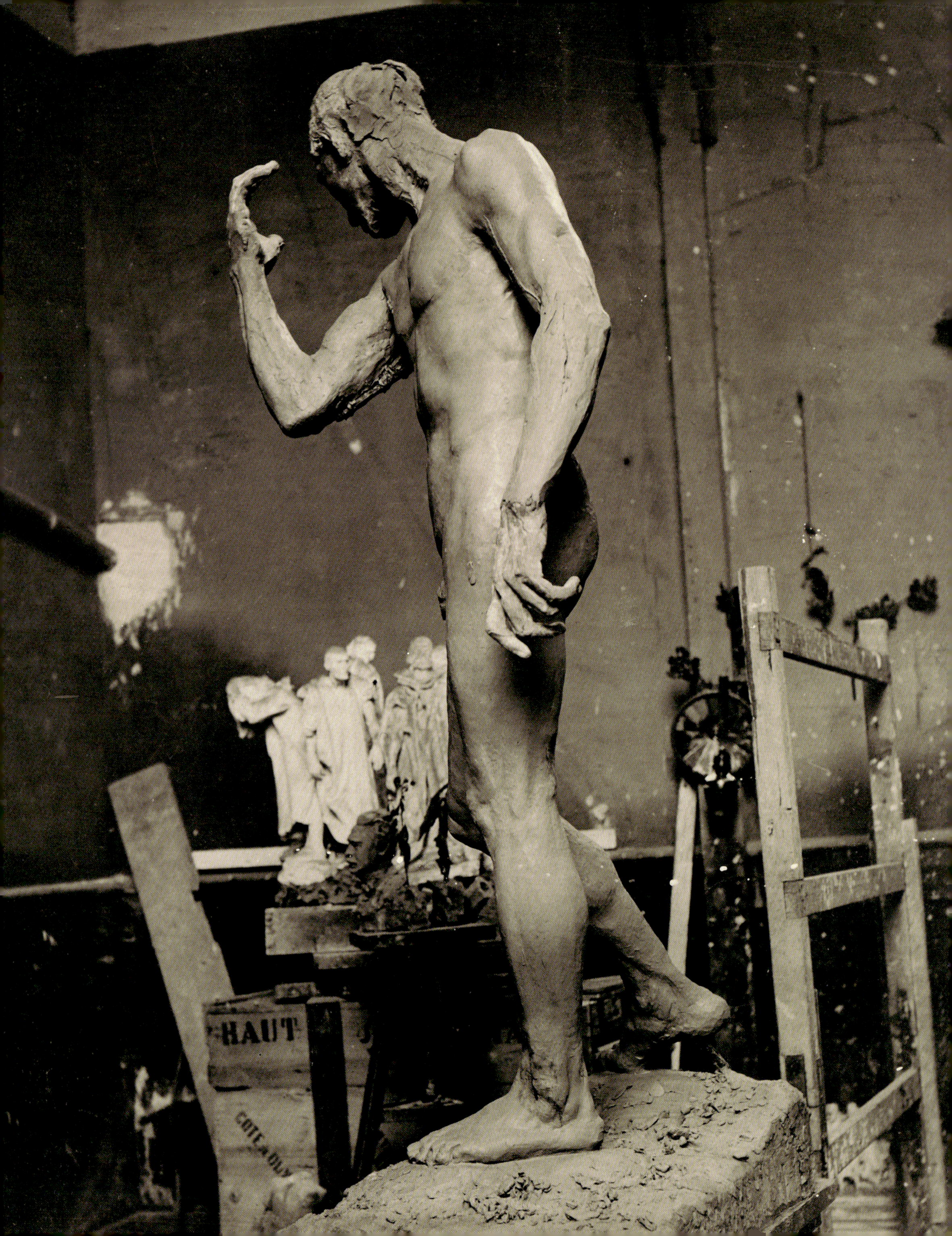
HAUT

4

THE BURGHERS OF CALAIS
A Monument in Reduction
(1884–1895)

One of Rodin's most famous monuments, *The Burghers of Calais* (pls. 23–30), was commissioned by the mayor of Calais, in northern France, to commemorate the sacrifice and patriotism of townsmen in 1347, during the Hundred Years' War. England's King Edward had offered to spare the starving, besieged city if its top leaders would surrender themselves to him. Rodin's monument portrays the six barefoot burghers with the keys to the city and ropes around their necks. His figures express their self-sacrifice as well as their internal anguish. As with so much of Rodin's work, this piece, too, became embroiled in controversy. It was criticized at the time for not being heroic enough, and the first cast of 1895 was placed, contrary to Rodin's wishes, on a high pedestal in the city's public park. Today, it is positioned as the sculptor intended, on a low base in front of Calais's city hall, where viewers can encounter the figures more directly.

The Legion holds five of the six figures in reduced-scale versions. These works provide an opportunity to view closely how Rodin expressed each subject's unique response to his fate—such as the plodding and forlorn figure of Eustache de Saint-Pierre, the downward-facing Pierre de Wiessant with his right arm raised in despair, and the stoic Jean d'Aire with his enormous hands and feet. The museum also possesses a plaster of the figure of Jean d'Aire that is dated 1906 when it was given to Loïe Fuller, and a plaster of the head of Pierre de Wiessant from about 1886 that is one of the few casts of this particular iteration. All of the *Burghers* were acquired from Rodin's founder Eugène Rudier, and records show that Alma Spreckels bought the reductions from Rudier in 1929 and then gave them to the museum officially in 1941. [xix]

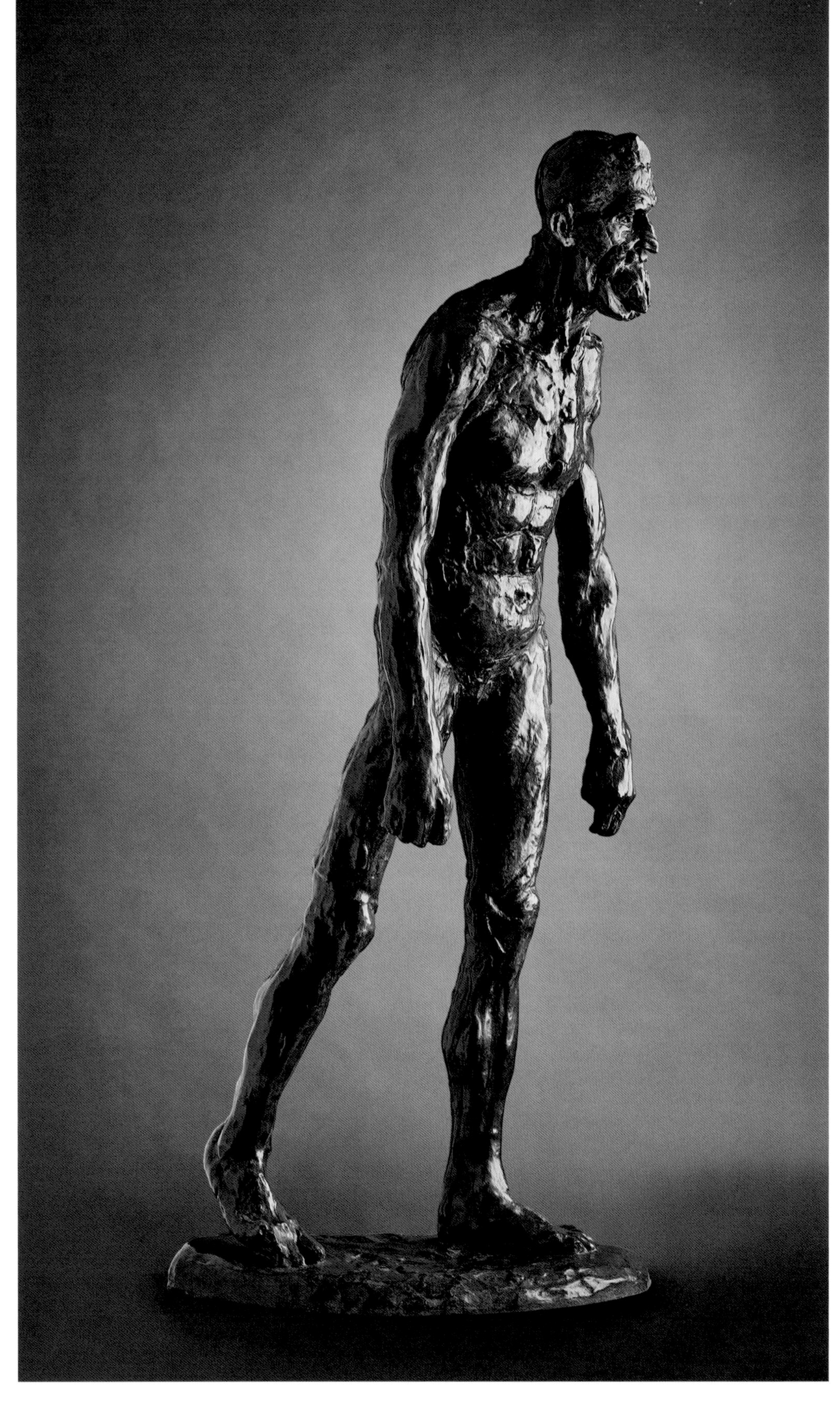

23. *Nude Study of Eustache de Saint-Pierre*, ca. 1885–1886 (cast 1965). Bronze, 38½ x 12½ x 15 in. (97.8 x 31.8 x 38.1 cm).
Inscribed: *A Rodin / No. 4* and *Georges Rudier / Fondeur. Paris* and © *by Musée Rodin 1965*. Gift of B. Gerald Cantor, 1968.7

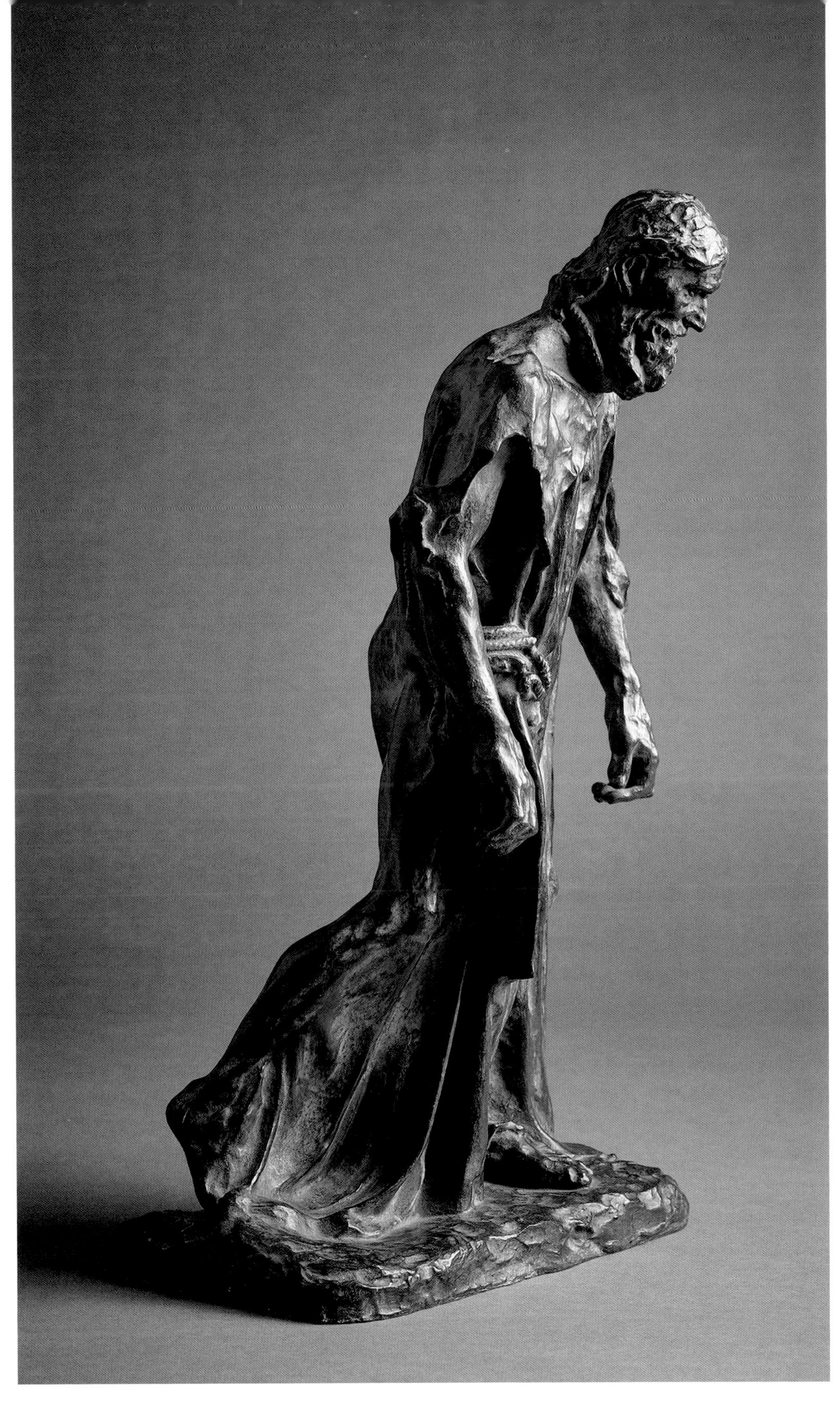

24. *Eustache de Saint-Pierre*, 1887 (reduced 1902, cast before 1929). Bronze, 18 ⅝ x 14 ½ x 8 ⅛ in. (47.3 x 36.8 x 20.6 cm).
Inscribed: *A. Rodin* and *ALEXIS RUDIER. FONDEUR PARIS.*
Gift of Alma de Bretteville Spreckels, 1941.34.12

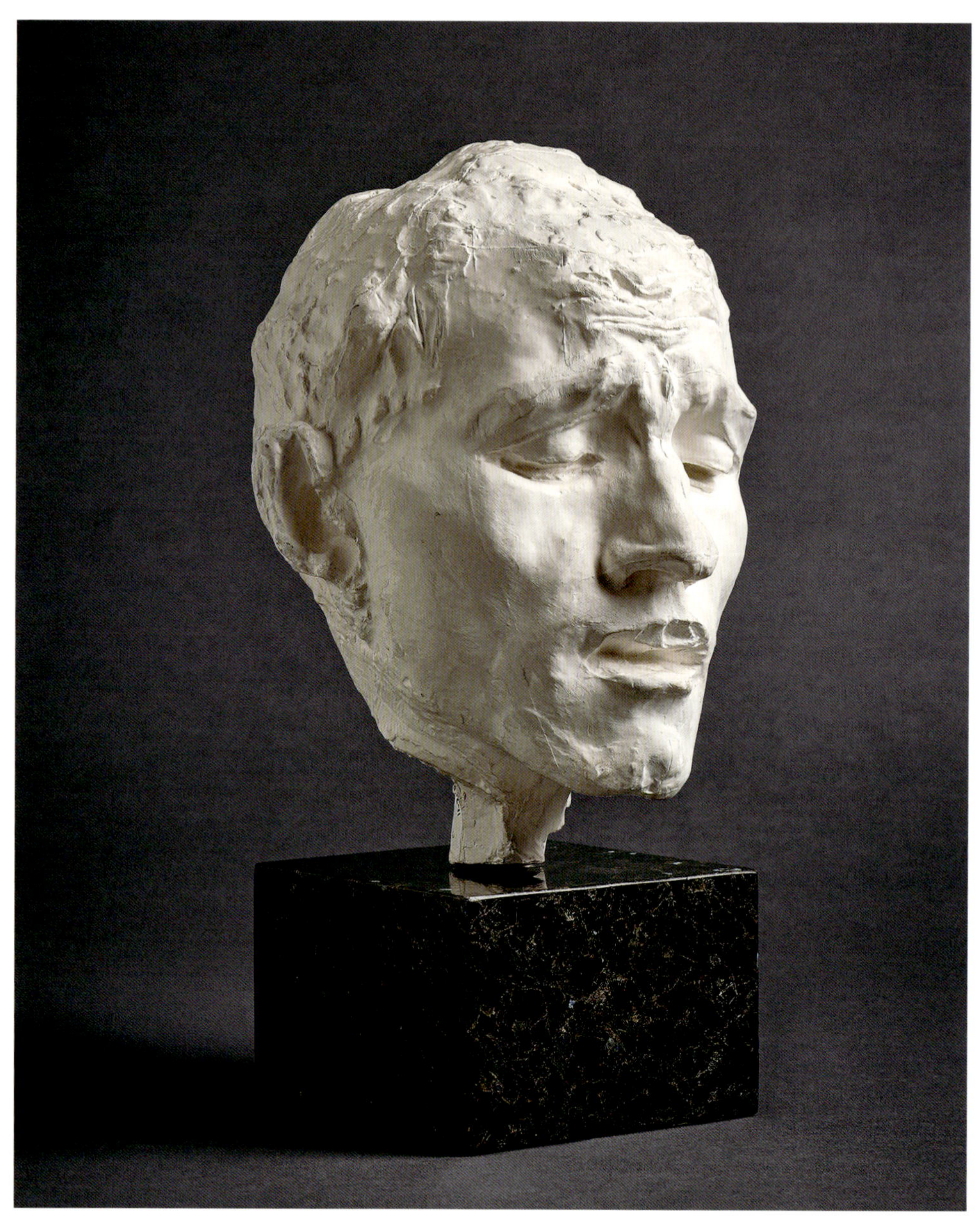

25. *Head of Pierre de Wiessant*, ca. 1886. Plaster, 11 ⅜ x 8 ⅝ x 9 ⅝ in. (28.9 x 21.9 x 24.3 cm).
Gift of Adolph B. Spreckels, Jr., 1933.12.11

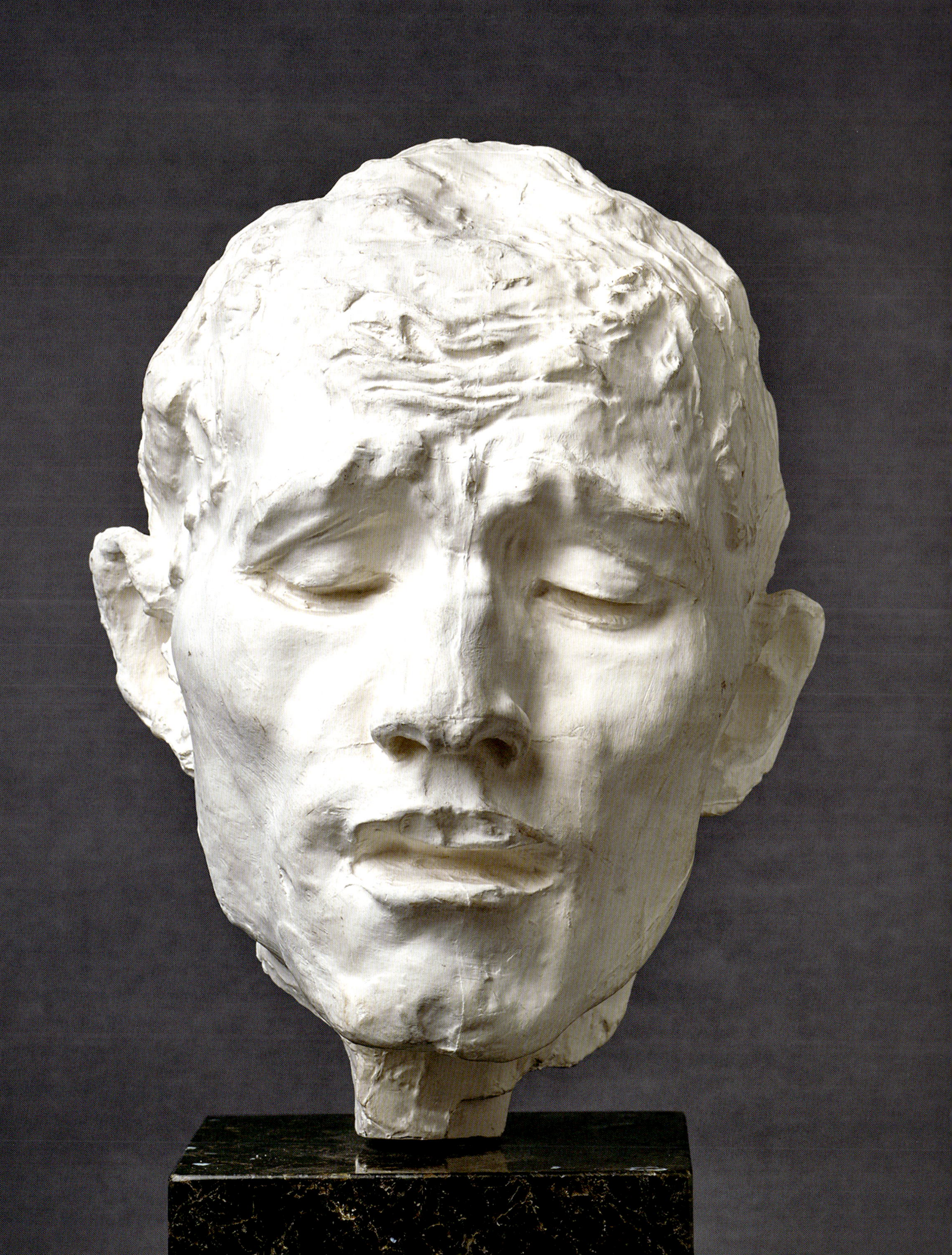

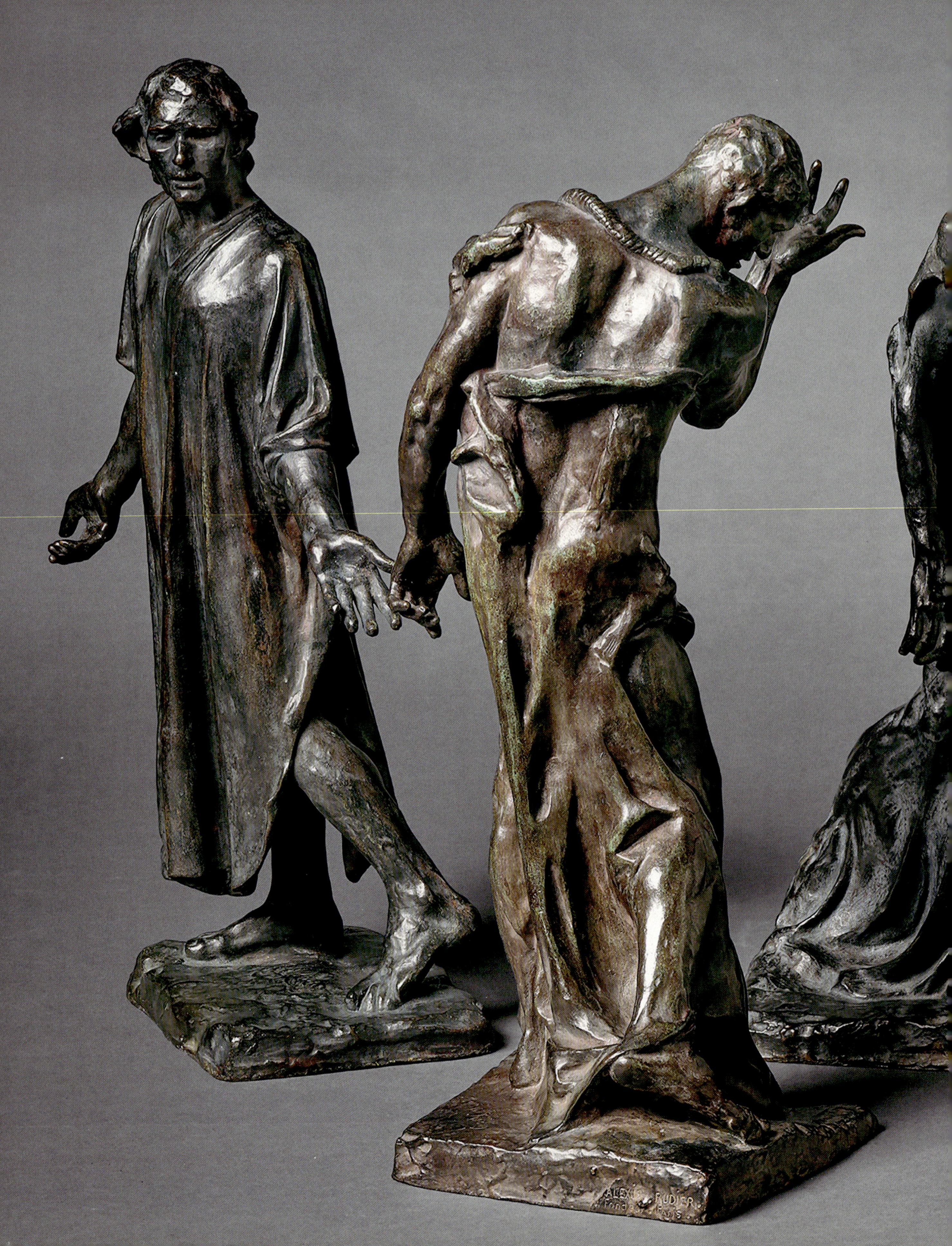

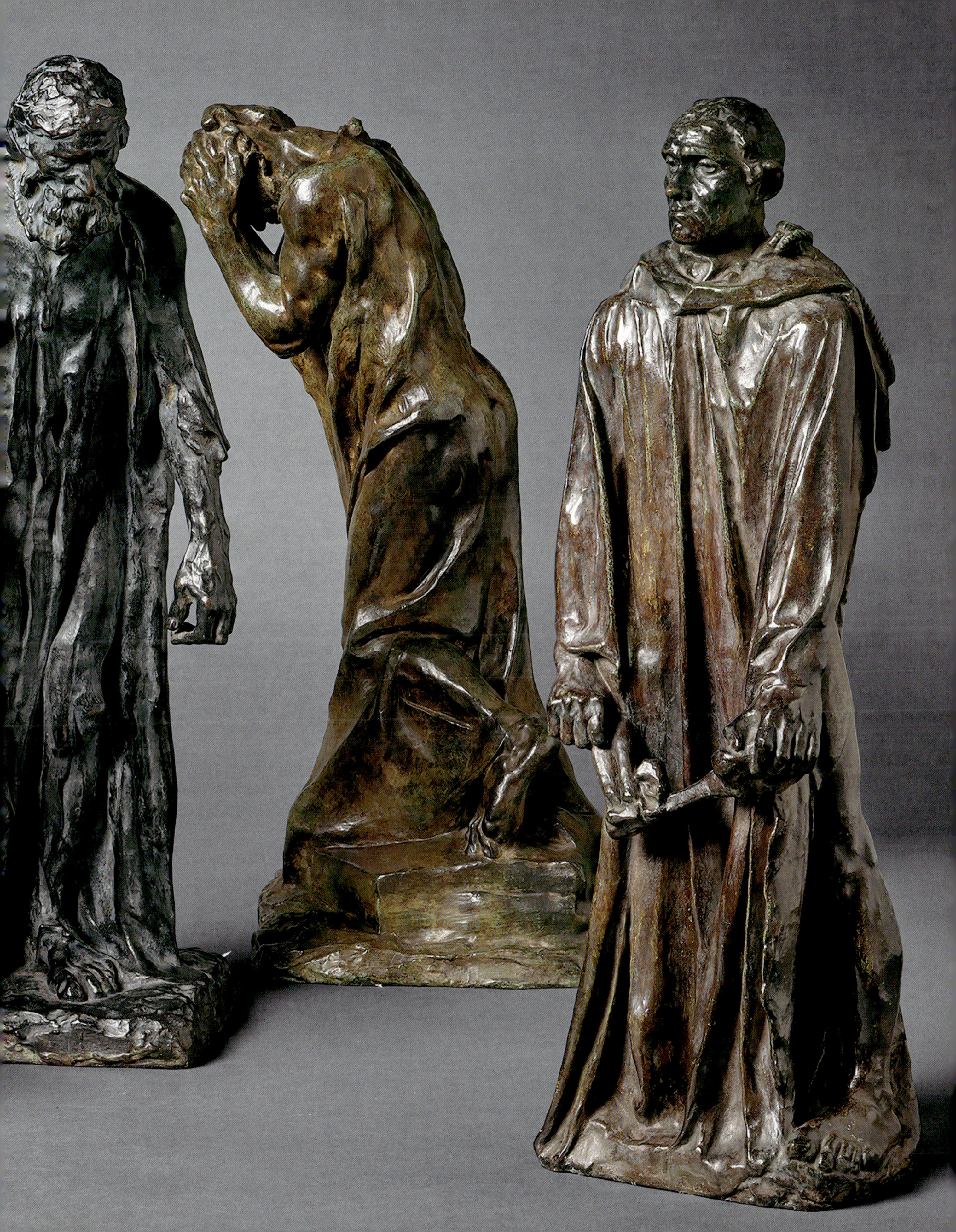

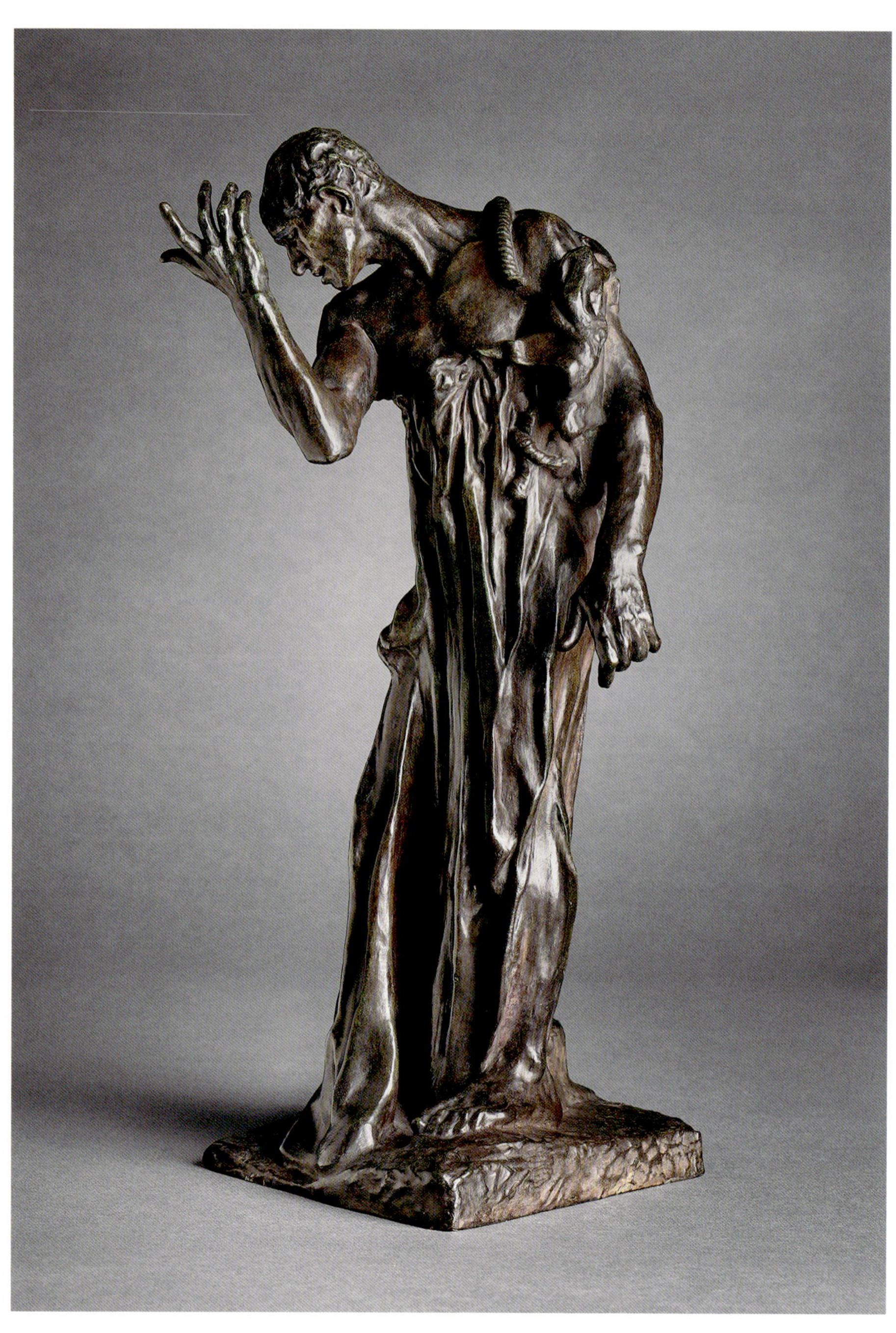

26. *Pierre de Wiessant*, 1886 (reduced 1886, cast before 1929). Bronze, 17 ¾ x 9 x 9 in. (45.1 x 22.7 x 22.7 cm).
Inscribed: *A. Rodin* and *ALEXIS. RUDIER. / FONDEUR. PARIS.*
Gift of Alma de Bretteville Spreckels, 1941.34.15

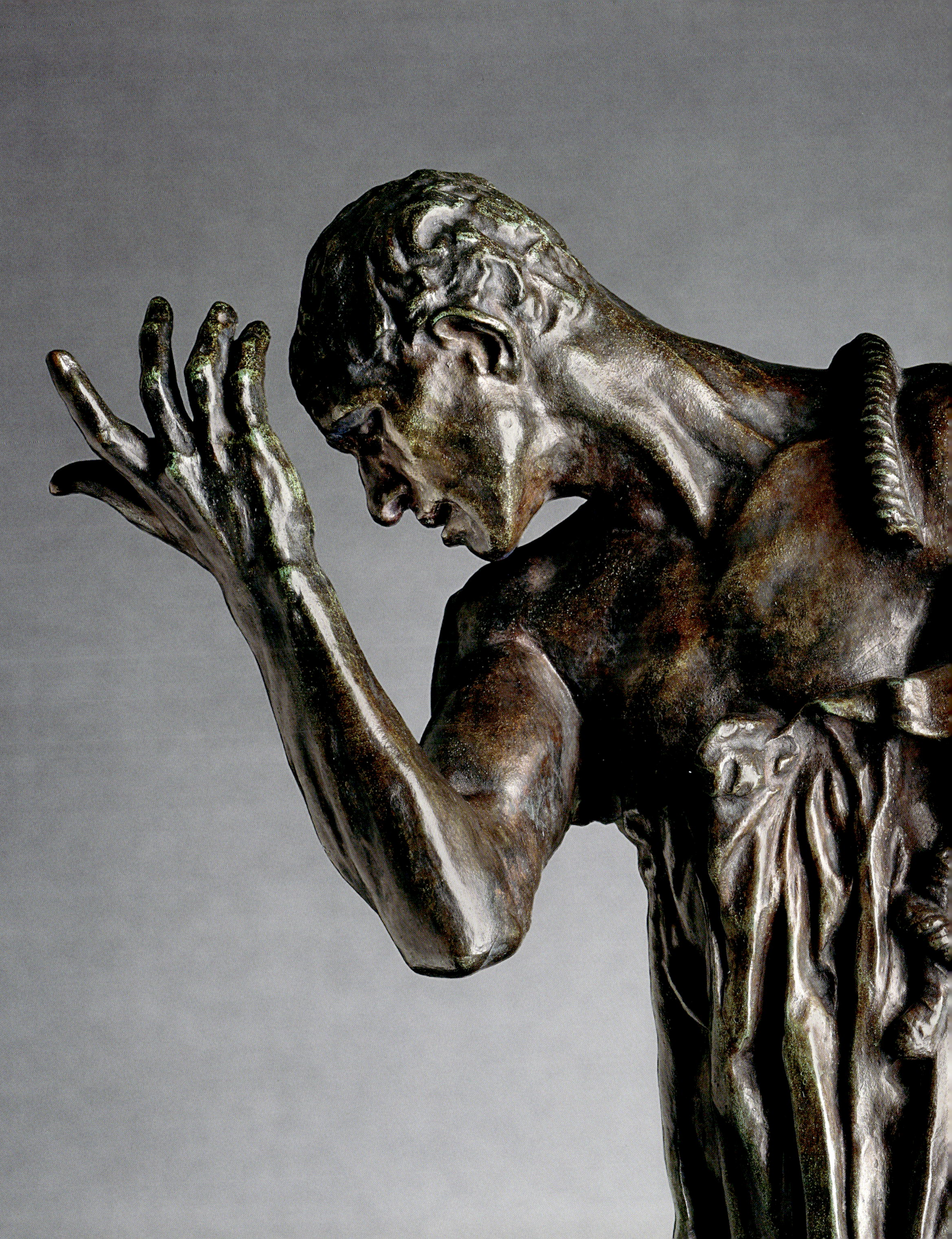

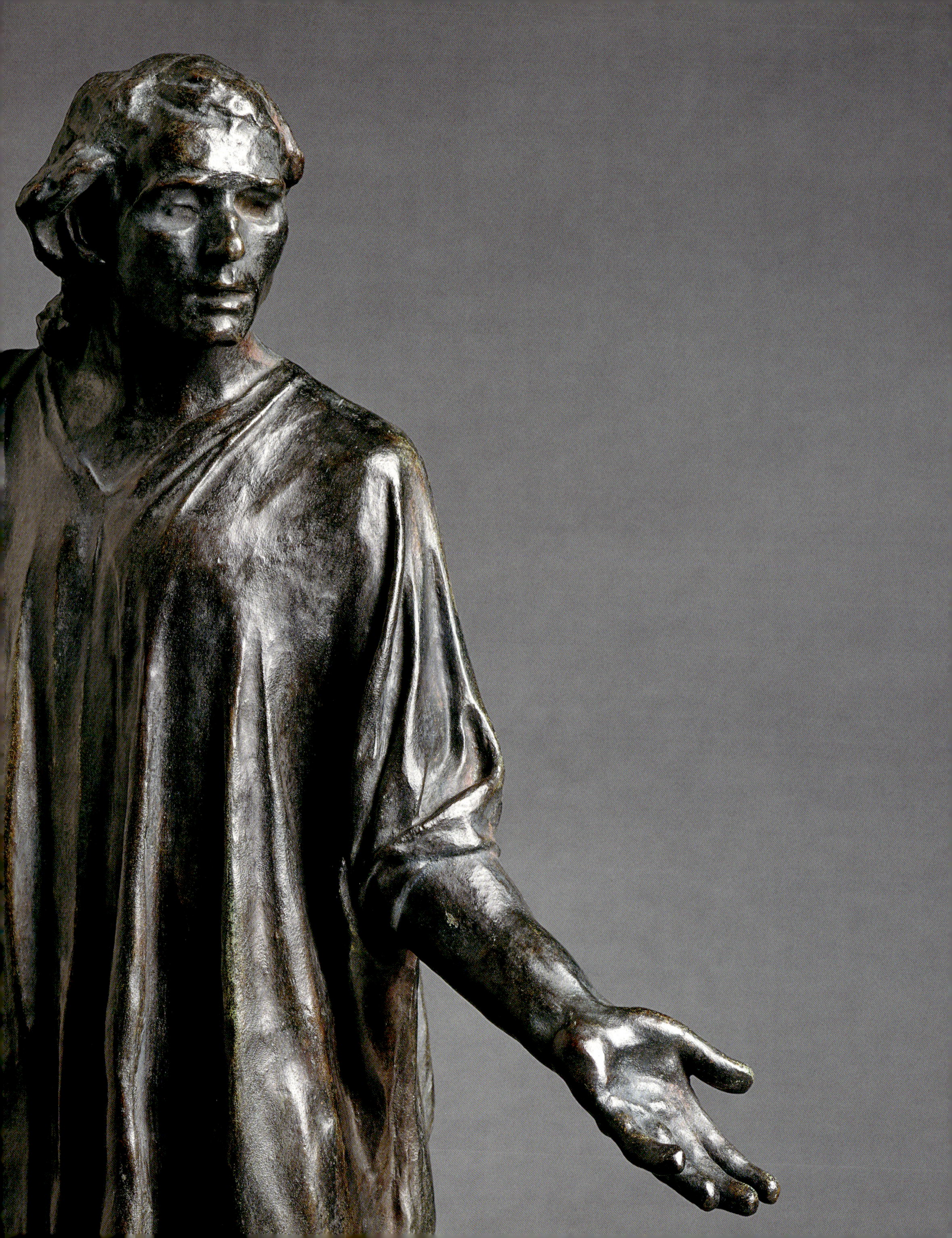

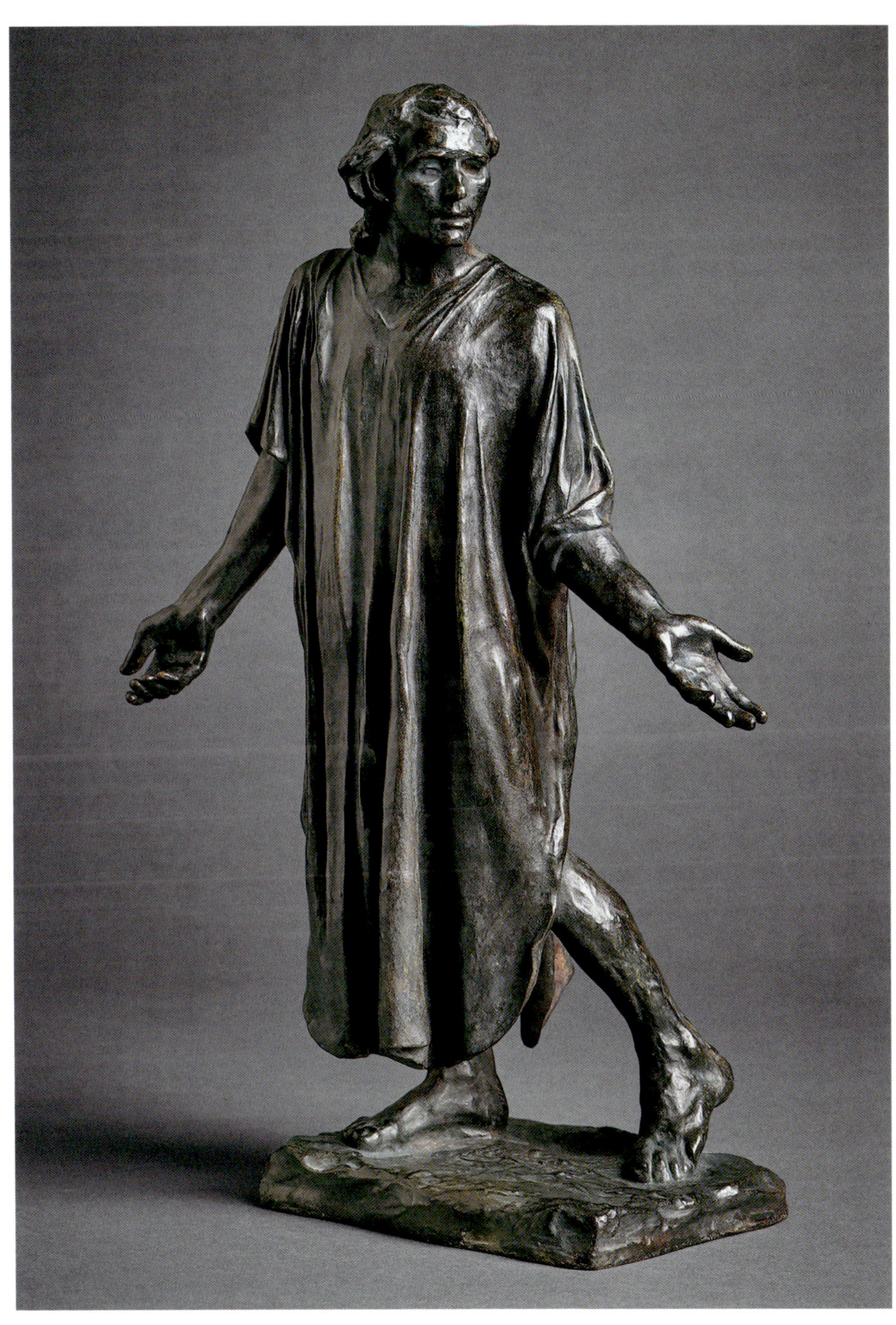

27. *Jean de Fiennes*, ca. 1887 (reduced 1899, cast before 1929). Bronze, 18 ⅛ x 11 ⅜ x 6 ⅜ in. (46 x 28.9 x 16.2 cm).
Inscribed: *A. Rodin* and *Alexis Rudier. / Fondeur Paris.*
Gift of Alma de Bretteville Spreckels, 1941.34.11

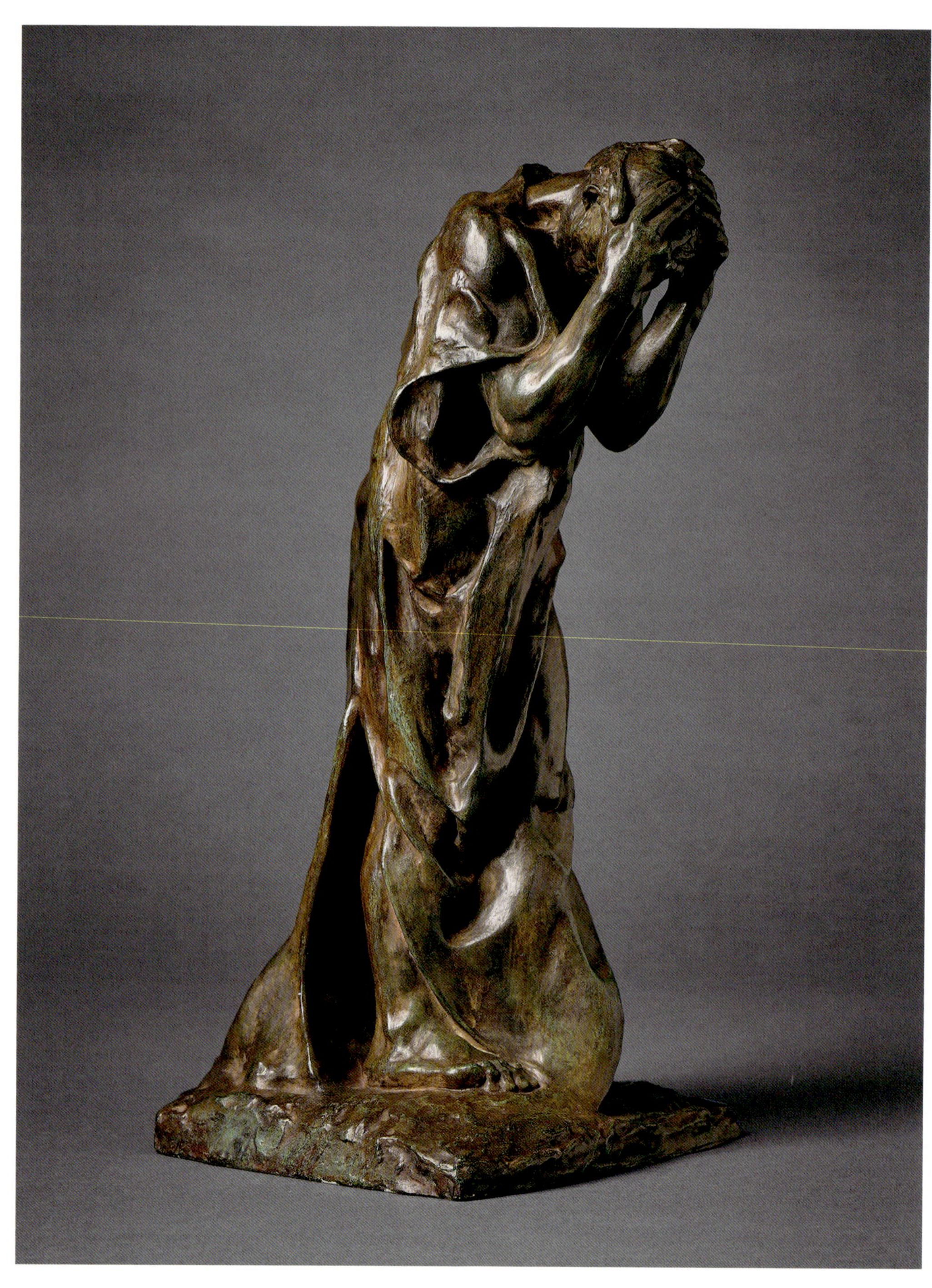

28. *Andrieu d'Andres*, 1888 (reduced 1900, cast before 1929). Bronze, 16 x 8⅝ x 9¾ in. (40.5 x 21.9 x 24.8 cm).
Inscribed: *A. Rodin* and *ALEXIS. RUDIER. FONDEUR PARIS.* Gift of Alma de Bretteville Spreckels, 1941.34.14

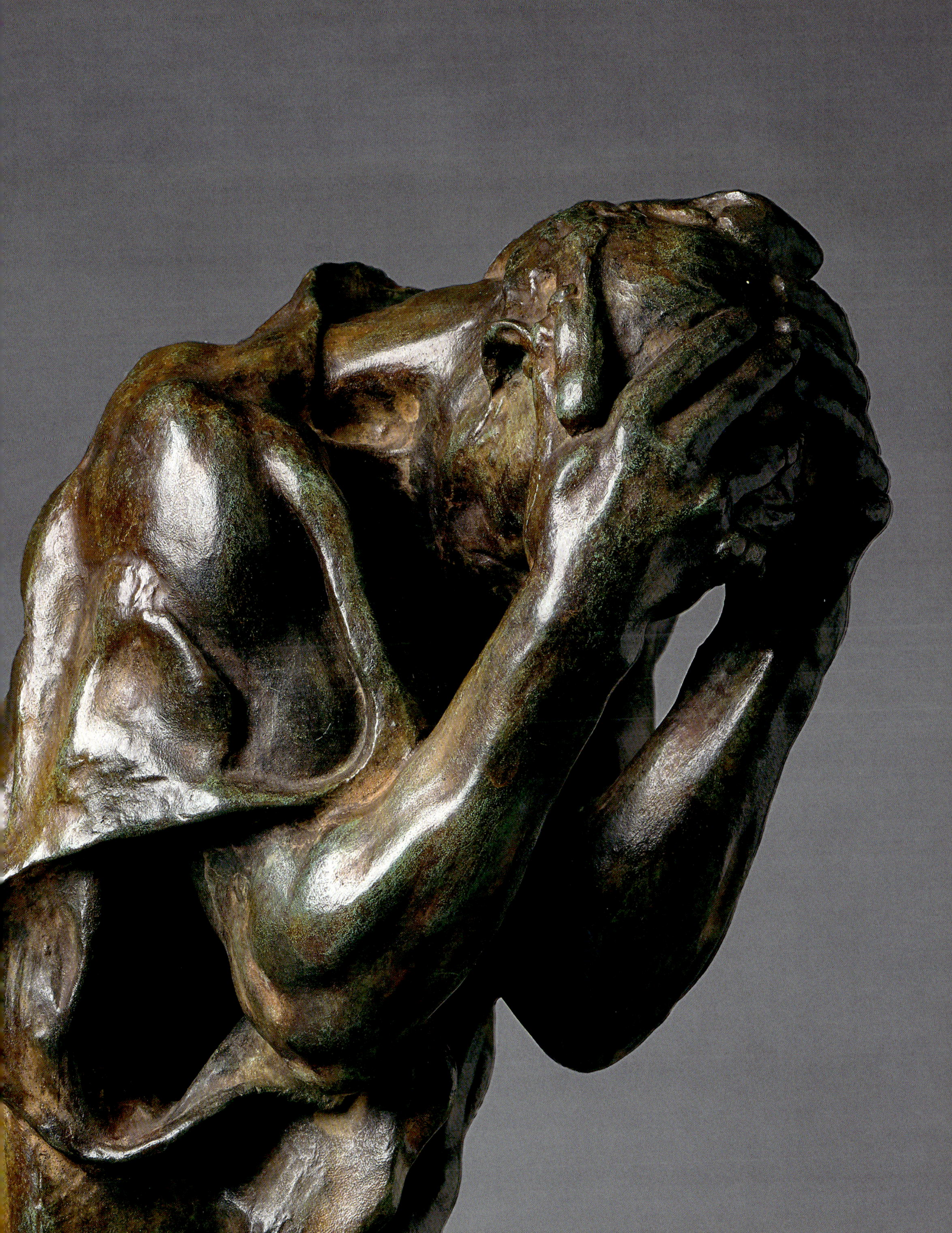

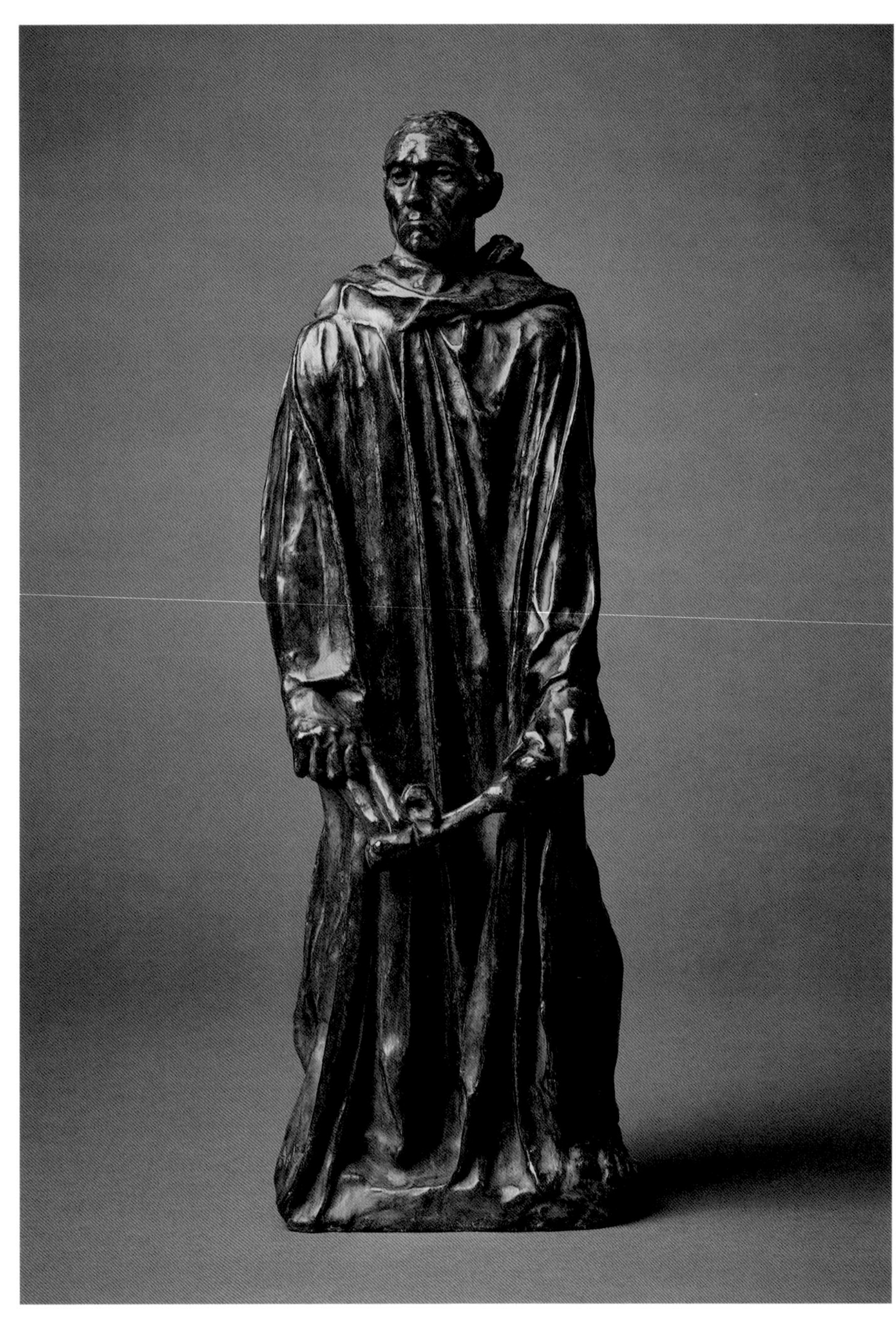

29. *Jean d'Aire*, 1887 (reduced 1895, cast before 1929). Bronze, 18 ⅜ x 6 ¾ x 6 ⅛ in. (46.7 x 17.1 x 15.7 cm).
Inscribed: *A. Rodin* and *Alexis. Rudier. / Fondeur. Paris.*
Gift of Alma de Bretteville Spreckels, 1941.34.13

30. *Jean d'Aire*, 1887. Plaster, 18 ⅝ x 6 ⅜ x 5 ¾ in. (47.1 x 16.3 x 14.6 cm).
Inscribed: *à loïe / Rodin* and *1906* [date given to Loïe Fuller]. Gift of Adolph B. Spreckels, Jr., 1933.12.1

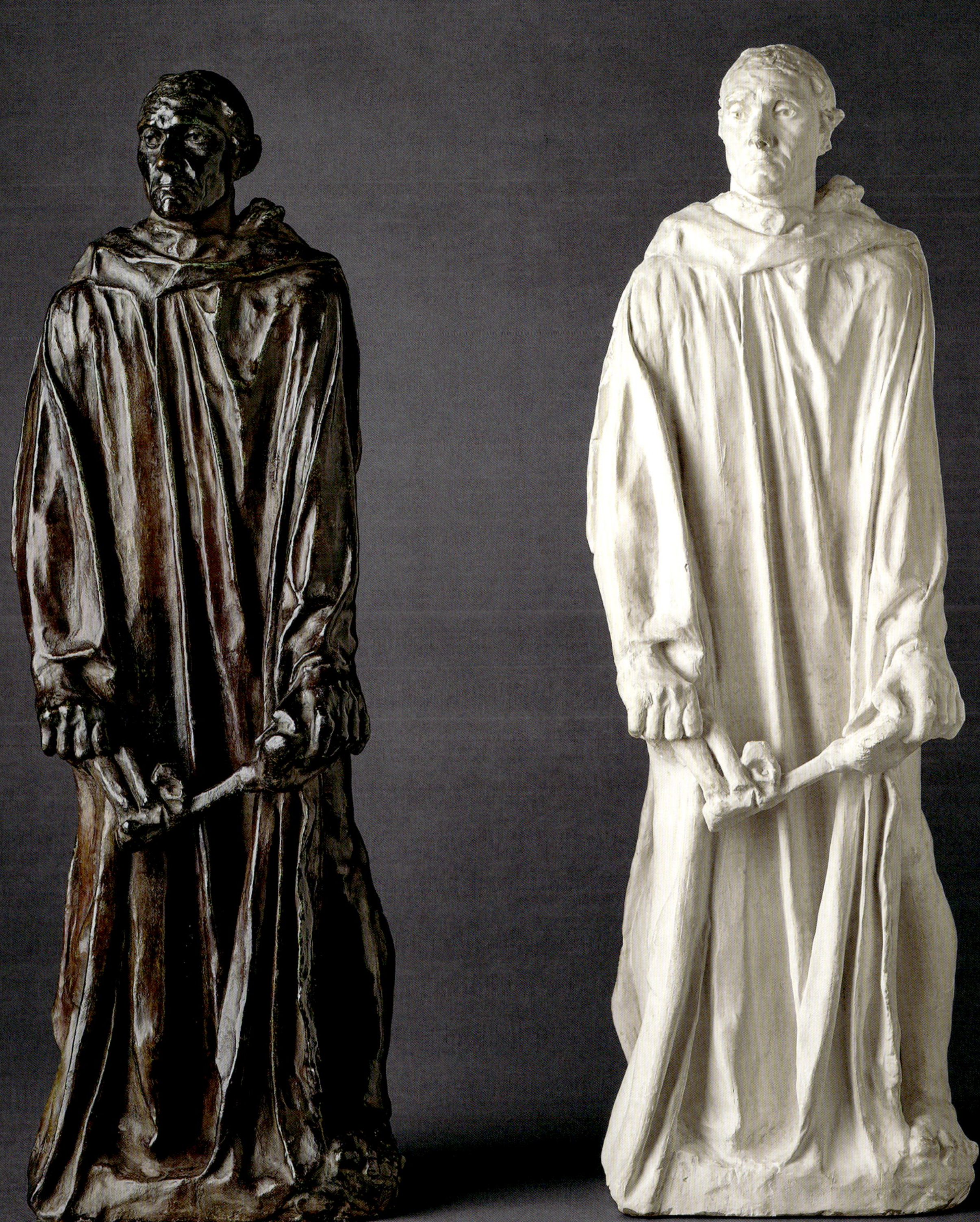

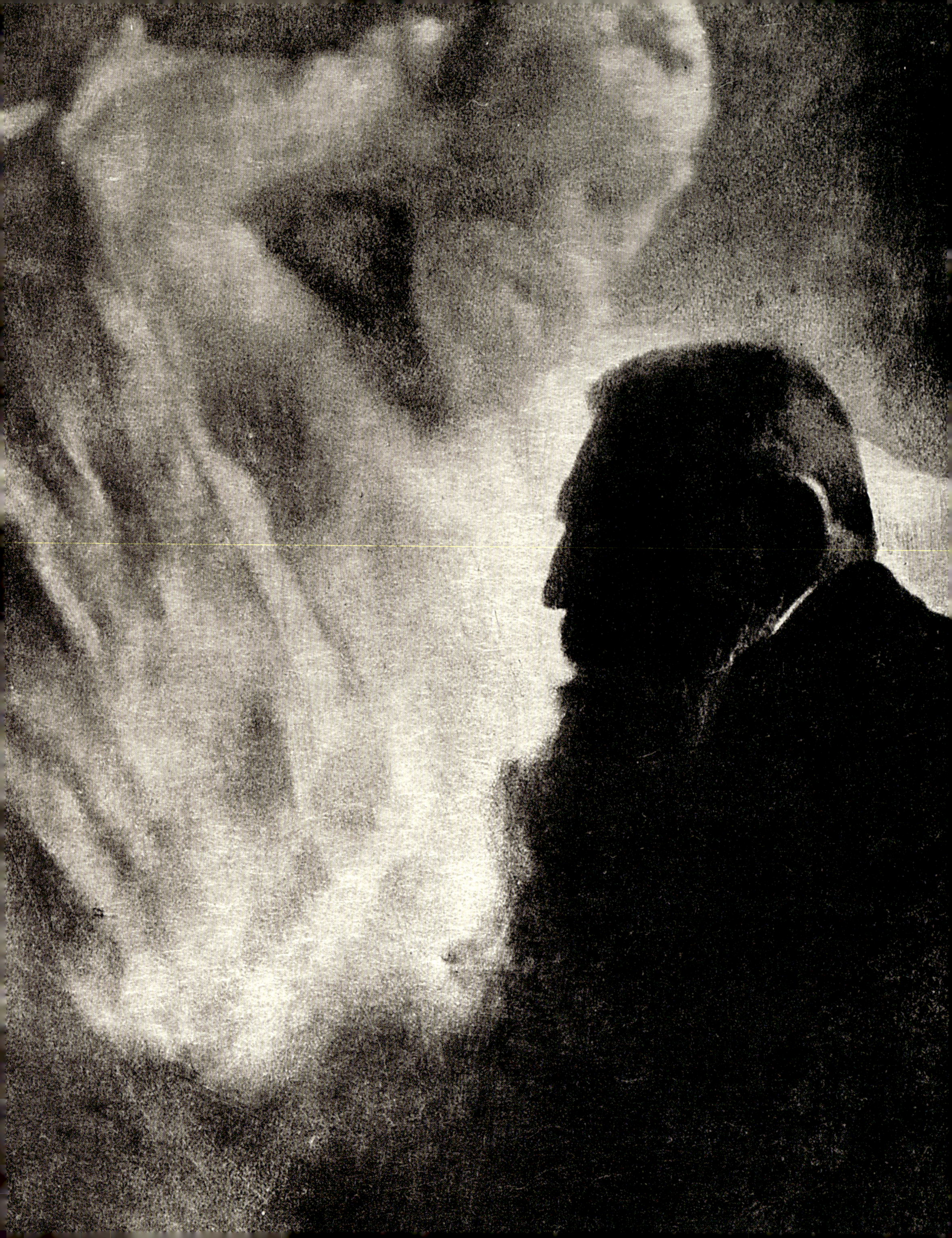

5

PORTRAITS
From Personal to Public Images
(1864–1917)

As Rodin became more successful, he received prominent portrait commissions. His more ambitious works in this genre, however, were the ones that he executed for his own interests and that expanded his own horizons as a sculptor. *Mignon* (pl. 31) portrays his lifetime companion and eventual wife, Rose Beuret (French, 1844–1917) as the Romantic character from a novel by Johann Wolfgang von Goethe (German, 1749–1832), with unruly hair, parted lips, and an angry, hurt expression in her eyes—perhaps reflecting the tension in their relationship due to Rodin's relationships with other women. His attachment to Camille Claudel (French, 1864–1943), a highly talented young sculptor who worked as the artist's assistant from 1885, led to the most famous and stormy of his love affairs. This relationship was more fulfilling for Rodin than others because, along with being lovers, the two sculptors inspired each other artistically. Unfortunately, Claudel became mentally unstable and separated from Rodin in 1893; she was committed to a mental institution in 1913, where she lived for thirty years until her death. Rodin's plaster *Head of Mademoiselle Camille Claudel* (pl. 32) is rendered in a direct and spontaneous manner, and shows the young artist in a bandeau with a large blob over one of her eyes. Such misshapen features remained uncorrected by Rodin, who liked to maintain elements of the accidental in his work. Working closely together in the 1880s, Claudel modeled for Rodin, and depictions of her head are featured in many of his larger projects, including figures in the *Gates of Hell*, *The Eternal Idol* (1891), and *La France* (1907–1908). Claudel sculpted only one portrait of Rodin (fig. 20). Although she began the work from life studies, it was abandoned for many years and the final piece, which captures Rodin's features in an intense, powerful, and highly personal manner, was apparently completed from her memory.

In 1883, when Rodin was first encouraged by the author Edmond Bazire (French, 1846–1892) to portray famous people he admired, the sculptor pursued the writer Victor Hugo (French, 1802–1885; fig. 21) and the revolutionary politician and journalist Henri Rochefort (French, 1831–1913) to sit for him.[xx] Hugo was reluctant and eventually refused to sit for the artist, so his portrait, made partly from memory, is more idealized than is typical of Rodin's work (pl. 33). The piece was very successful, however, and Rodin made multiple versions of it. In the second iteration, the same bronze bust is taken from its socle and inserted into a drilled block of marble, showing the artist's interest in the relationship between a sculpture and its pedestal (pl. 34).

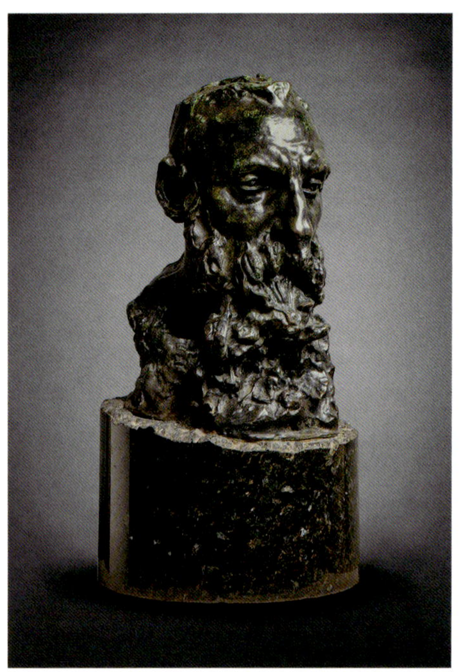

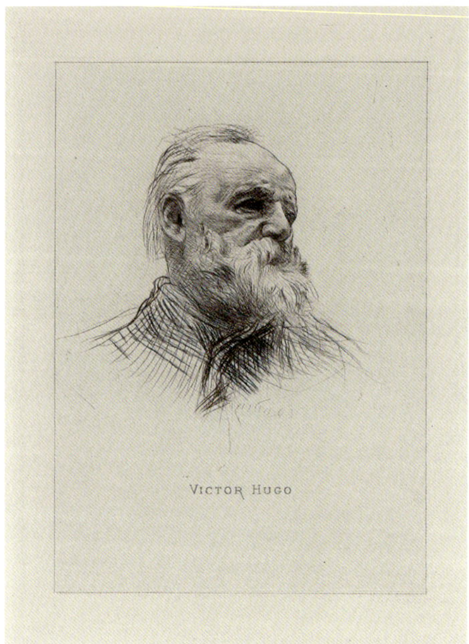

As popular interest in Hugo grew after his death in 1885, Rodin was commissioned in 1889 by the French state to create a monument to the writer. This project led to the undertaking of two public works and, toward the end of Rodin's career, the creation of the larger-than-life-size marble portrait that is housed in the Legion's collection (pl. 41). Based on the earlier portraits of Hugo, this highly dramatic bust is captured within a grand unfinished marble block, in the manner of Michelangelo's "unfinished" *Slaves* or *Captives* of the 1520s to 1534.

Rodin portrayed the flamboyant and controversial figure Henri Rochefort, who was exiled several times for his political agitation, with an intense, challenging gaze (pl. 35). Rochefort, like Hugo, was dismayed by the artist's slow working methods and abandoned the sittings before the bust was completed, which may account for the contrast between his highly finished face shown deep in thought and the sketchiness of his coat and shock of wavy hair. Regardless, Rodin was pleased with the result and even thought it superior to *The Age of Bronze*. [xxi] Declaring that the piece surpassed ancient sculpture, Rodin later stated, "I have never found the Latin classic type as pure as in Rochefort." [xxii]

As his international reputation grew in the early 1900s, Rodin received many portrait commissions, including those of English society figures. He met the Yorkshire beauty Eve Fairfax (British, 1871–1978; fig. 23) in 1901, when her fiancé, Ernest Beckett, commissioned the artist to sculpt her portrait prior to their marriage. [xxiii] Rodin was fascinated by Fairfax, and she sat for him many times in Paris between 1901 and 1909. Although he was never paid for the commission, Rodin made several busts of Fairfax "out of the same [block of] marble," [xxiv] perhaps because she struck him as "a woman who resembles in expression as well as in form, one of the faces of Michelangelo." [xxv] Laced with strong Symbolist overtones in its melancholic and dreamlike expression, Rodin's unique portrayal of Fairfax in the Legion's collection is not a straightforward portrait (pl. 40). [xxvi] In this allegorical work, Fairfax's long braided tresses transform into large ears of wheat, which might refer to Ceres, the goddess of agriculture, who was often portrayed with the

Fig. 20 Camille Claudel, *Bust of Auguste Rodin*, 1886–1892 (cast ca. 1900). Bronze, 16 ¼ x 9 ¾ x 11 ¼ in. (41.3 x 24.8 x 28.6 cm). Inscribed: *Camille Claudel*. Fine Arts Museums of San Francisco, Gift of Alma de Bretteville Spreckels, 1968.26.7

Fig. 21 Auguste Rodin, *Victor Hugo*, 1885. Drypoint, 8 ¾ x 5 ⅞ in. (22.2 x 14.9 cm). Fine Arts Museums of San Francisco, Achenbach Foundation for Graphic Arts, 1963.30.1501

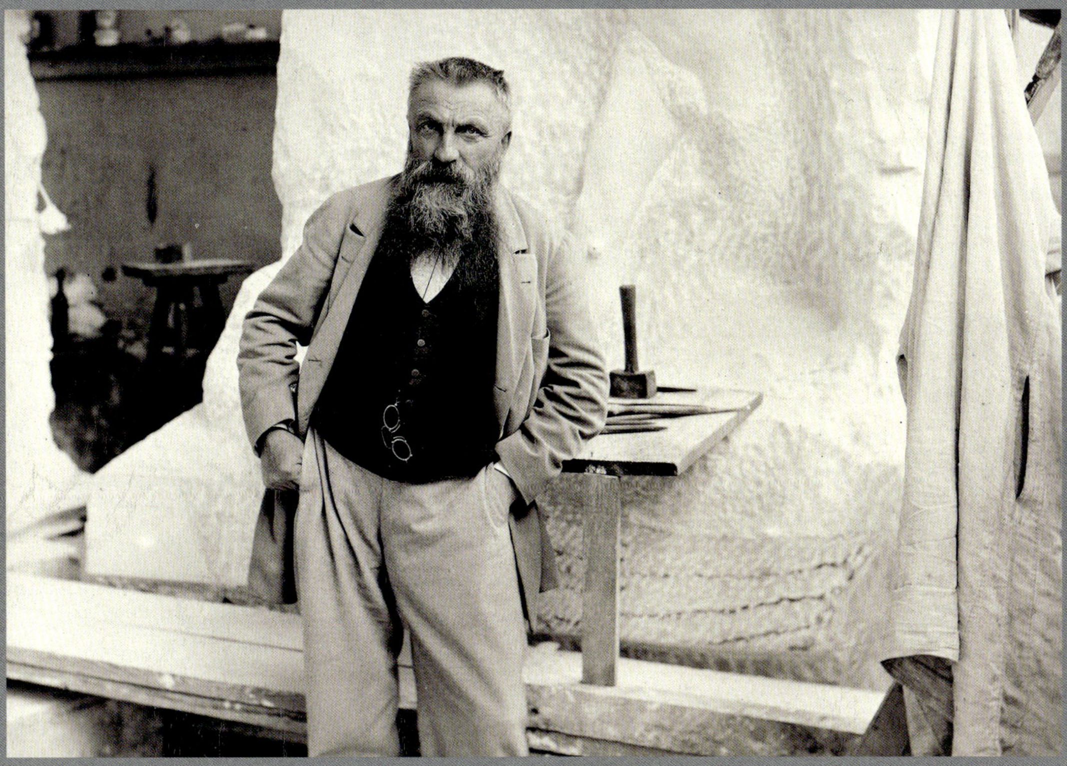

RODIN AND MARBLE

Marble is an important aspect of Rodin's mature work. In the nineteenth century it was regarded as the most elevated of media for sculpture due to its association with the academic tradition from the eighteenth century and stretching back through the Renaissance to classical antiquity; it was also the most monetarily valuable material in Rodin's time. Many of the sculptor's popular bronze models held in the Legion's collection, such as *The Kiss* and *The Hand of God* (before 1898), were also executed in marble. Rodin loved marble, admiring its use in ancient works and particularly in Michelangelo's sculptures. The French artist sought to emulate the refined finish of the snowy white marble employed in the Renaissance sculptor's output, and he intentionally left some of his pieces unfinished, reflecting the quality of Michelangelo's later works. However, because of the long process involved to carve, chisel, and finish a marble, Rodin did not execute these examples himself, but rather depended on the work of specialized craftsmen.[xxvii] This system problematized the attribution of Rodin's marbles by later generations, although today these objects are considered as relevant in the artist's oeuvre as the bronzes that he consigned to founders and other practitioners (see sidebar, p. 103, this volume). The carver of the dreamlike *Siren of the Sea* (pl. 11) has not been identified. The marble shows a strange fishlike woman depicted as she emerges from the waters. Lacking a bronze counterpart, it is the primary version of this composition and was acquired by Alma Spreckels from the group brought by Loïe Fuller to the PPIE in 1915.[xxviii] Other significant marbles in the collection are *La Nature, Miss Eve Fairfax* (pl. 40) and the *Bust of Victor Hugo* (pl. 41).

———
Fig. 22 Pol Marsan Dornac, Rodin in front of *Monument to Sarminento*, 1898. Albumen print, 4 ⅞ x 7 ⅛ in. (12.5 x 18 cm). Musée Rodin, Paris, Ph.185

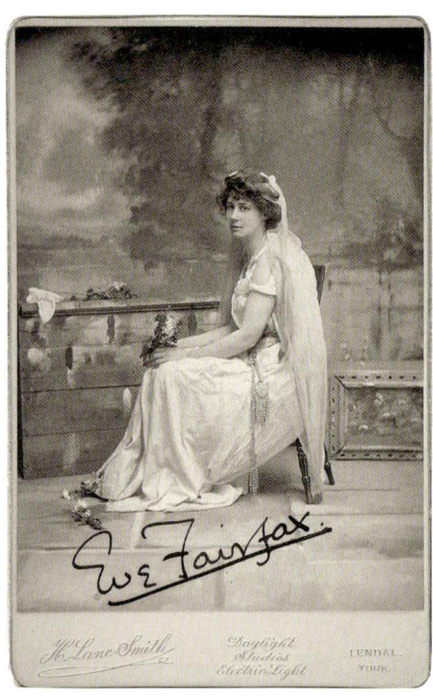

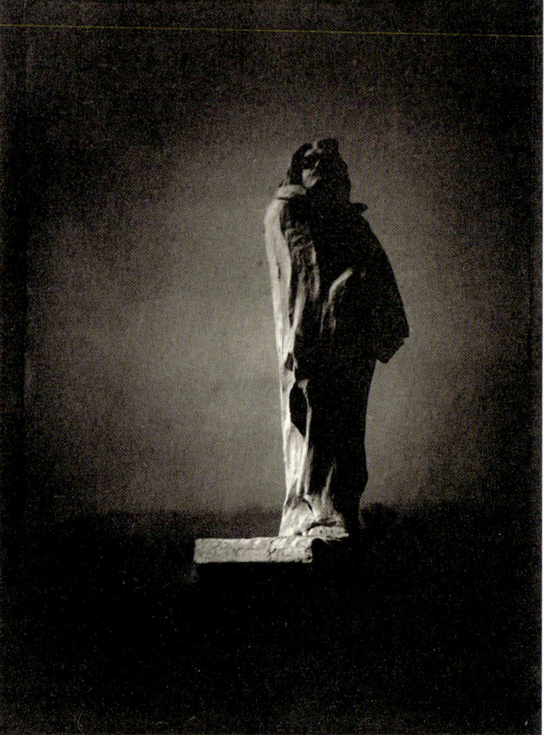

attributes of grain. In a rare but unsigned surviving note about the sculpture, presumably penned by Loïe Fuller, she claimed that she "watched the sculptor day after day putting on the finishing touches and when it was partly finished I found the lines so beautiful that I asked the master to leave it as it is today, so he agreed and left the lines as they are. This was in June 1916."[xxix] The sculpture, inscribed to Fuller by the artist, was acquired from the dancer by Alma Spreckels in the following year (pl. 40, detail).[xxx]

Rodin's project to create a monument to the writer Honoré de Balzac (French, 1799–1850) was the most ambitious and controversial of his career. Commissioned in 1891 by the Société des Gens de Lettres, Paris, and exhibited in 1898 at the Salon, the sculpture was rejected by the group. After studying Balzac's written works, Rodin produced an interpretation of the writer that was more psychological and abstracted than traditional portraiture. The piece created such a stir that other artists, including Paul Cézanne (French, 1839–1906), Claude Monet (French, 1840–1926), and Eugène Carrière (French, 1849–1906), voiced support of it, while more conservative factions decried it. The work's surprising absence of detail contrasted with its highly expressive face has given it the distinction of being the first truly modern piece of sculpture (fig. 24). The Legion holds two studies for the head of Balzac, one in plaster (pl. 36) and one in bronze (pl. 37). The plaster is mounted with Balzac's head tilted back as it is in the completed sculpture.

Fig. 23 H. Lane Smith, *Portrait of Eve Fairfax*, ca. 1905. Aristotype on matt collodion paper, 5 ⅝ x 4 ⅛ in. (14.3 x 10.4 cm). Musée Rodin, Paris, Ph.1620

Fig. 24 Edward Jean Steichen, *Rodin's Balzac*, 1908. Photogravure, 8 ¼ x 6 ¼ in. (21 x 15.9 cm). Fine Arts Museums of San Francisco, Museum purchase, George Fuchs Memorial Fund, 1994.85

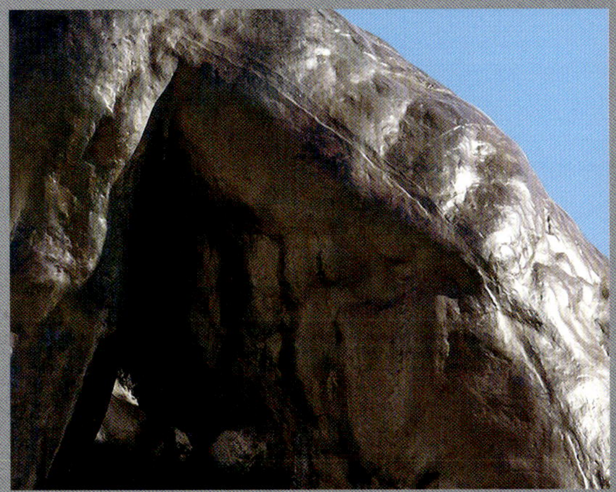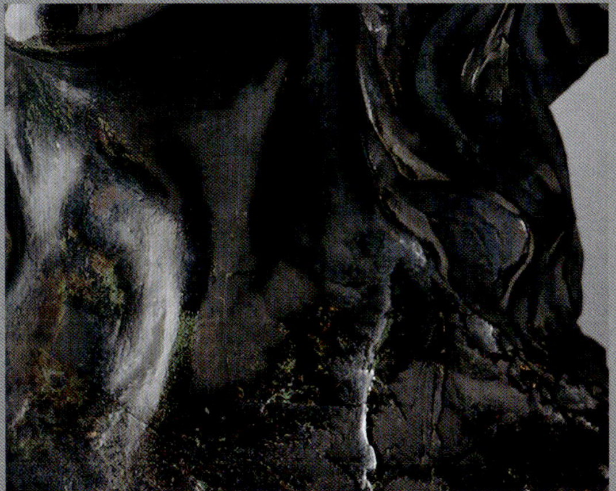

RODIN AND BRONZE

Of the two bronze-casting methods, lost wax and sand, Rodin preferred the latter, which was less expensive and gave him the results he desired. From about 1902, Rodin consigned most of his casts to Eugène Rudier (French, 1878–1952) of the foundry named for his father, Alexis Rudier (French, 1844–1897), who specialized in the sand-casting method. By 1917, more than five hundred casts were made by Rudier in the sand-casting method, including five casts of the monumental version of *The Thinker* (see pp. 53 and 56, this volume).[xxxi] In the sand-casting method a plaster model is covered in a slippery brown shellac substance so that the plaster can be easily released from the sand mold that is formed under it. The brown stain, which is evident on the Legion's plasters of *Eve* (pl. 14) and *Mother and Child* (pl. 42), signifies that these works were active models for casting bronzes. The molten bronze, heated in a crucible, is poured into the sand mold, which is contained within a box or frame. After the bronze cools, the piece is removed from the mold. Bronzes are usually cast in sections, to avoid undercuts or projections, and then the sections are soldered together to make a complete sculpture. This is the case for the Legion's *Thinker* and *Three Shades*, both of which have visible joins (fig. 25). After a cast is soldered together, it is filed to remove any extraneous bronze and then chased all over its surface to obtain the desired finish, whether rough or smooth. This technique is evident on the Legion's cast of *The Age of Bronze*, which has a very subtle and complex textured surface with bumps and pits to resemble human skin. A finished cast is then sent to a specialized patinator, who applies a variety of techniques to give the surface liveliness and color, ranging from a dark glossy brown to a coppery green. Rodin's favorite patinator from 1900 was Jean Limet (French, 1855–1941), who was also a photographer—he, in fact, used the same chemicals for both processes.[xxxii] Limet introduced unusual colors into his patinations, and he was doubtlessly responsible for the varied tints of orange, red, and turquoise found on the Legion's cast of *Mignon* (fig. 26). He also used copper acid to break a work's surface down to resemble an archeological bronze. This treatment can be seen on the "skin" of *Saint John the Baptist Preaching* (pl. 4). The wide range of effects of Limet's patination on many of the Legion's bronzes contribute to their characterful qualities and distinguish them from later casts.

Fig. 25 Detail of *The Thinker* (pl. 12)
Fig. 26 Detail of *Mignon* (pl. 31)

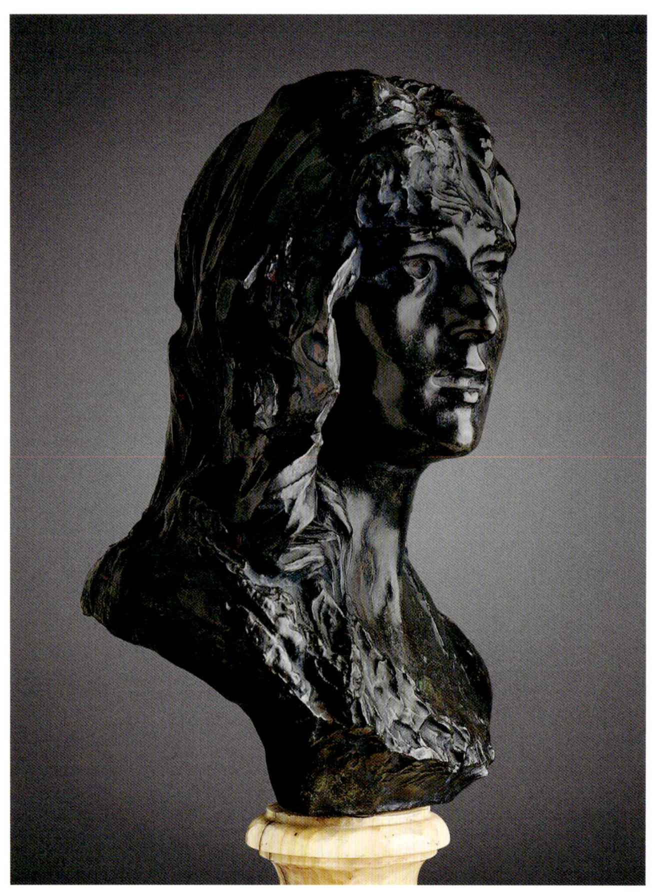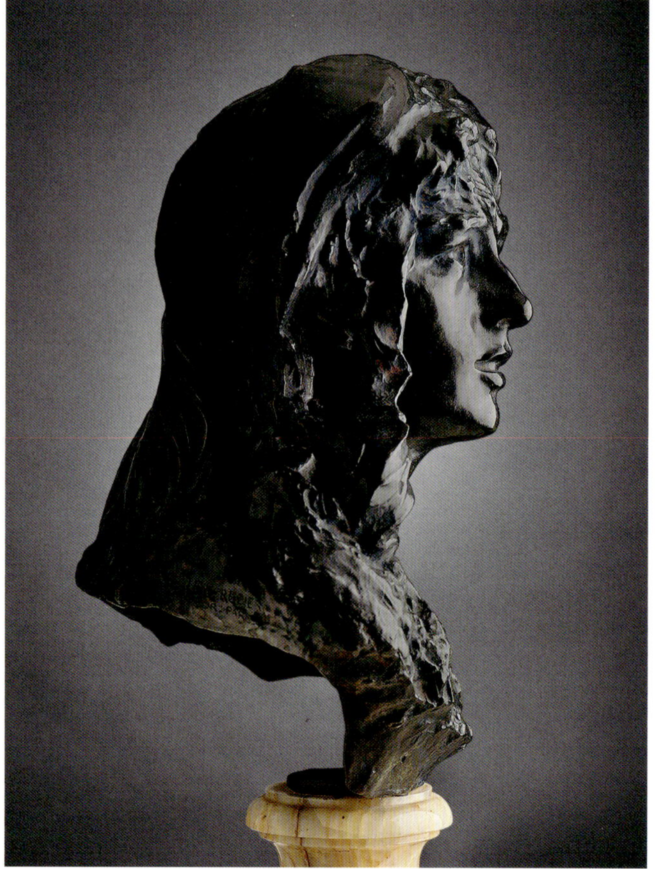

31. *Mignon*, 1870. Bronze on marble base, 16 ½ x 12 ⅝ x 10 ⅞ in. (41.9 x 32.1 x 27.6 cm).
Inscribed: *A. Rodin* and *Auguste Rodin* and *ALEXIS RUDIER. / FONDEUR. PARIS.*
Gift of Alma de Bretteville Spreckels, 1941.34.9

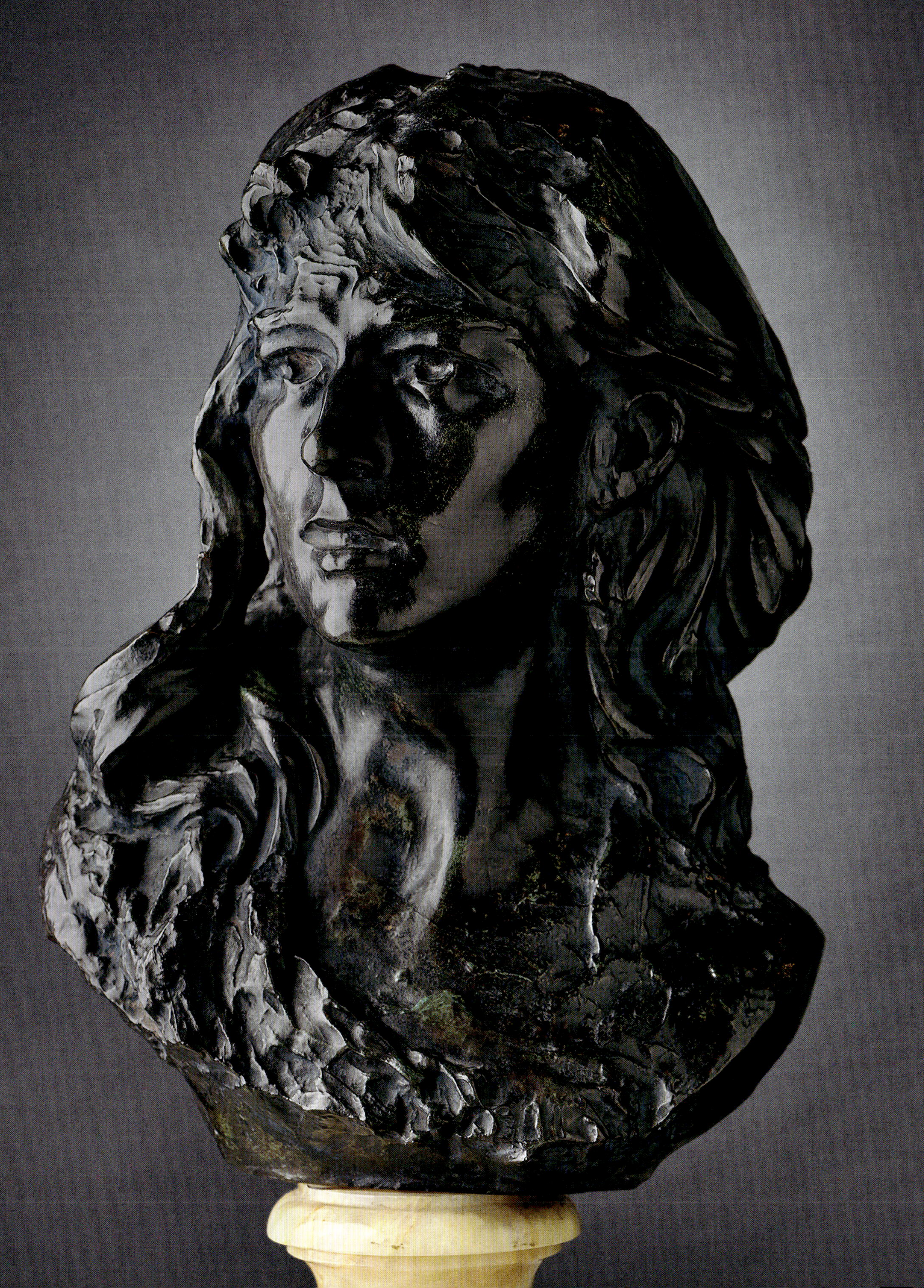

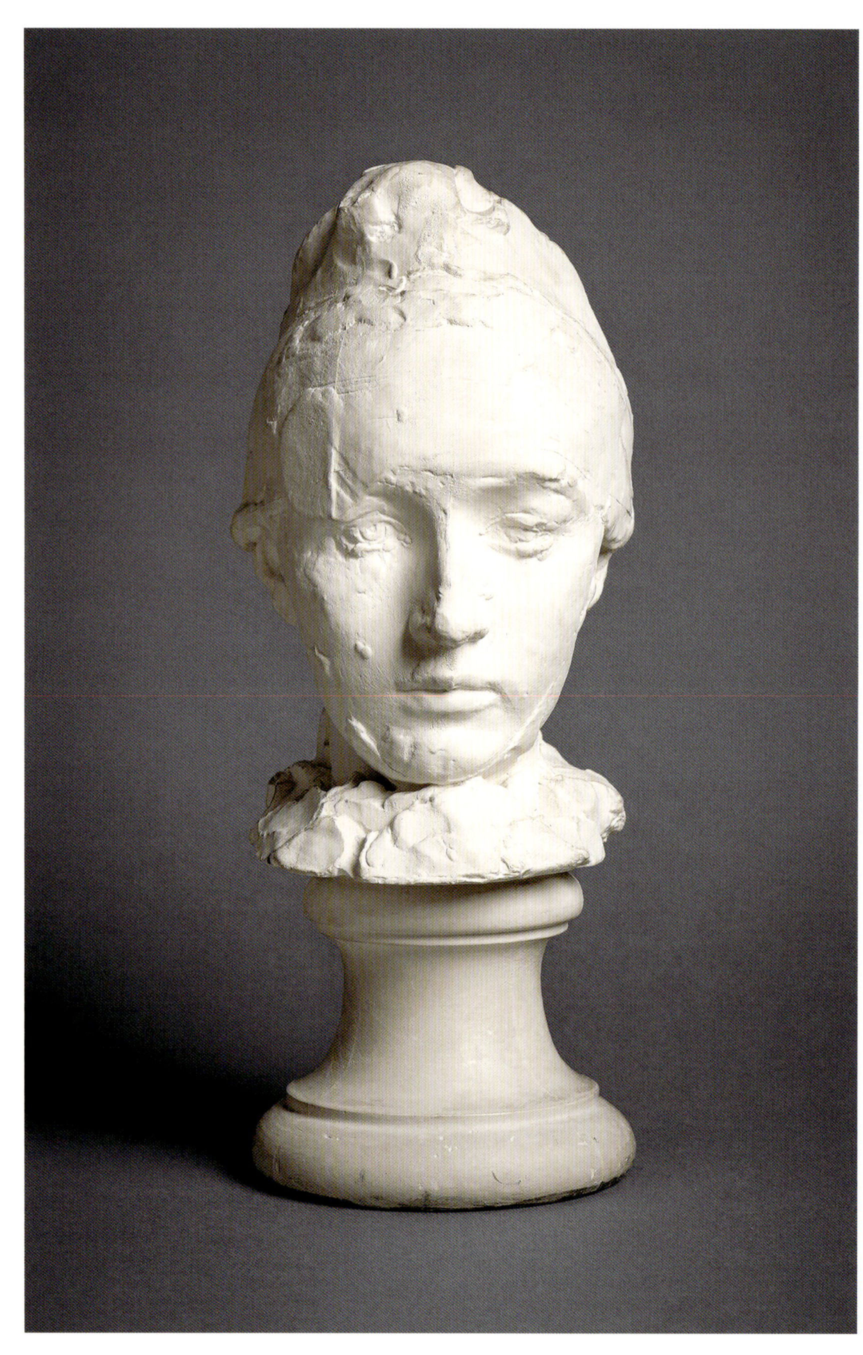

32. *Head of Mademoiselle Camille Claudel*, 1880s. Plaster, 10 x 6 x 7 ¼ in. (25.4 x 15.2 x 18.4 cm).
Gift of Adolph B. Spreckels, Jr., 1933.12.7

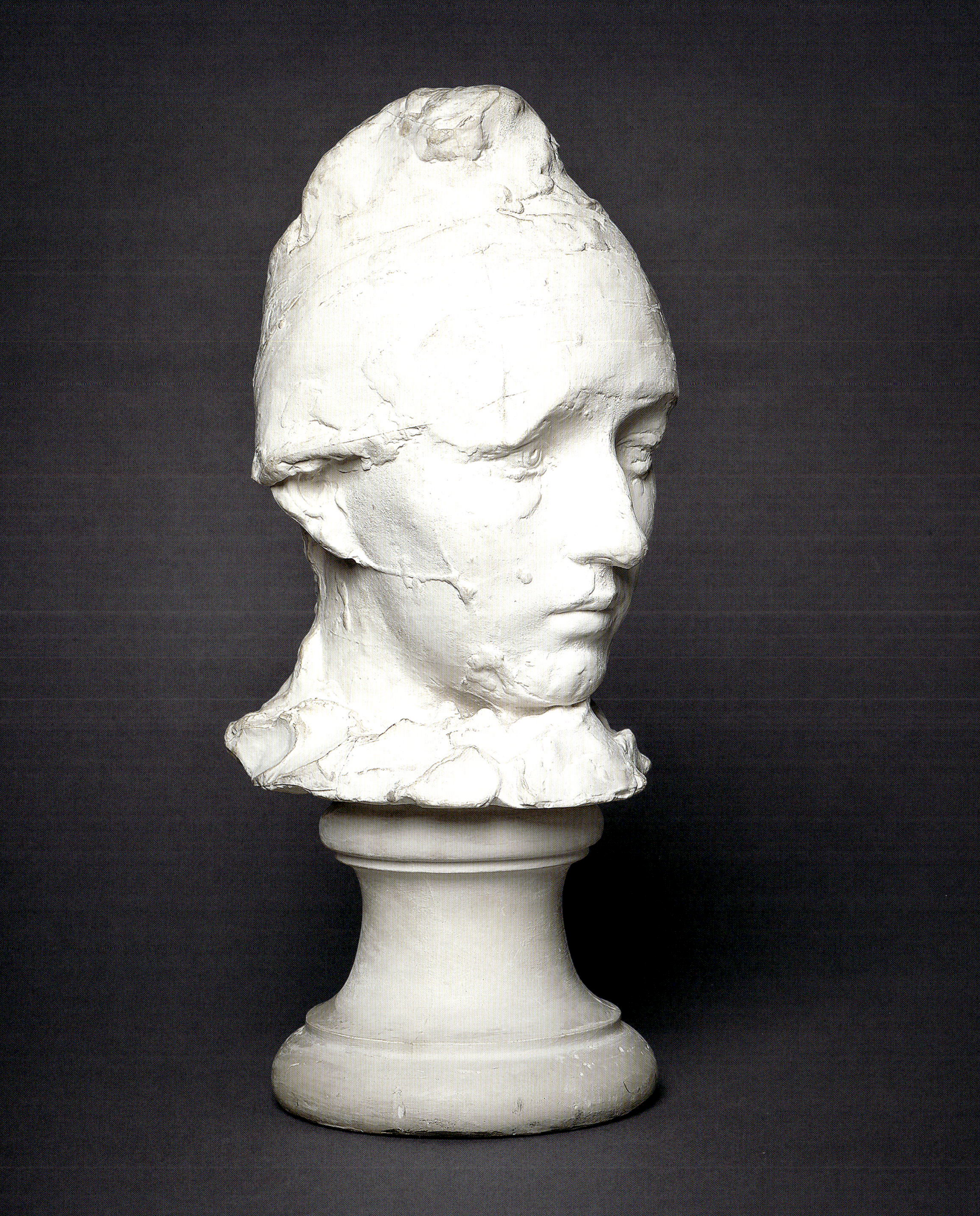

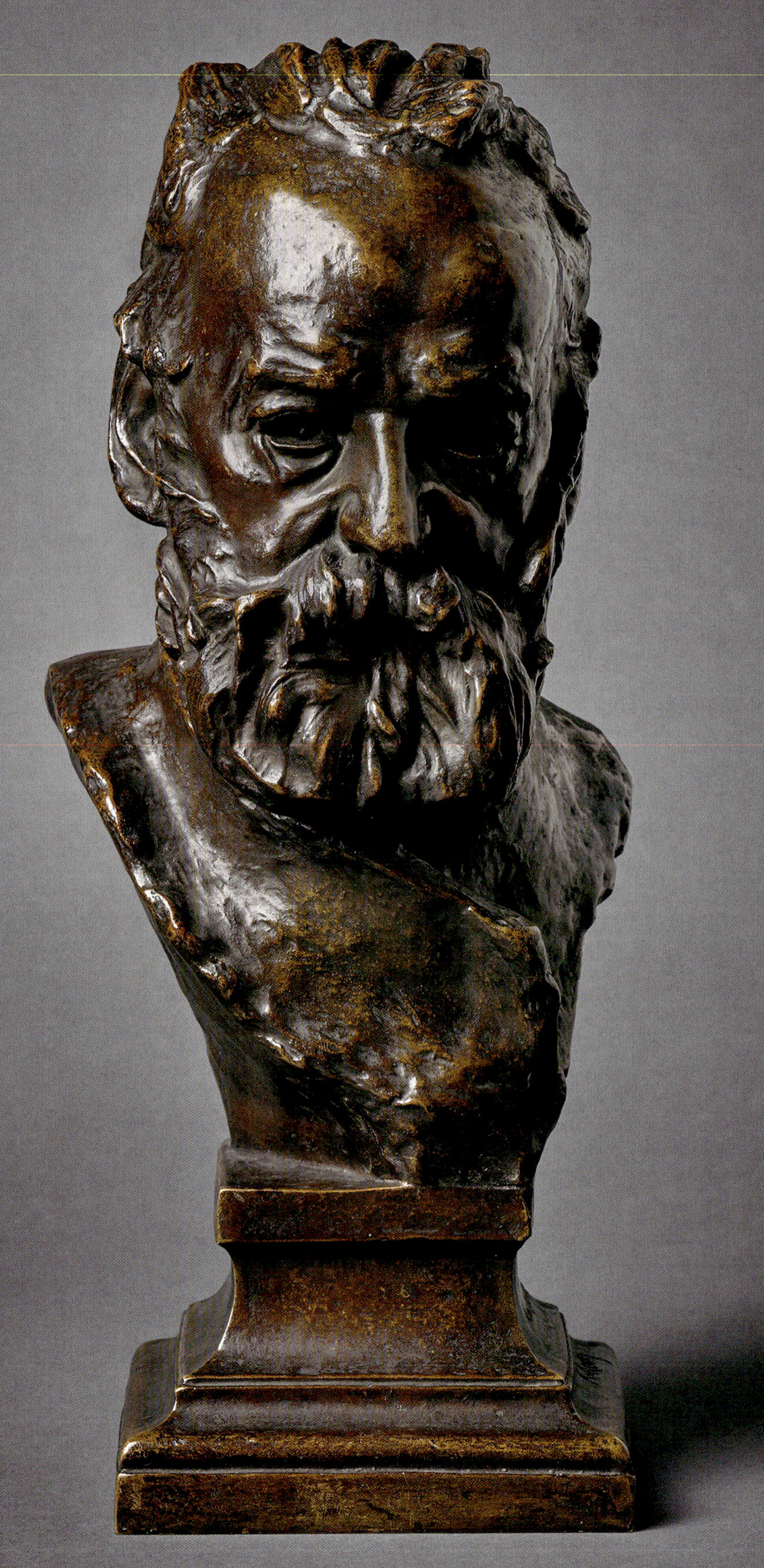

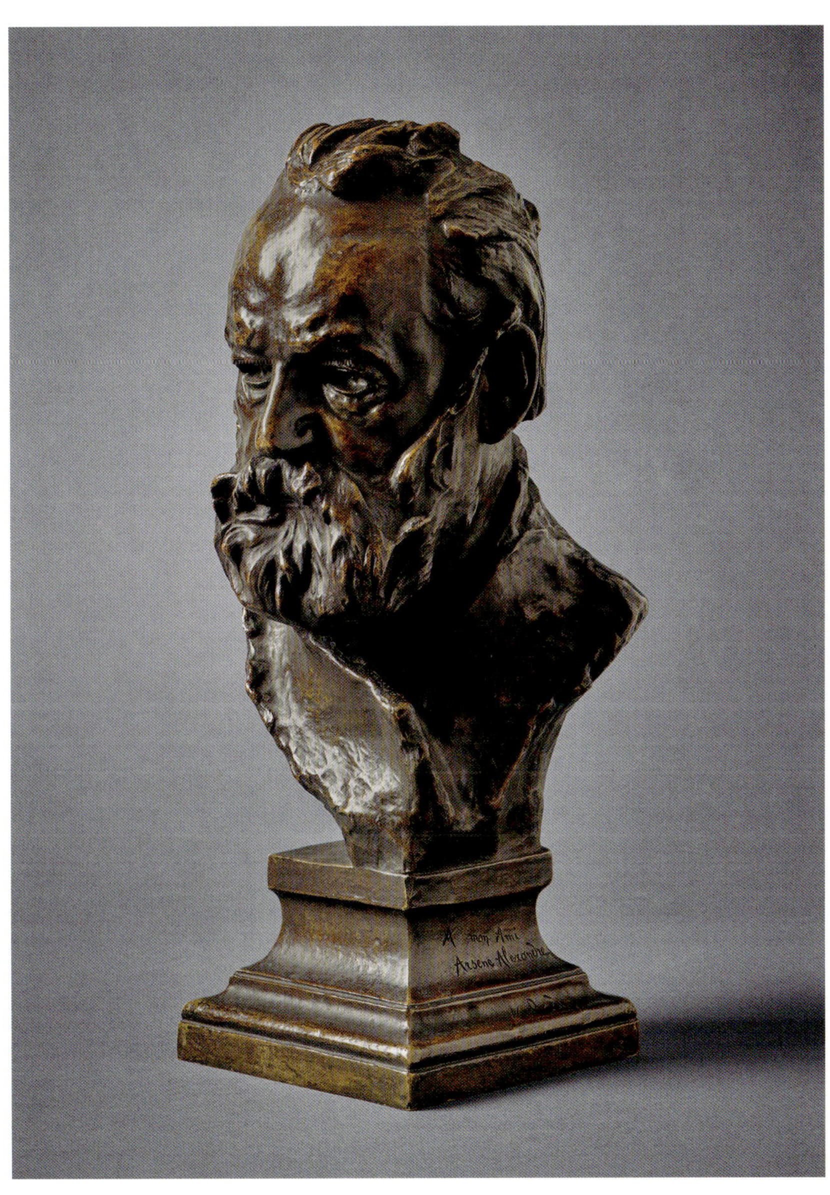

33. *Victor Hugo*, 1883 (reduced 1885, cast before 1891). Bronze, 15 x 6 ⅝ x 6 ¾ in. (38.1 x 16.8 x 17.1 cm).
Inscribed: *1891* [probably the date of the gift] and *A mon Ami /Arsene* [*sic*] *Alexandre* and *A. Rodin*. Gift of Alma de Bretteville Spreckels, 1942.38

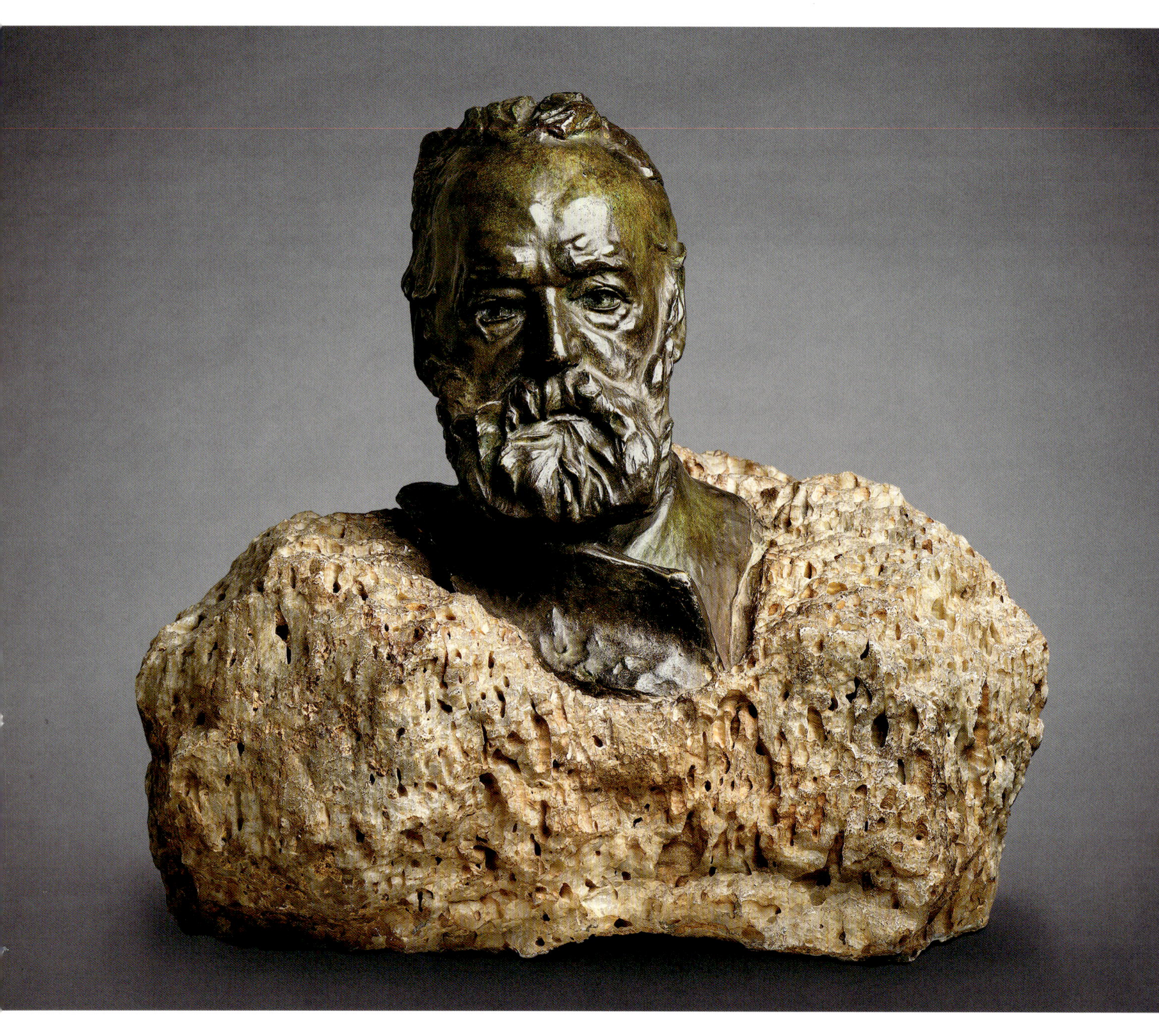

34. *Victor Hugo*, 1883 (cast before 1915). Bronze with marble base, 15 ⅞ x 10 ⅜ x 9 ⅜ in. (40.3 x 26.5 x 23.8 cm). Inscribed: *A. Rodin*. Gift of Alma de Bretteville Spreckels, 1942.37

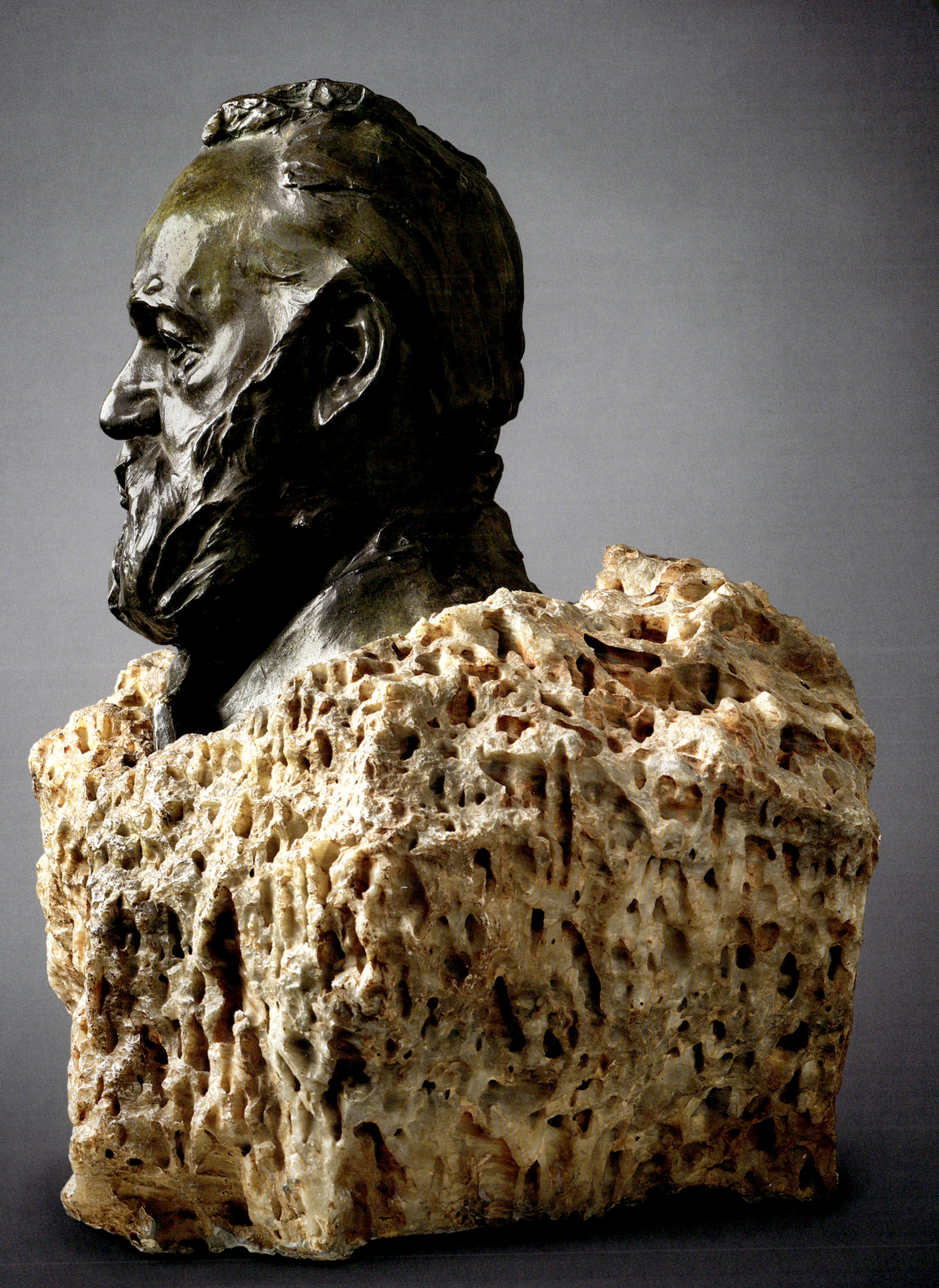

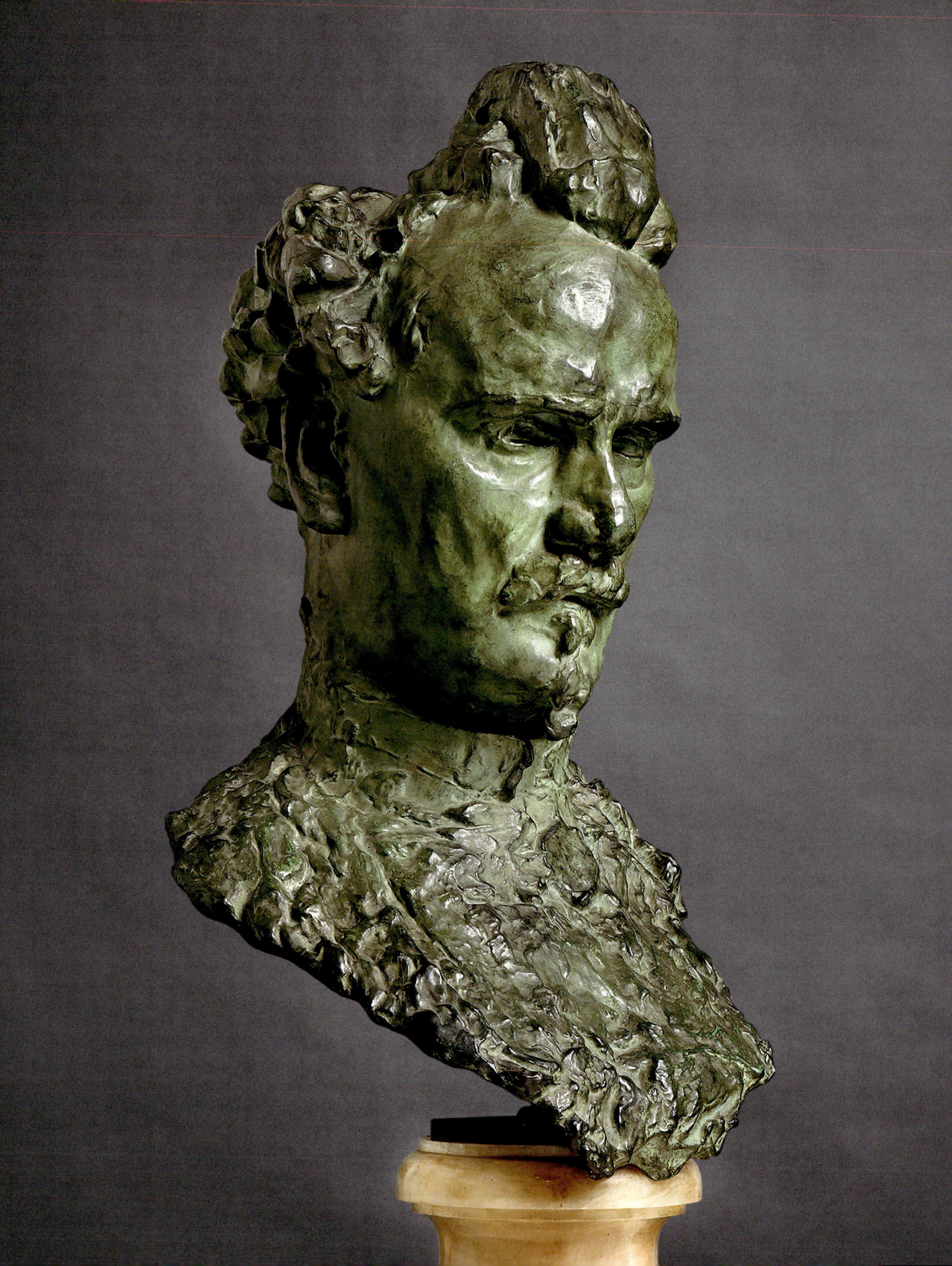

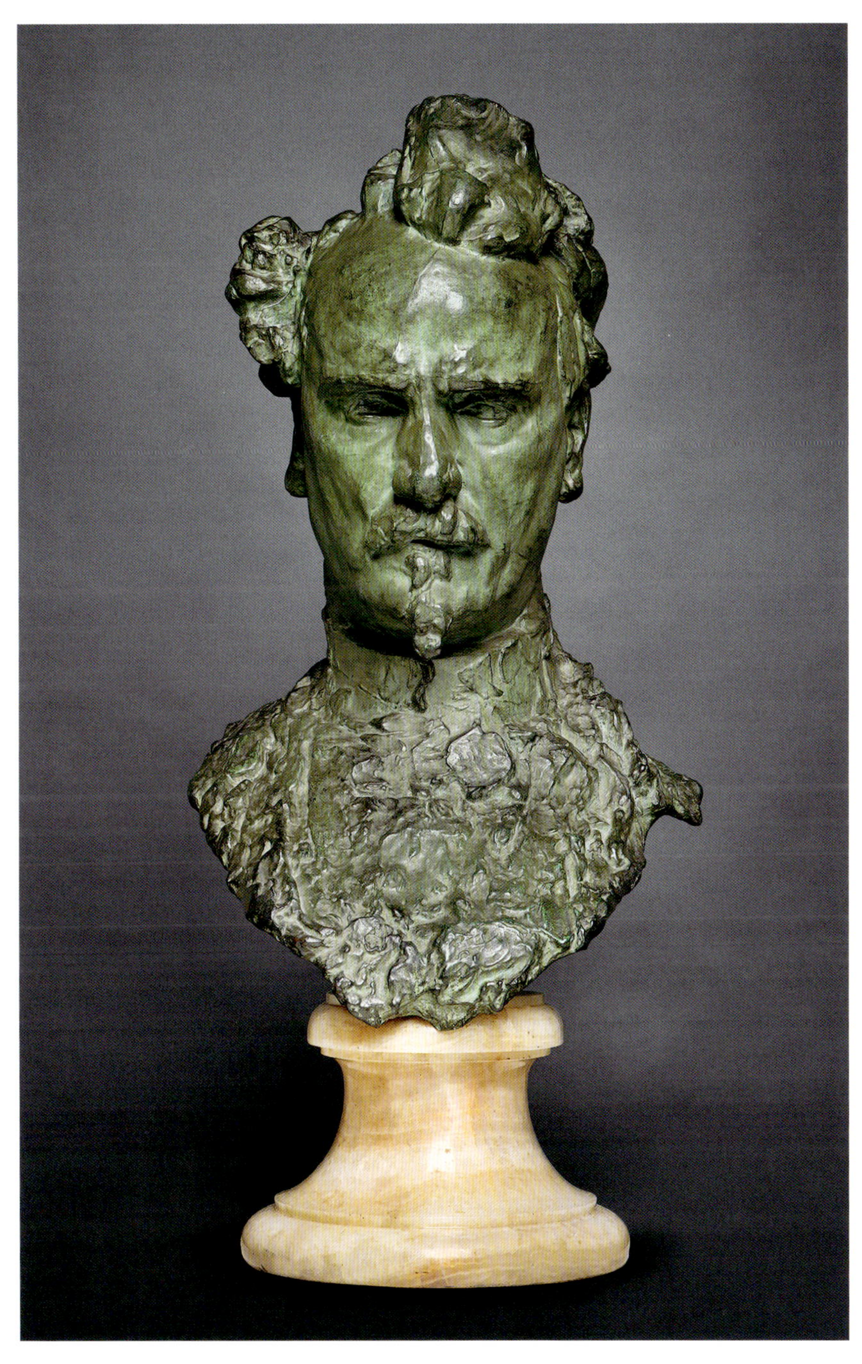

35. *Henri Rochefort*, 1884–1886 (cast ca. 1914). Bronze on marble base, 27 ⅝ x 16 ⅛ x 15 ¼ in. (70.2 x 41 x 38.6 cm). Inscribed: *A. Rodin* and *ALEXIS. RUDIER / FONDEUR. PARIS*. Gift of Alma de Bretteville Spreckels, 1941.34.4

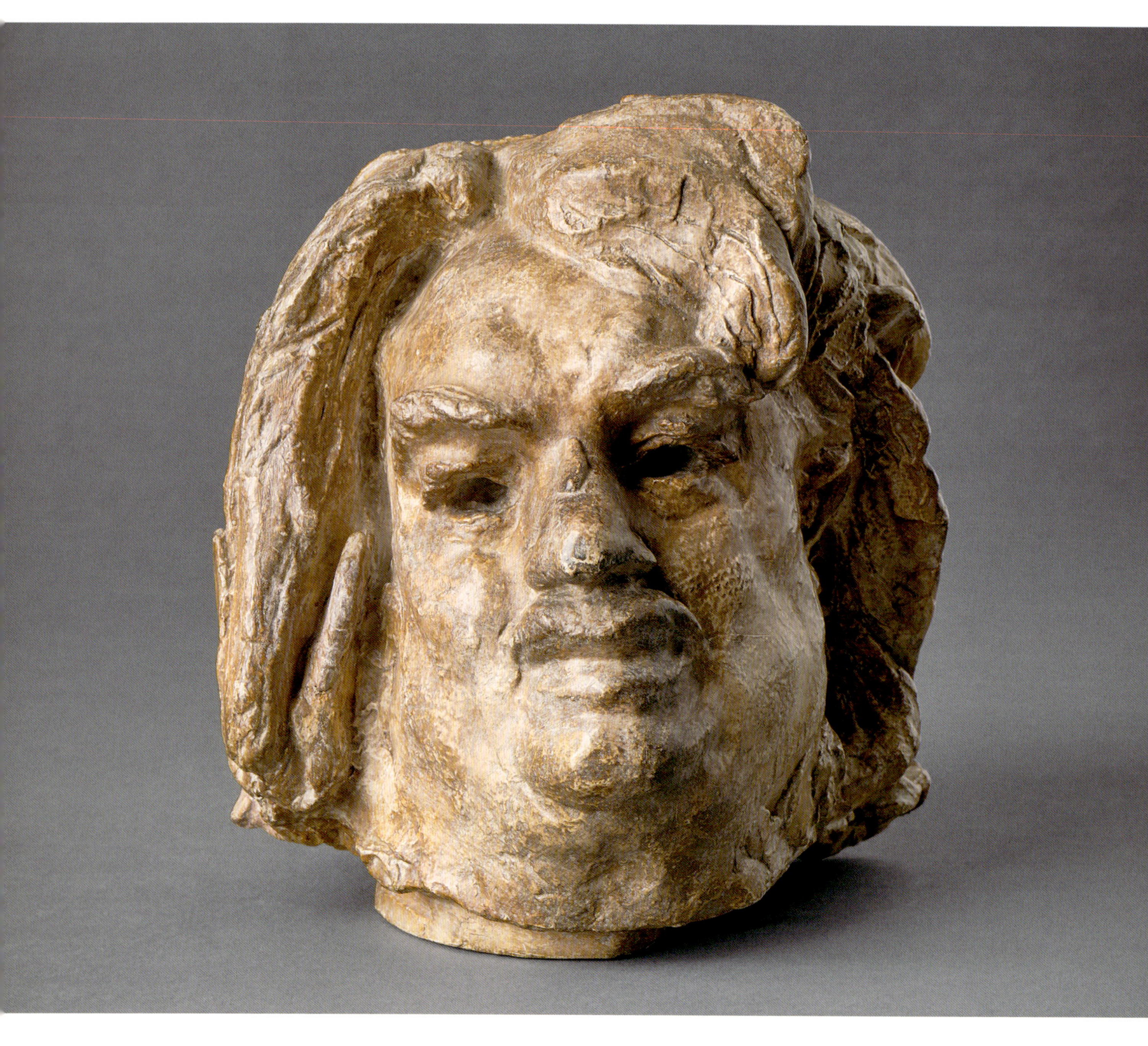

36. *Head of Balzac*, ca. 1897. Plaster, 7 ⅛ x 6 ⅞ x 6 ⅞ in. (18 x 17.5 x 17.3 cm).
Inscribed: *R.* Gift of Adolph B. Spreckels, Jr., 1933.12.17

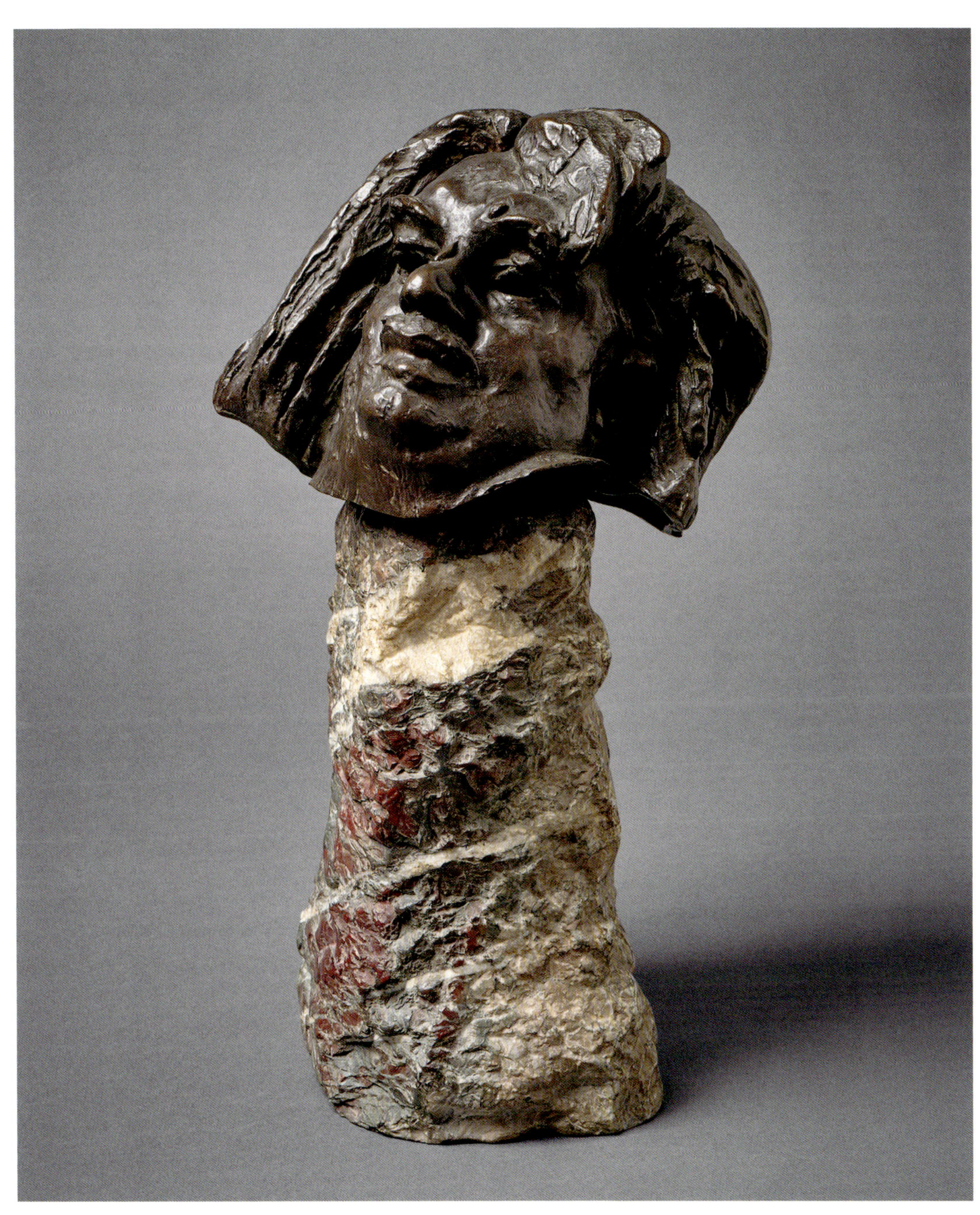

37. *Head of Balzac*, 1897 (cast before 1915). Bronze, 6 ½ x 7 ⅞ x 7 ⅝ in. (16.5 x 20 x 19.4 cm).
Inscribed: *A. Rodin*. Gift of Alma de Bretteville Spreckels, 1941.34.5

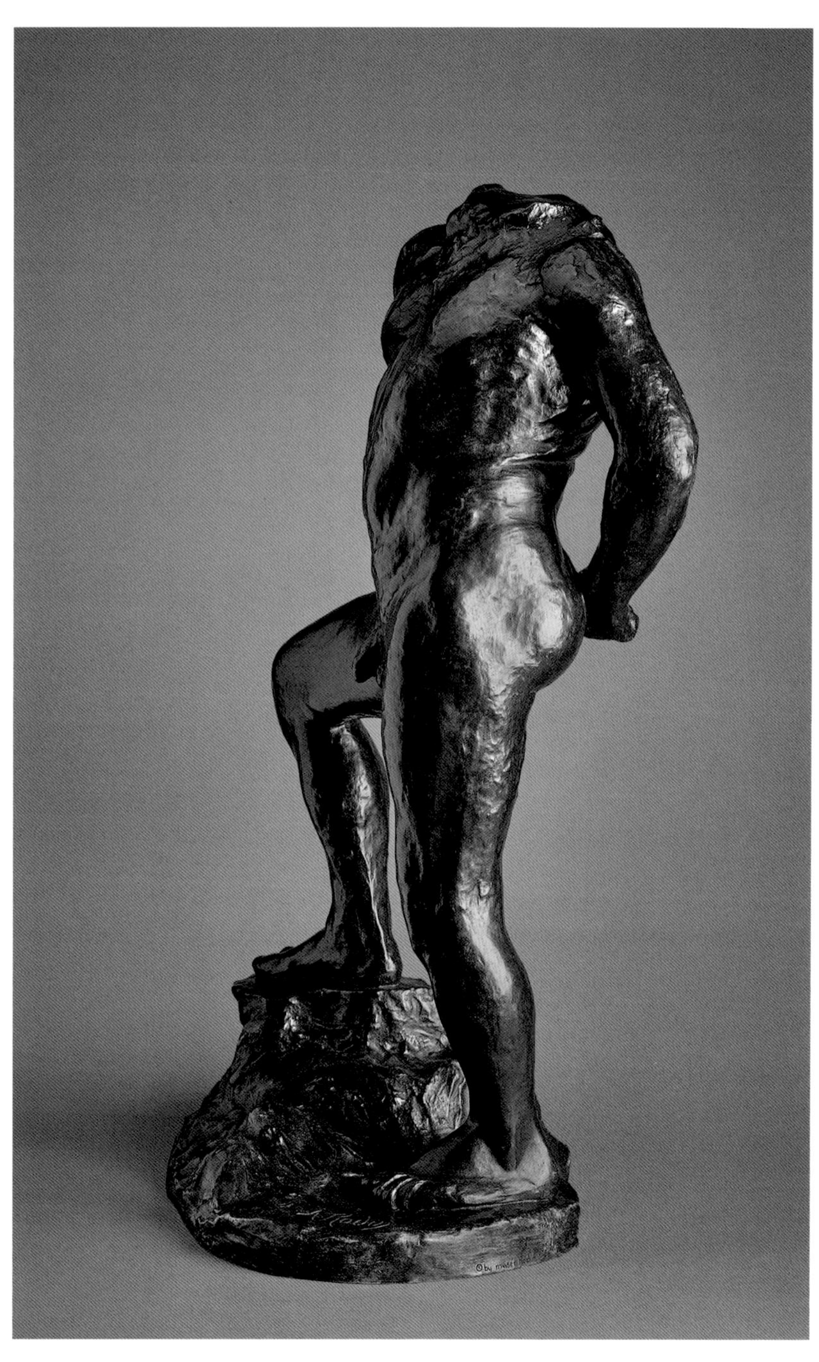

38. *Nude Study for Balzac "G,"* ca. 1893 (cast 1975). Bronze, 32 ⅛ x 21 ¾ x 13 ⅞ in. (81.6 x 55.2 x 35.2 cm).
Inscribed: *A. Rodin No 3 © by musée Rodin 1975 Georges Rudier. Fondeur. PARIS.*
Gift of the B. G. Cantor Art Foundation, 1978.9

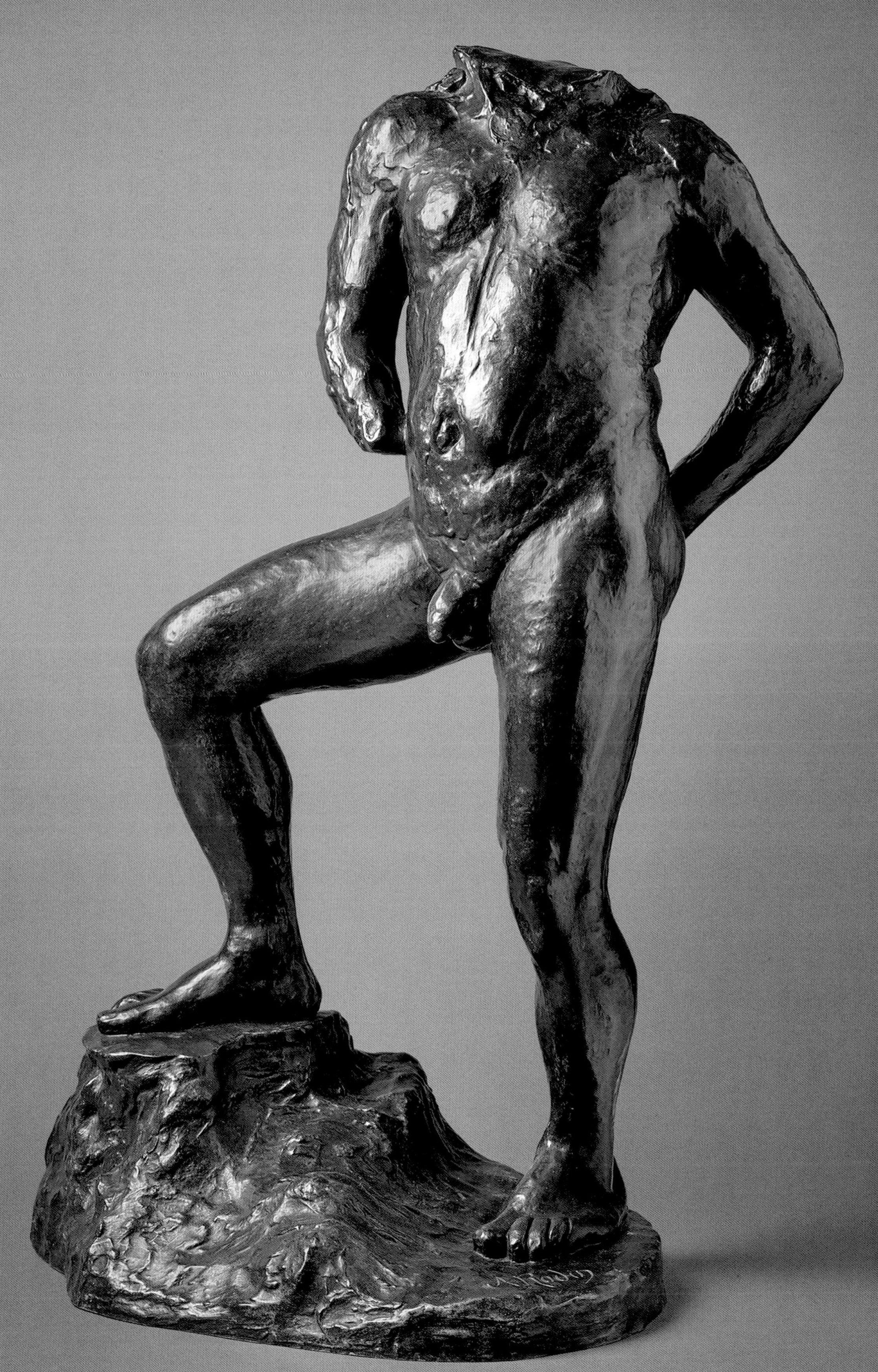

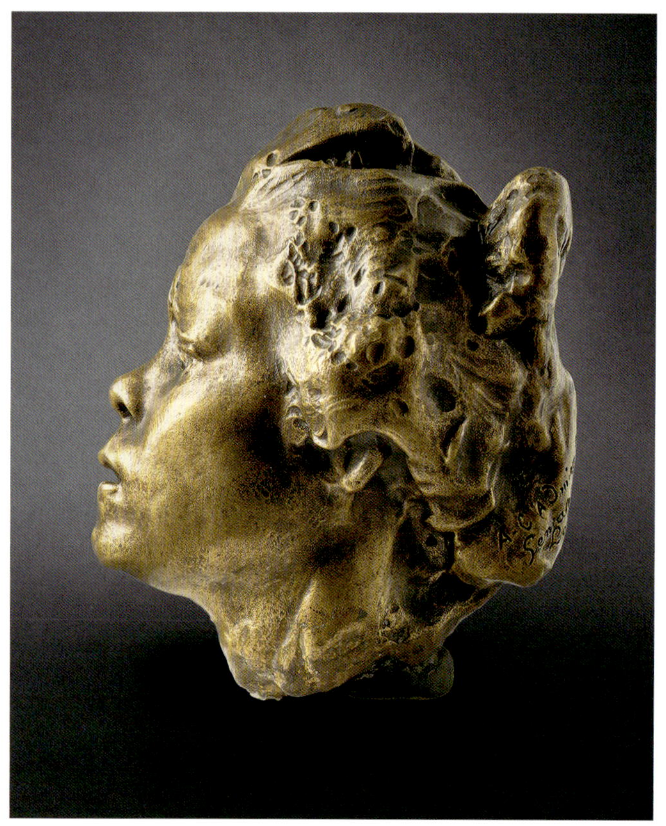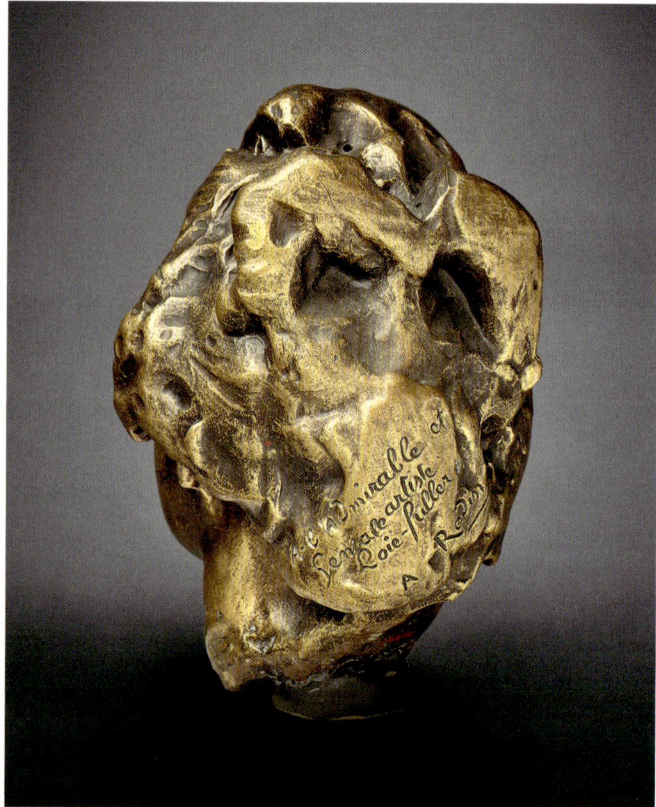

39. *Hanako*, 1907 (cast before 1919). Gilt bronze, 6 ½ x 5 x 5 ⅝ in. (16.5 x 12.7 x 14.3 cm).
Inscribed: *A–l'Admirable et / Geniale* [*sic*] *artiste / Loie-fuller / A Rodin.* Gift of Alma de Bretteville Spreckels, 1941.34.7

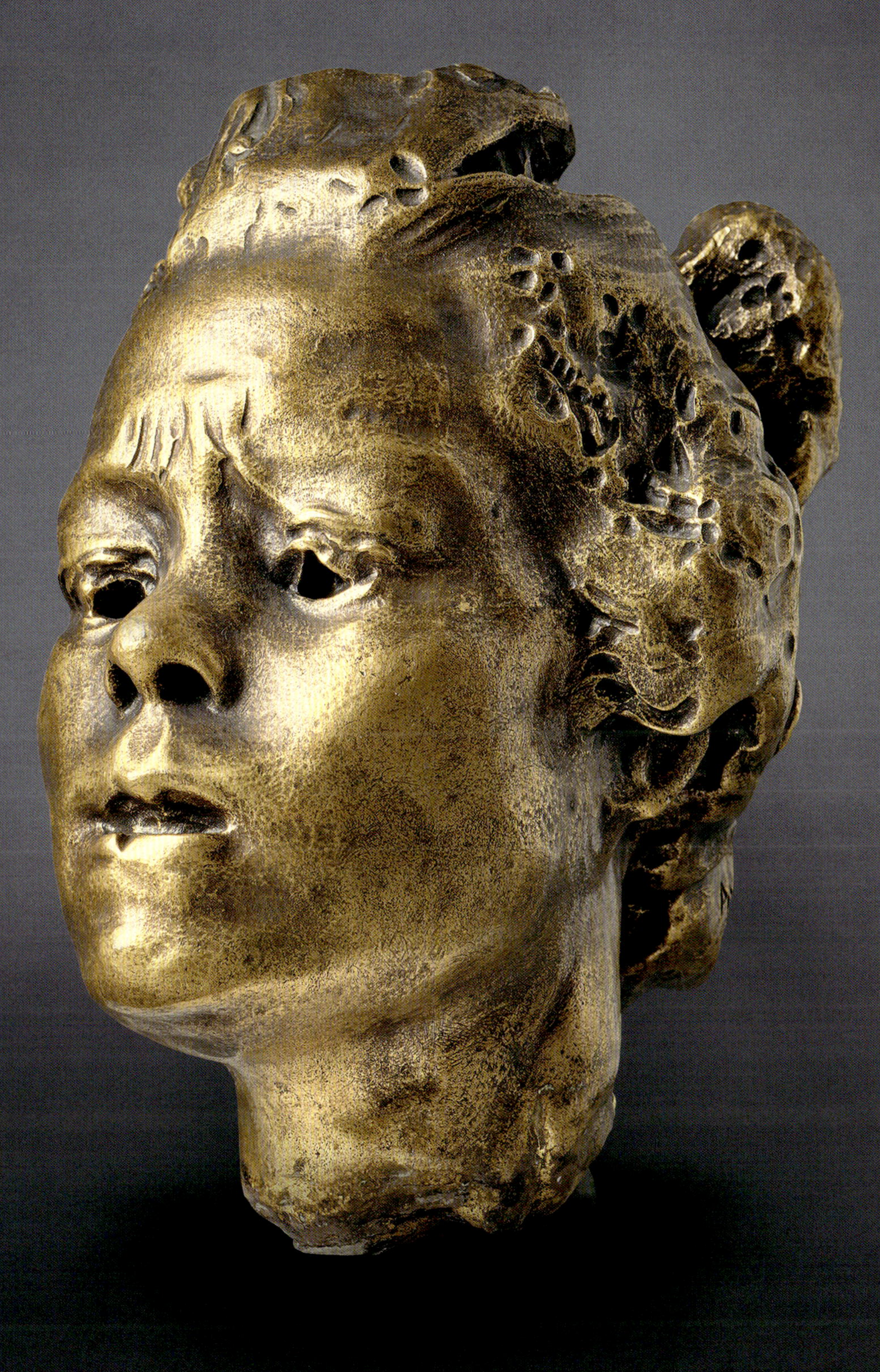

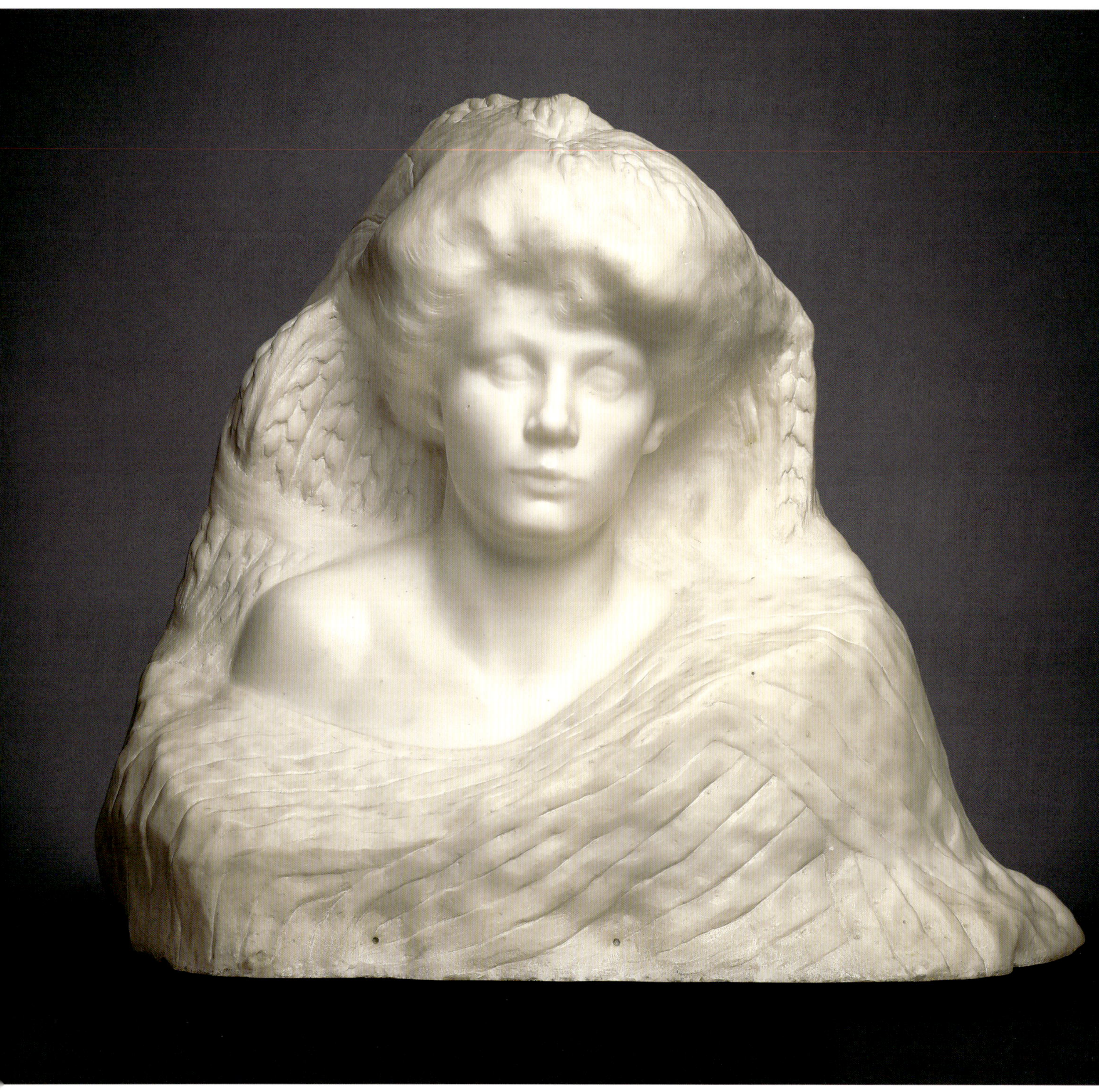

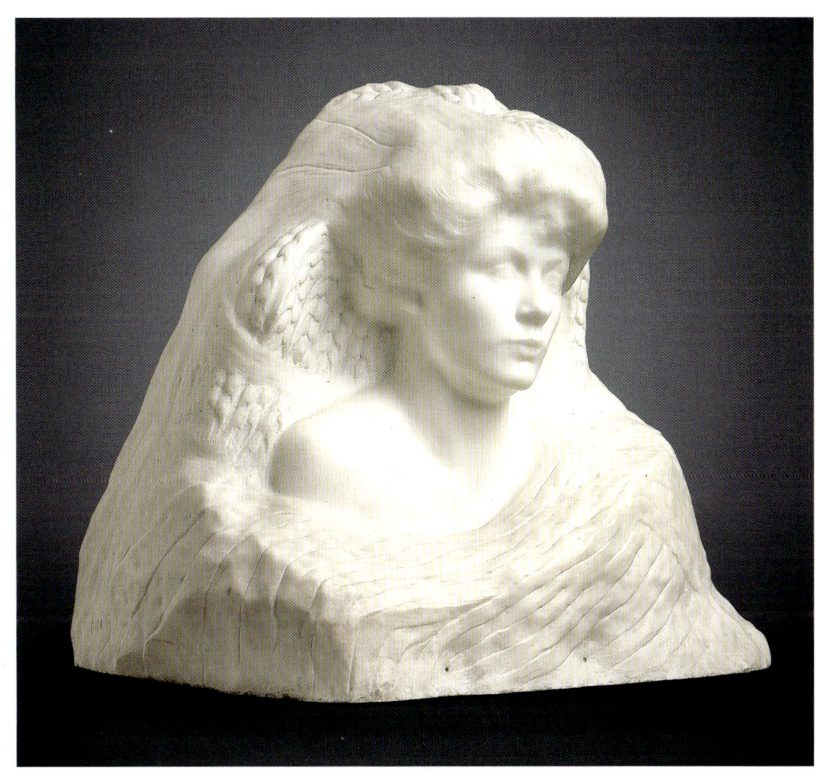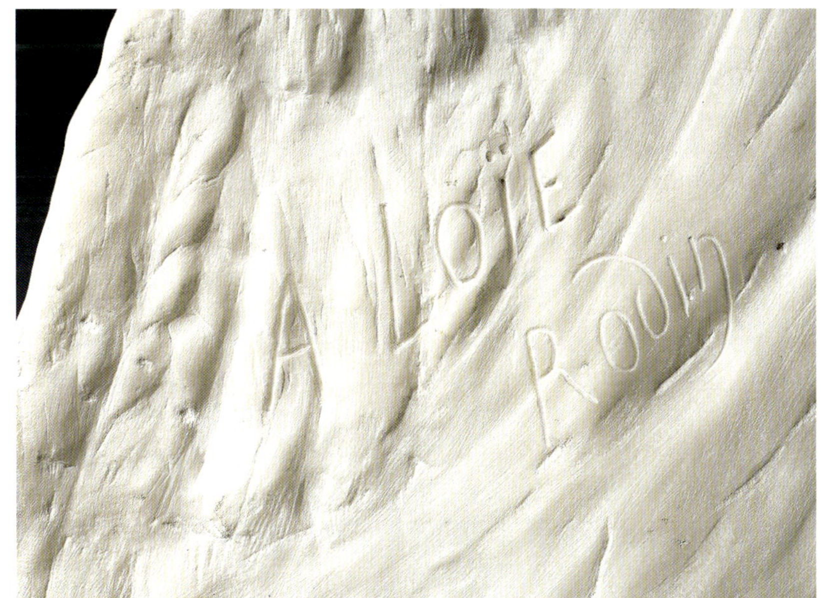

40. *La Nature, Miss Eve Fairfax*, ca. 1907–1916. Marble, 22 ⅝ x 27 ⅛ x 20 ⅛ in. (57.5 x 68.9 x 51.1 cm). Inscribed: *A LOÏE / Rodin*. Gift of Alma de Bretteville Spreckels, 1941.34.17

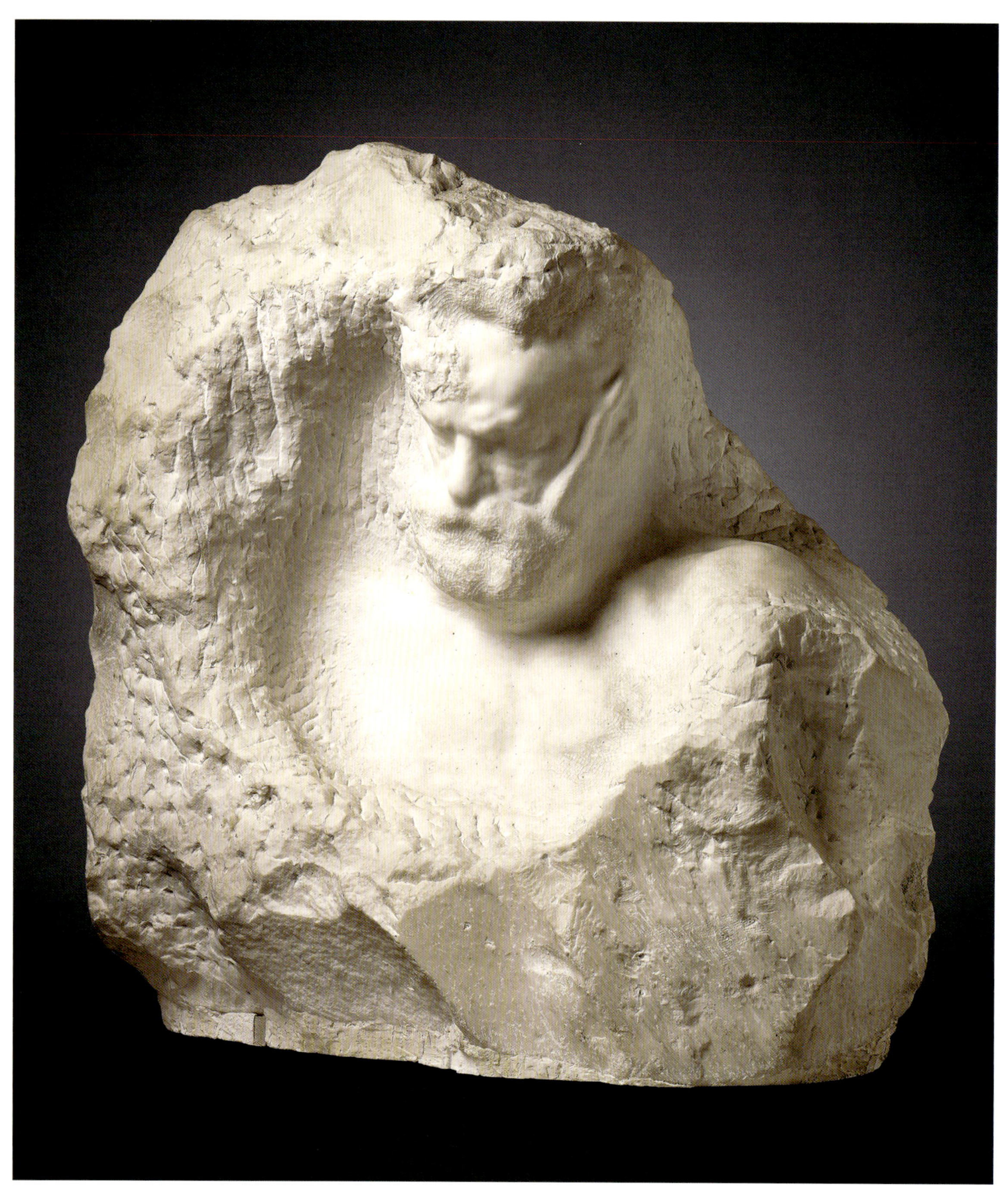

41. *Bust of Victor Hugo*, ca. 1917. Marble, 41 ½ x 41 ⅞ x 27 ½ in. (105.4 x 106.4 x 69.9 cm).
Inscribed: *3886* [probably a quarry number]. Anonymous gift, 1962.28

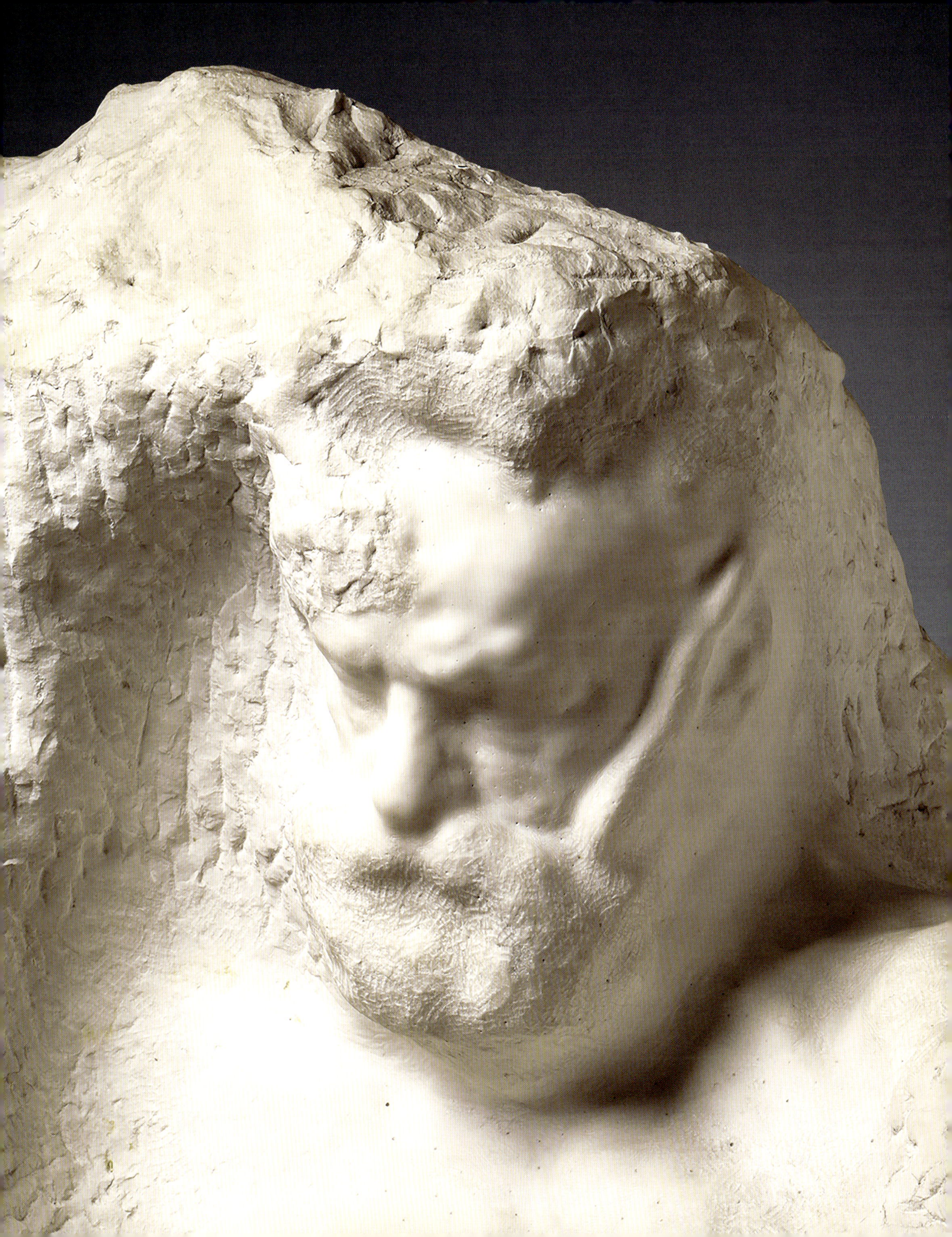

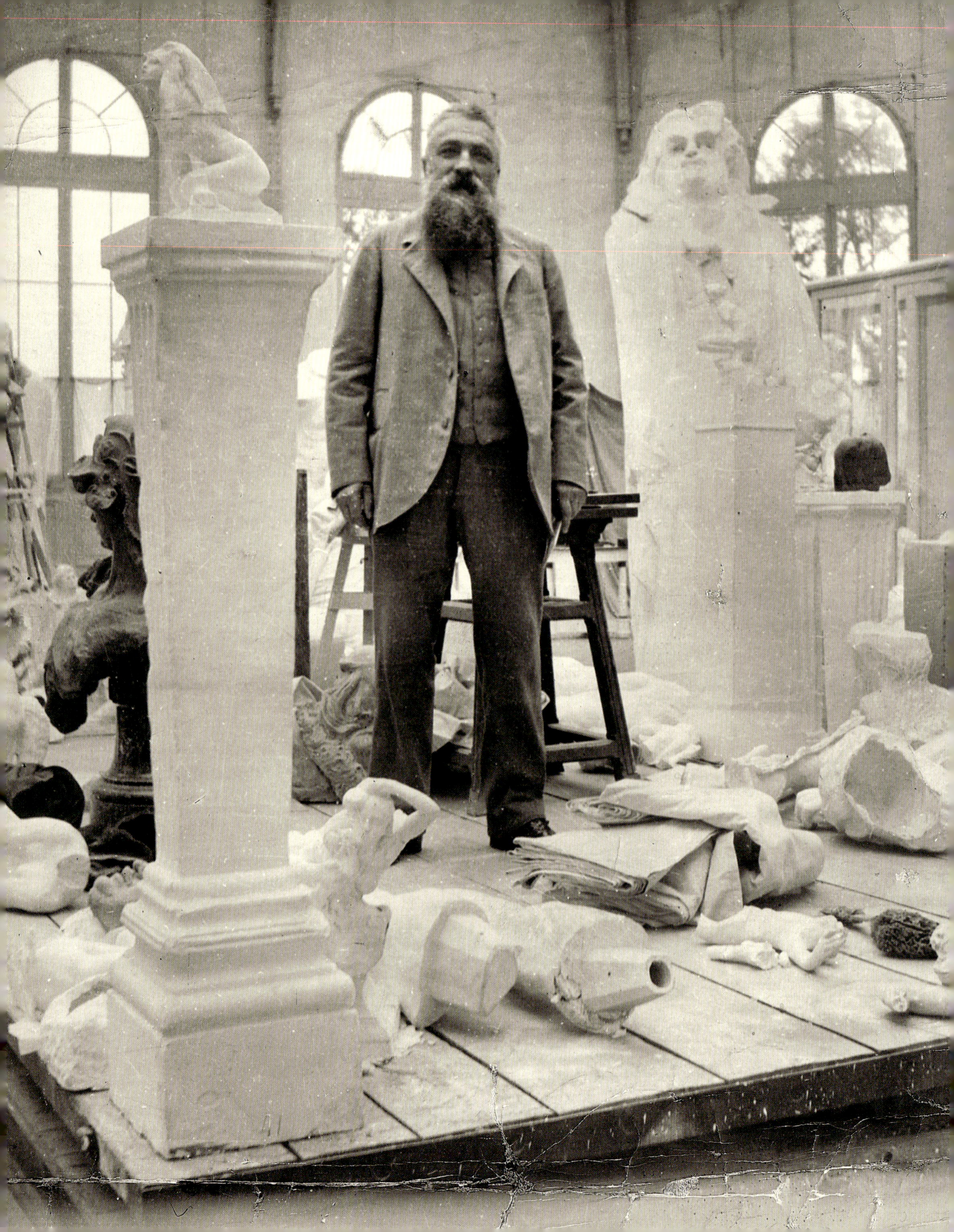

6

MODELS, PLASTERS, AND FRAGMENTS
Essential Tools for Rodin's Sculpture
(1860s–1917)

Models were an essential part of Rodin's working process, which involved first working in wet clay, then taking plaster casts, and finally casting the piece in bronze or carving it in marble (see sidebars on pp. 101 and 103, this volume). Rodin's models and fragments are keys to understanding the sculptor's work and the evolution of his finished sculptures. Most important were the plasters cast from the clay models, which themselves were prone to drying out and falling apart (such as happened with the back of the head in the *Man with the Broken Nose* [pl. 3]). Plasters served as faithful reproductions of clay models and could be embellished if necessary; they could also be regarded as freestanding works of art. Before the versions in bronze and marble were made, plasters represented more exactly what the artist wanted and effectively became the original model. At Rodin's studio in Meudon, outside Paris, there exists today a pavilion full of plasters that the sculptor used as reference works (fig. 27).

Rodin, like many other nineteenth-century sculptors, exhibited plaster models of his most famous works before they were cast in bronze, including *The Age of Bronze* (pl. 1) and *Saint John the Baptist Preaching* (pl. 4). Famously, the *Gates of Hell* only existed as a plaster in Rodin's lifetime (fig. 14), which enabled him to continually adapt and change parts of the massive project (see pp. 53–56, this volume). Two of his plasters in the Legion's collection, *Mother and Child* (pl. 42) and *Brother and Sister* (pl. 43), were clearly models for bronzes because they are both tinted brown for casting.[xxxiii] Plasters could also be used at earlier stages to develop a final sculpture. Rodin's models for *Nude Study for Balzac "G"* (pl. 38) and *Nude Study of Eustache de Saint-Pierre* (pl. 23) are both bronzes cast from the plaster models that show how the artist made nude figures before adding the clothing to the final sculptures.

Plasters could be adapted to make different models. For example, *Crying Girl Disheveled* (pl. 21), originally one of the figures planned for the *Gates of Hell*, was created after Rodin placed the plaster head of the girl in a marble basin to form a new composition. They could also serve as starting points for larger versions in other materials. The plaster *The Hand of God* (pl. 44) is one of Rodin's most compelling small sculptures, showing the Creator's hand opening up to reveal the bodies of Adam and Eve struggling out of a mass. This sculpture was translated into bronze and marble and made in different sizes, but the plaster holds the sculpture's meaning with the greatest immediacy and significance. Though typically used at the beginning

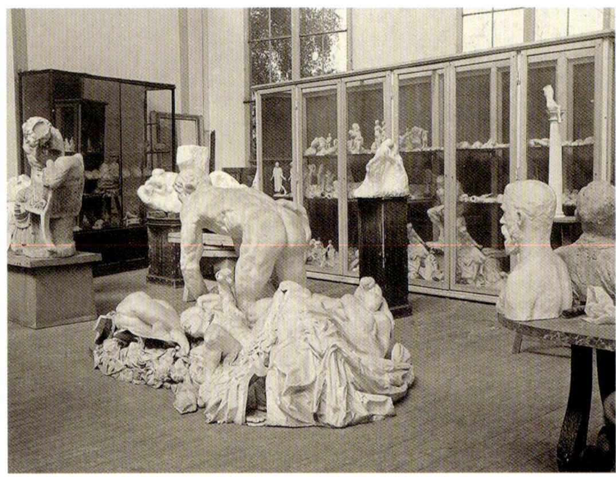

of a work's process, a plaster can also record a sculptor's final composition after its translation into bronze or marble. Plaster versions are especially meaningful as documents for marble works, as the latter have variations in each iteration based on the nuances of carving. *The Temptation of Saint Anthony* (pl. 46) and *Christ and the Magdalene* (pl. 45) are both examples of plasters that show the compositions' realizations in the completed marbles.

Rodin also retained a library of fragments that he could draw upon to make complete works. *The Mighty Hand* is one of his most powerful creations, showing a massive tensed hand, which was probably created at the time of the *Gates of Hell* and *The Burghers of Calais* but only took on its true significance when it was enlarged. This fragment exists in several versions, including the Legion's bronze rendition (pl. 48), cast directly from the plaster (fig. 28). On the opposite end of the scale are tiny feet and hands, including twenty versions of *Right Feet*, some mounted on wires so that the artist could adjust the positions and angles for new compositions (pl. 52).

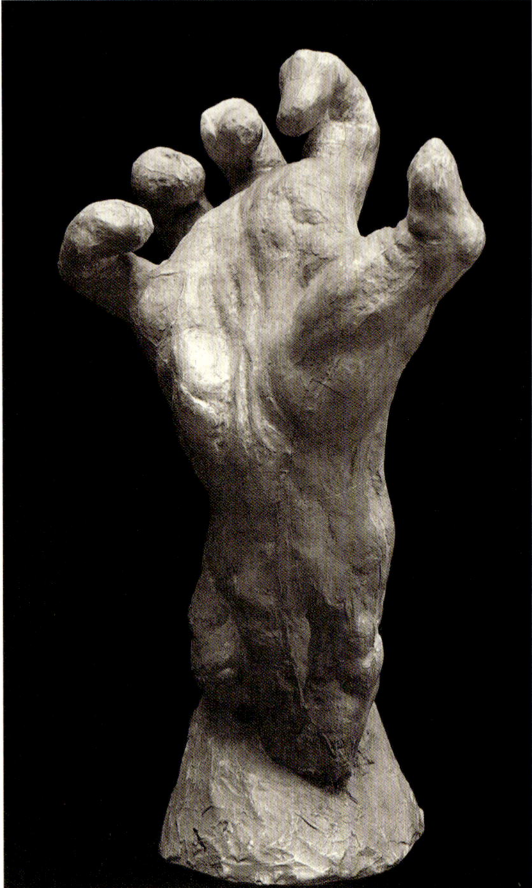

Fig. 27 Claude Lemery, *Rodin's Studio in Pavilion of Alma, Meudon*, ca. 1912. Gelatin silver print, 5 x 6 ¾ in. (12.6 x 17.2 cm). Fine Arts Museums of San Francisco, Museum purchase, Gift of Mrs. George S. Wong, 1994.12.1

Figs. 28 and 29 Pages from the photographic album of Rodin sculptures in Rudier's foundry, later acquired by Alma Spreckels, 1920–1930. Gelatin silver prints mounted on paper in a bound leather album, 10 ⅝ x 7 ½ x 1 ⅛ in. (27 x 19 x 3 cm). Fine Arts Museums of San Francisco, Gift of Alma de Bretteville Spreckels, 2005.59.1–24

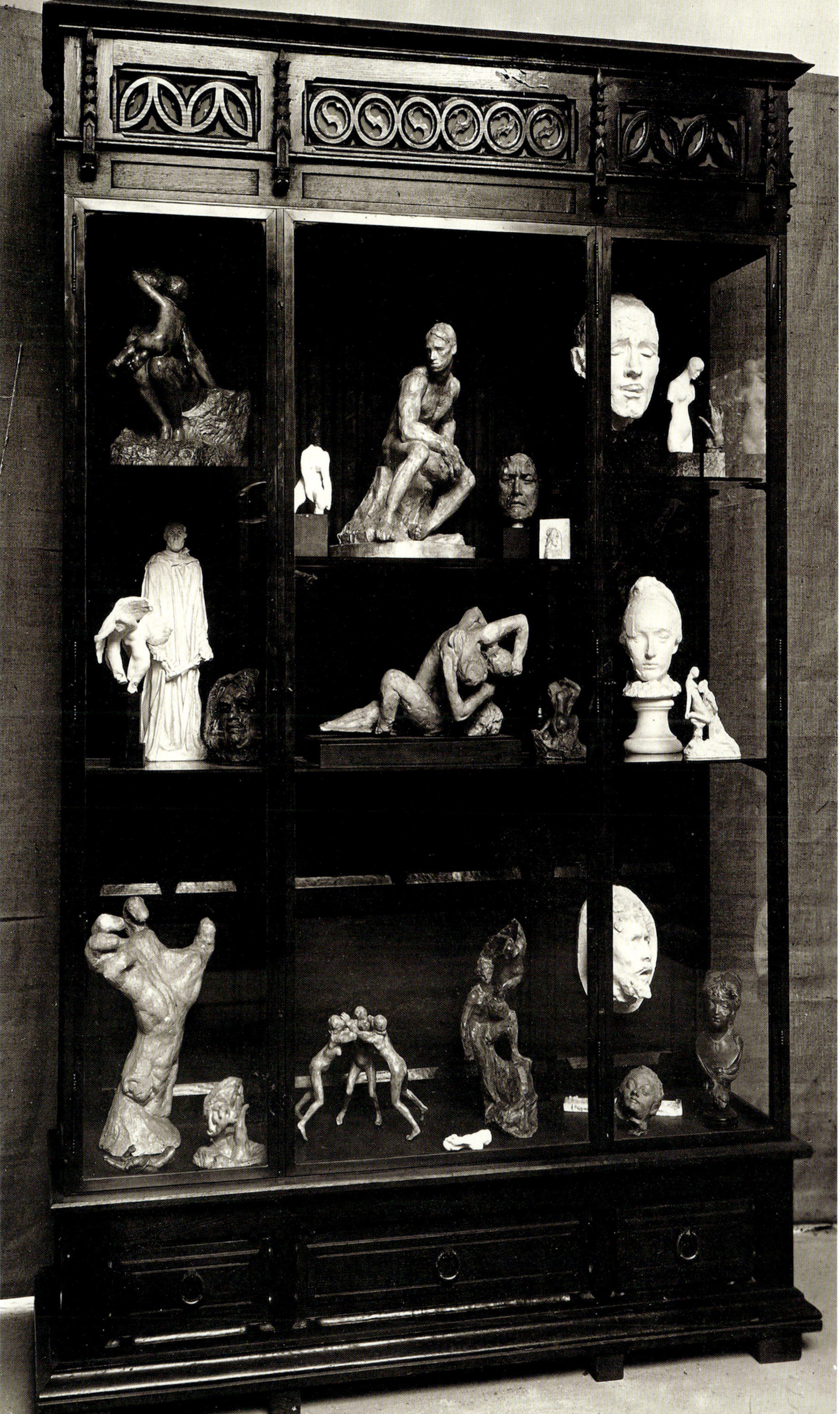

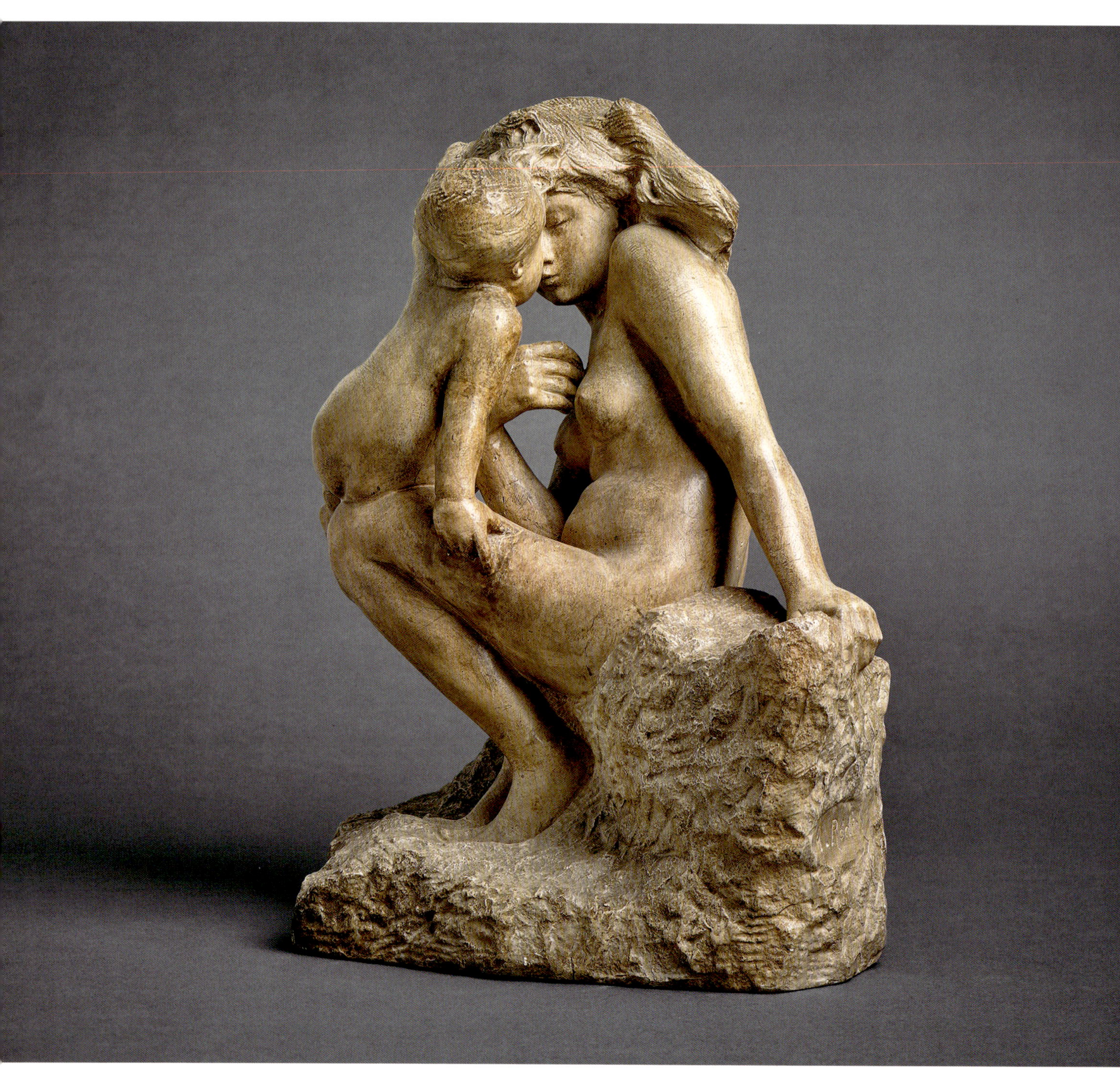

42. *Mother and Child* or *Young Mother*, ca. 1885. Plaster, 15 ⅜ x 14 ⅝ x 9 ⅞ in. (39.1 x 37.1 x 25.2 cm).
Inscribed: *Modele* [*sic*] */ pour le Bronze*. Gift of Alma de Bretteville Spreckels, 1947.17

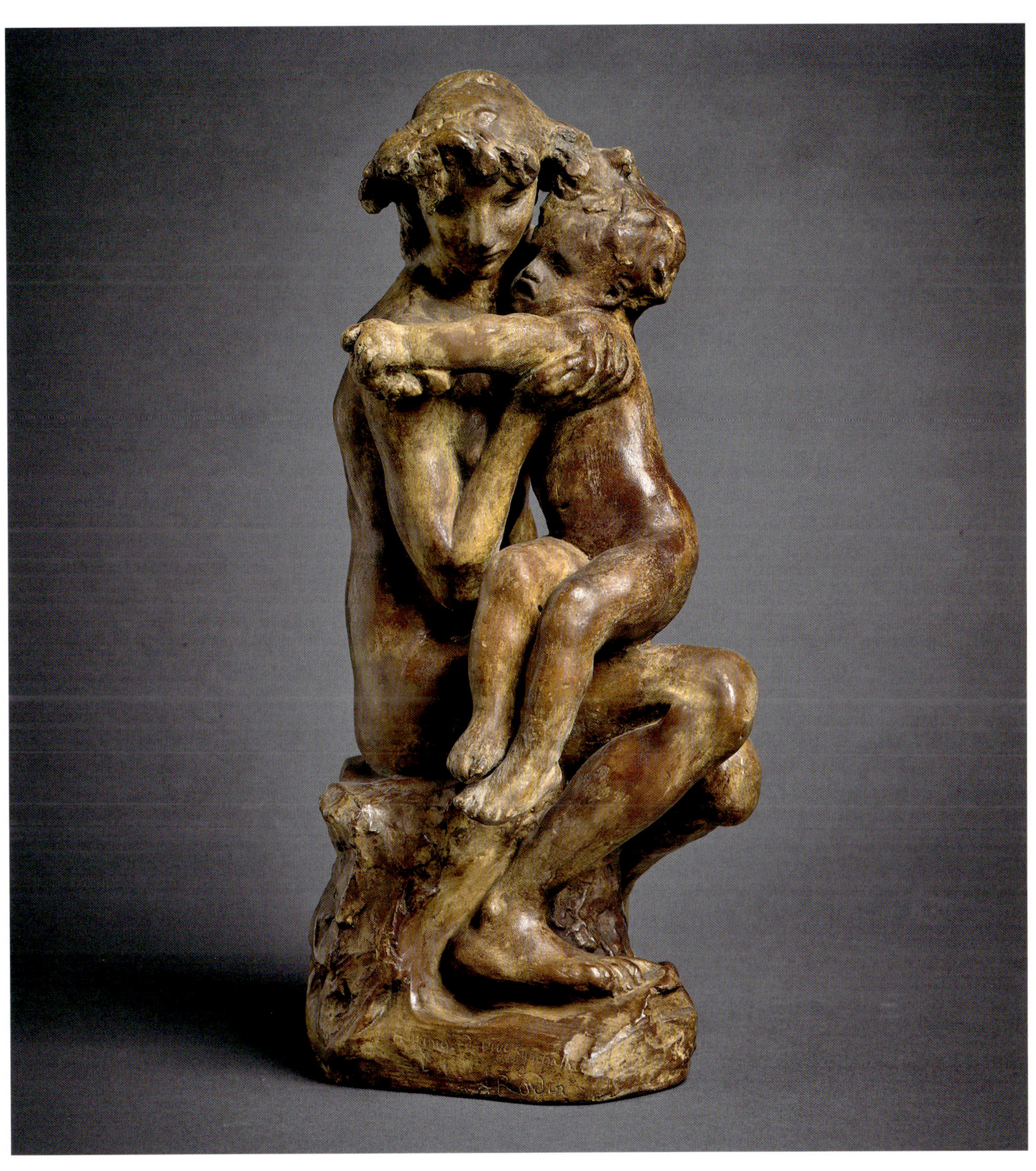

43. *Brother and Sister*, ca. 1890. Plaster, 15 ¼ x 7 ⅜ x 8 ½ in. (38.7 x 18.6 x 21.7 cm).
Inscribed: *Hommage de Vive Sympathie / A Rodin*. Gift of Alma de Bretteville Spreckels, 1924.18.2

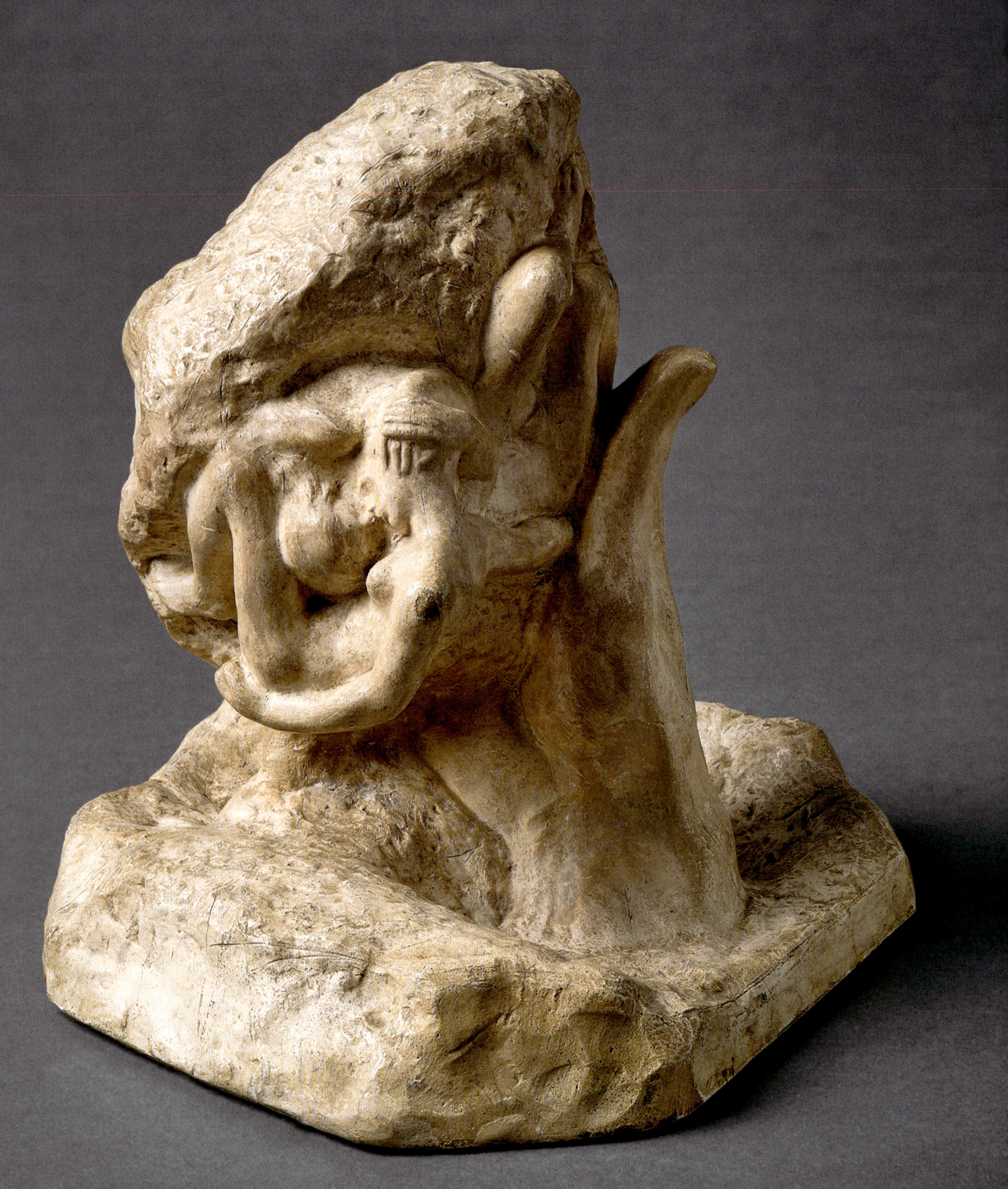

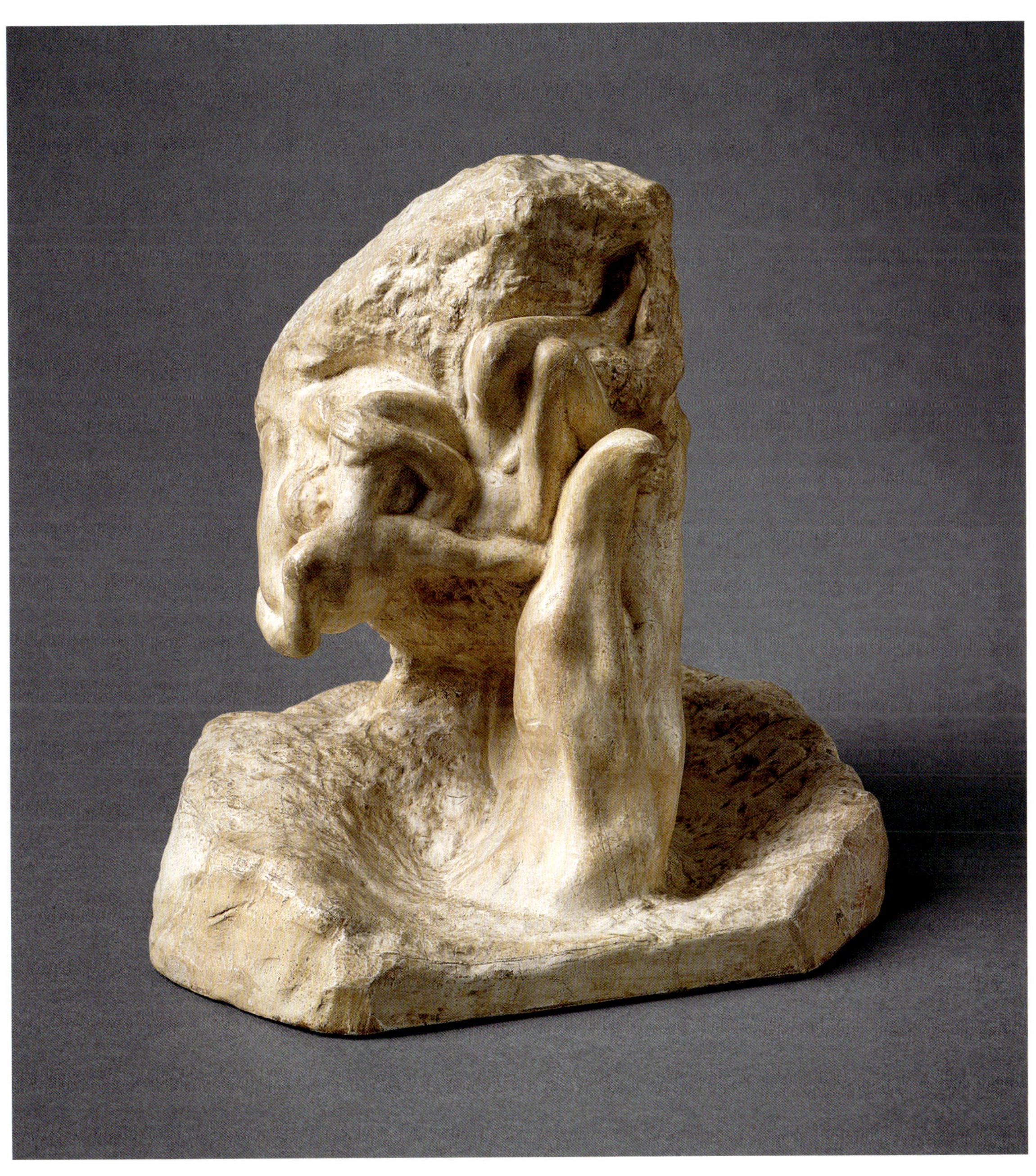

44. *The Hand of God*, ca. 1895. Plaster, 6 ⅛ x 6 ⅞ x 5 ½ in. (15.5 x 17.5 x 14 cm).
Gift of Adolph B. Spreckels, Jr., 1933.12.19

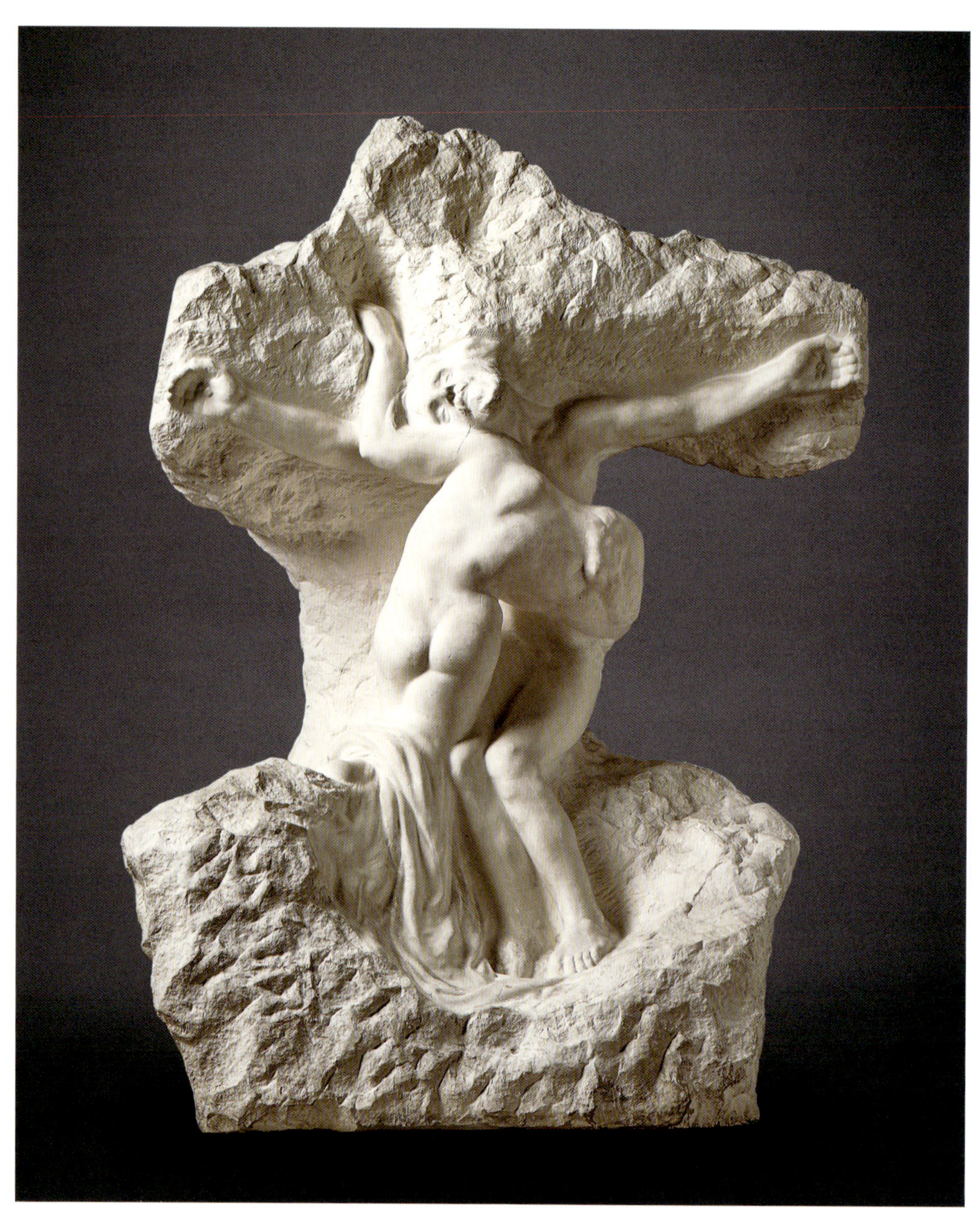

45. *Christ and the Magdalene*, ca. 1894 (cast ca. 1919). Plaster, 41 x 23 x 27 in. (104.1 x 58.4 x 68.6 cm).
Inscribed: *A. Rodin*. Gift of Alma de Bretteville Spreckels, 1949.18

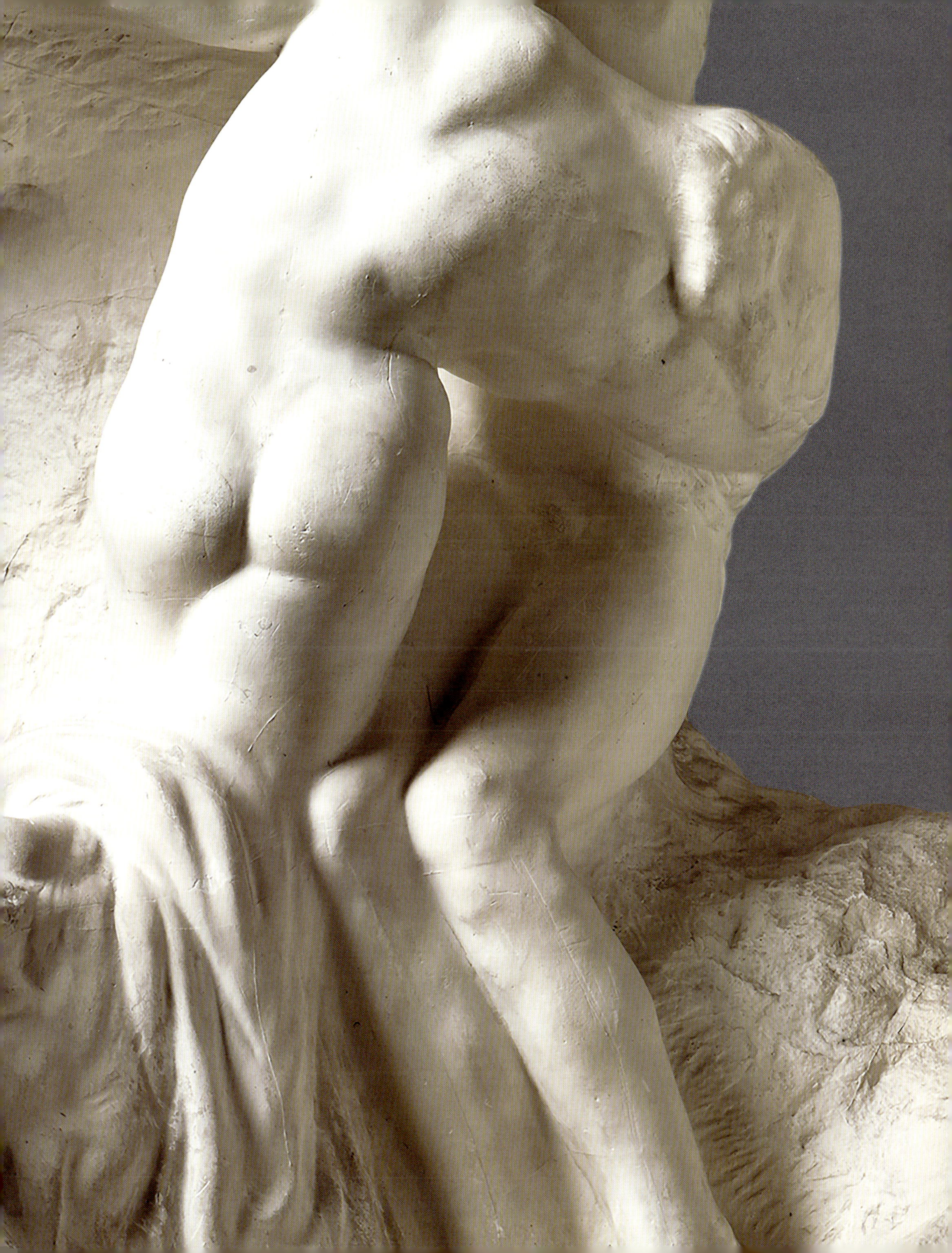

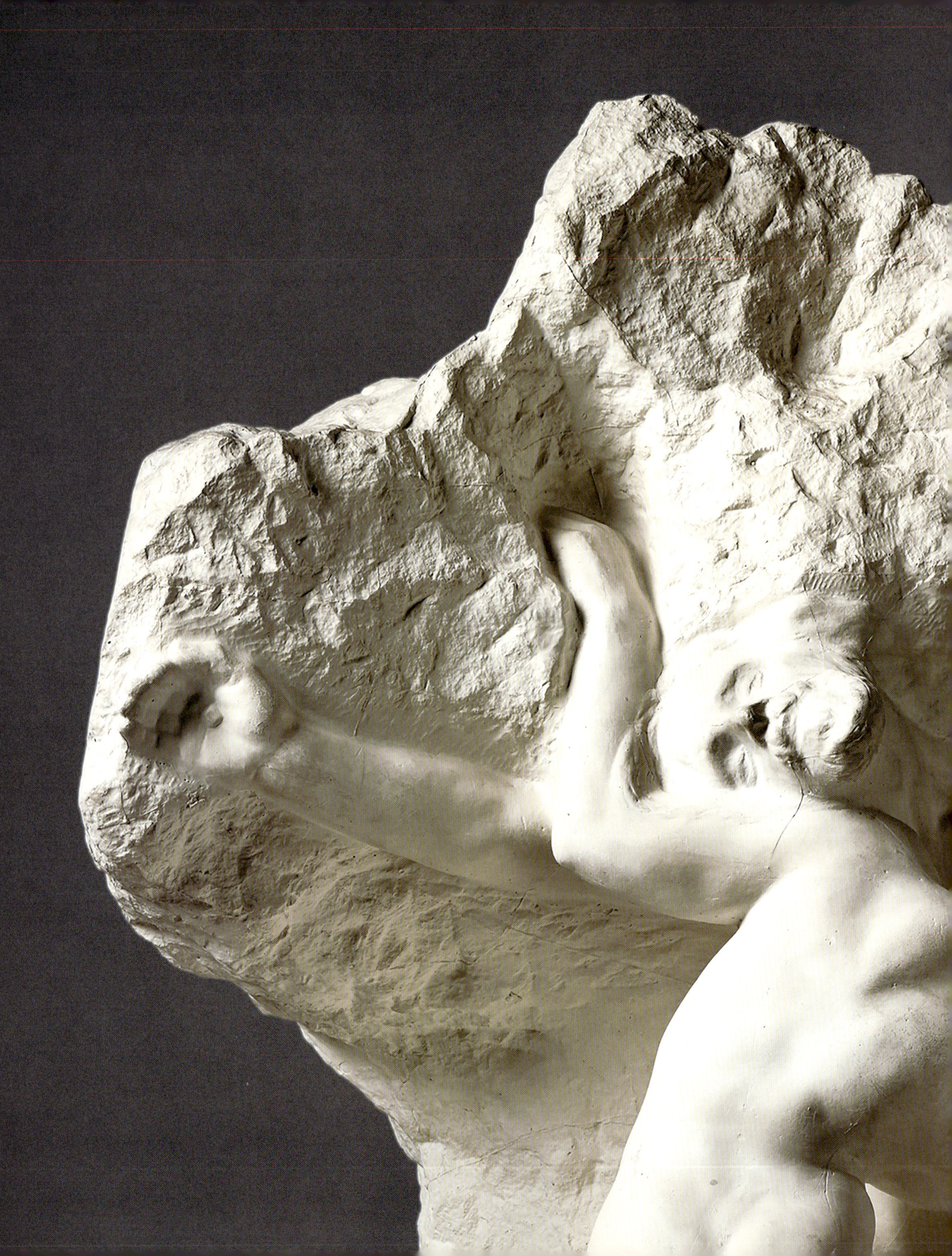

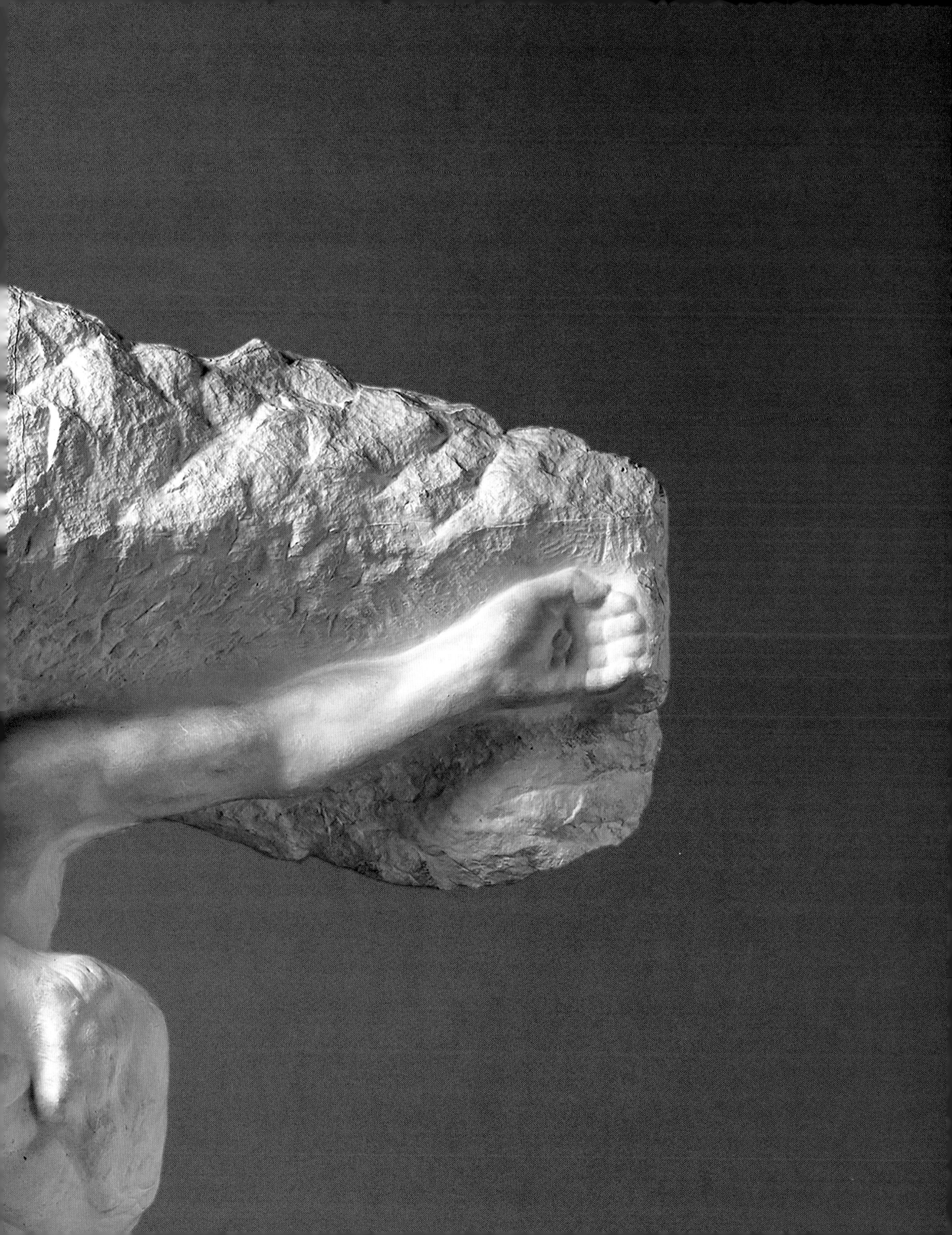

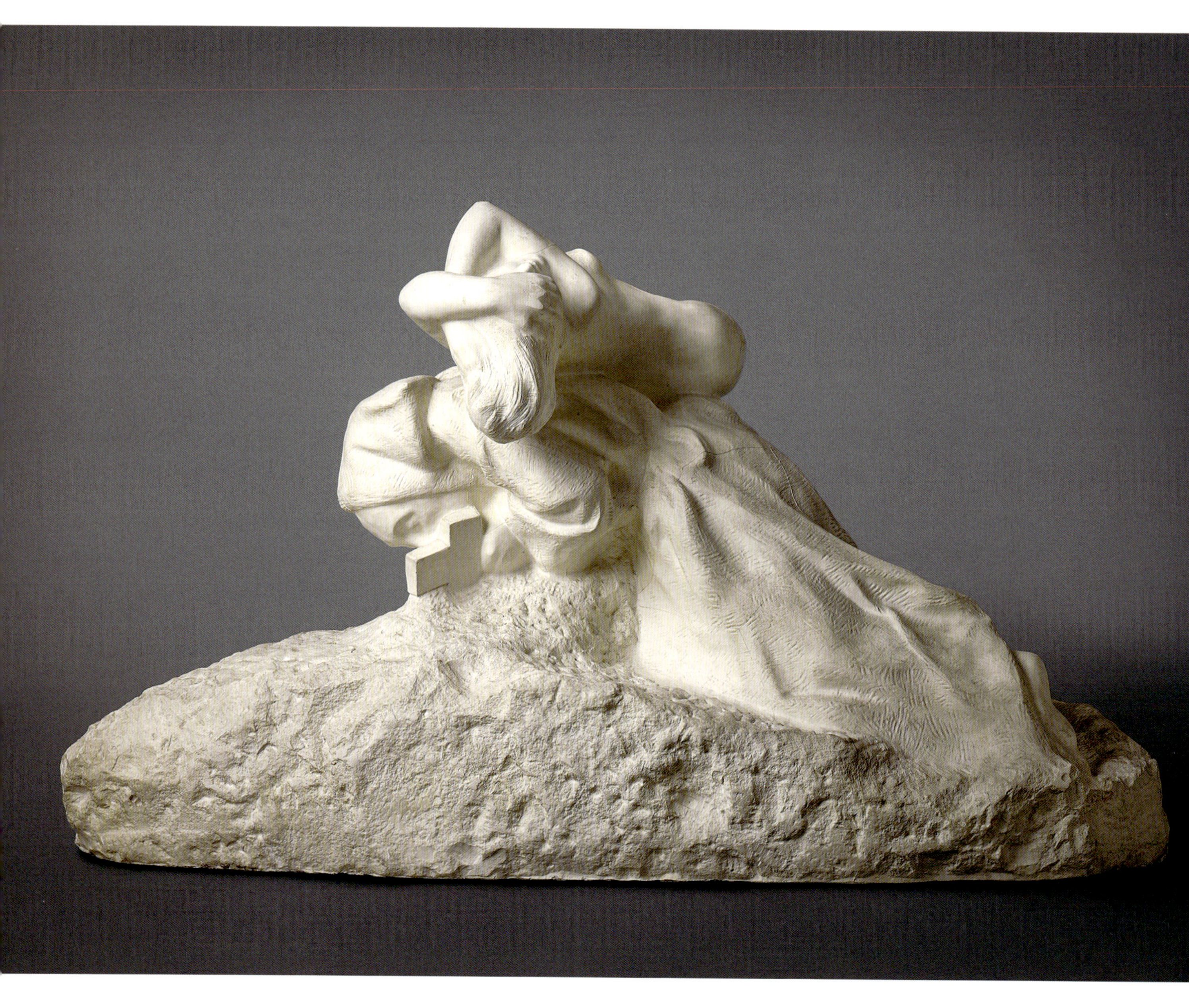

46. *The Temptation of Saint Anthony*, before 1900. Plaster, 24 ⅜ x 38 ½ x 29 ½ in. (61.9 x 97.8 x 74.9 cm).
Inscribed: *Rodin*. Gift of Alma de Bretteville Spreckels, 1962.27

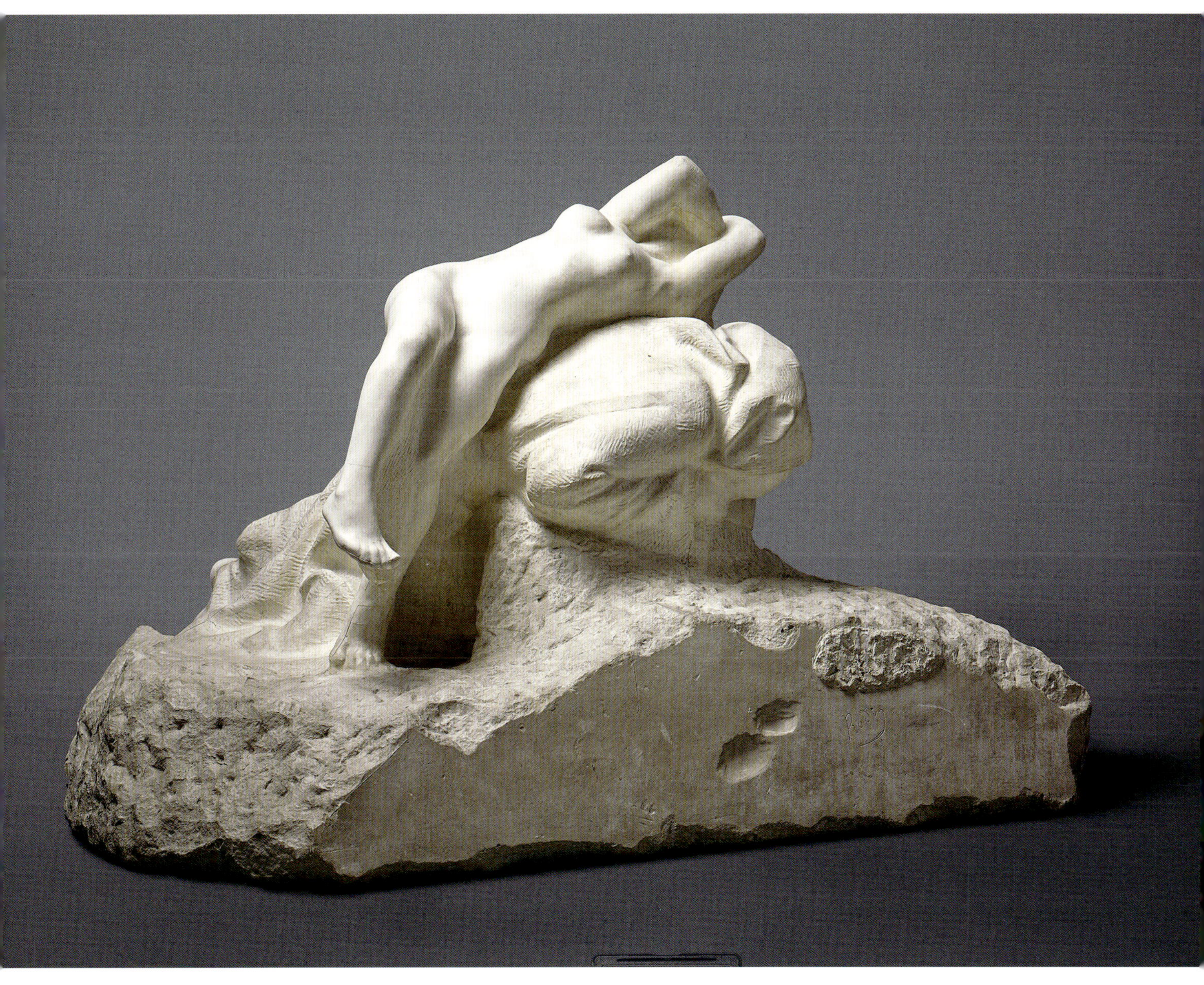

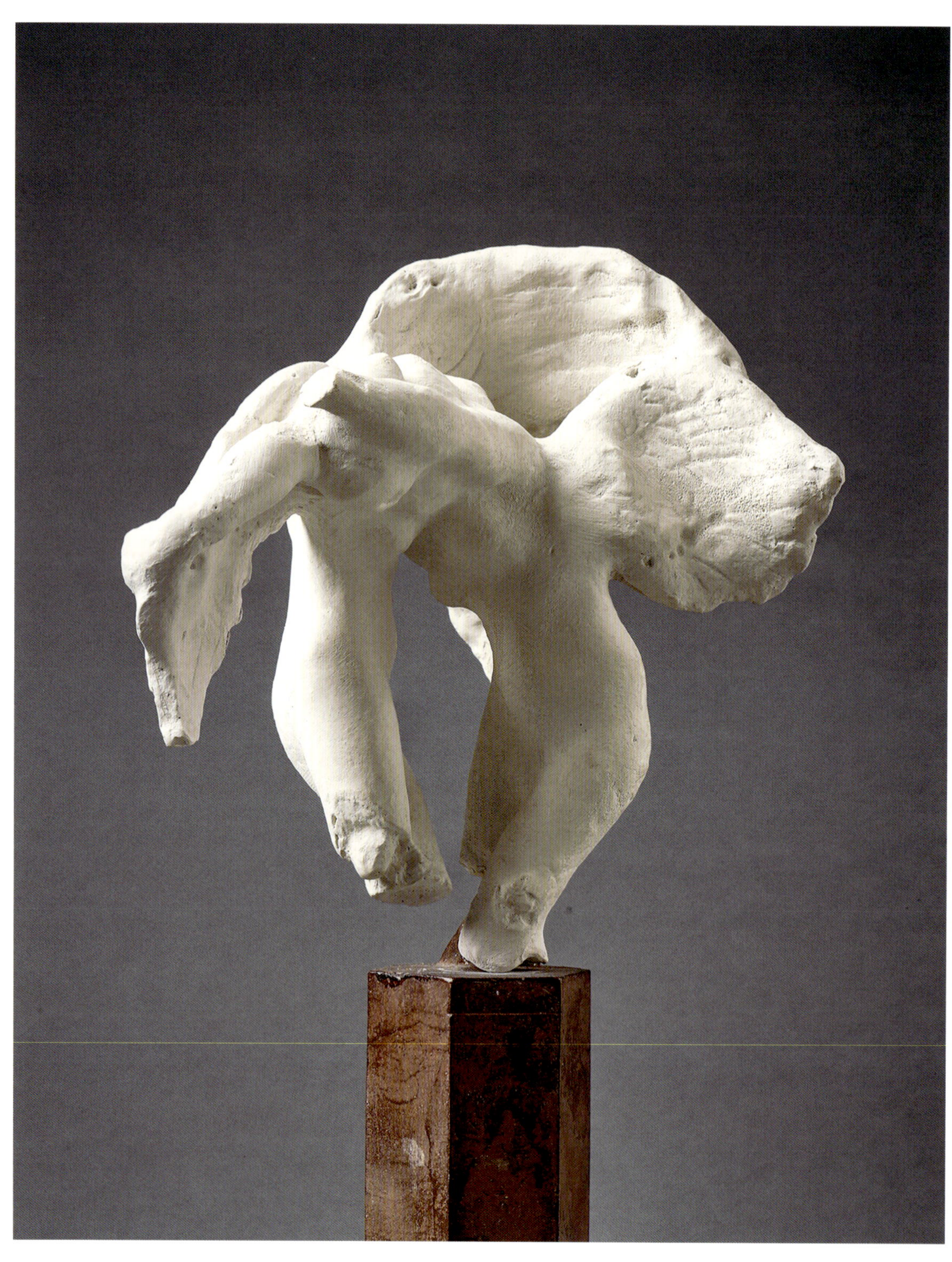

47. *Study for "The Benedictions,"* 1890s. Plaster, 7 x 7 ⅛ x 5 in. (17.8 x 18.1 x 12.7 cm).
Inscribed: *esquisse* / . . . [illegible] / *Benedictions* [sic].
Gift of Adolph B. Spreckels, Jr., 1933.12.16

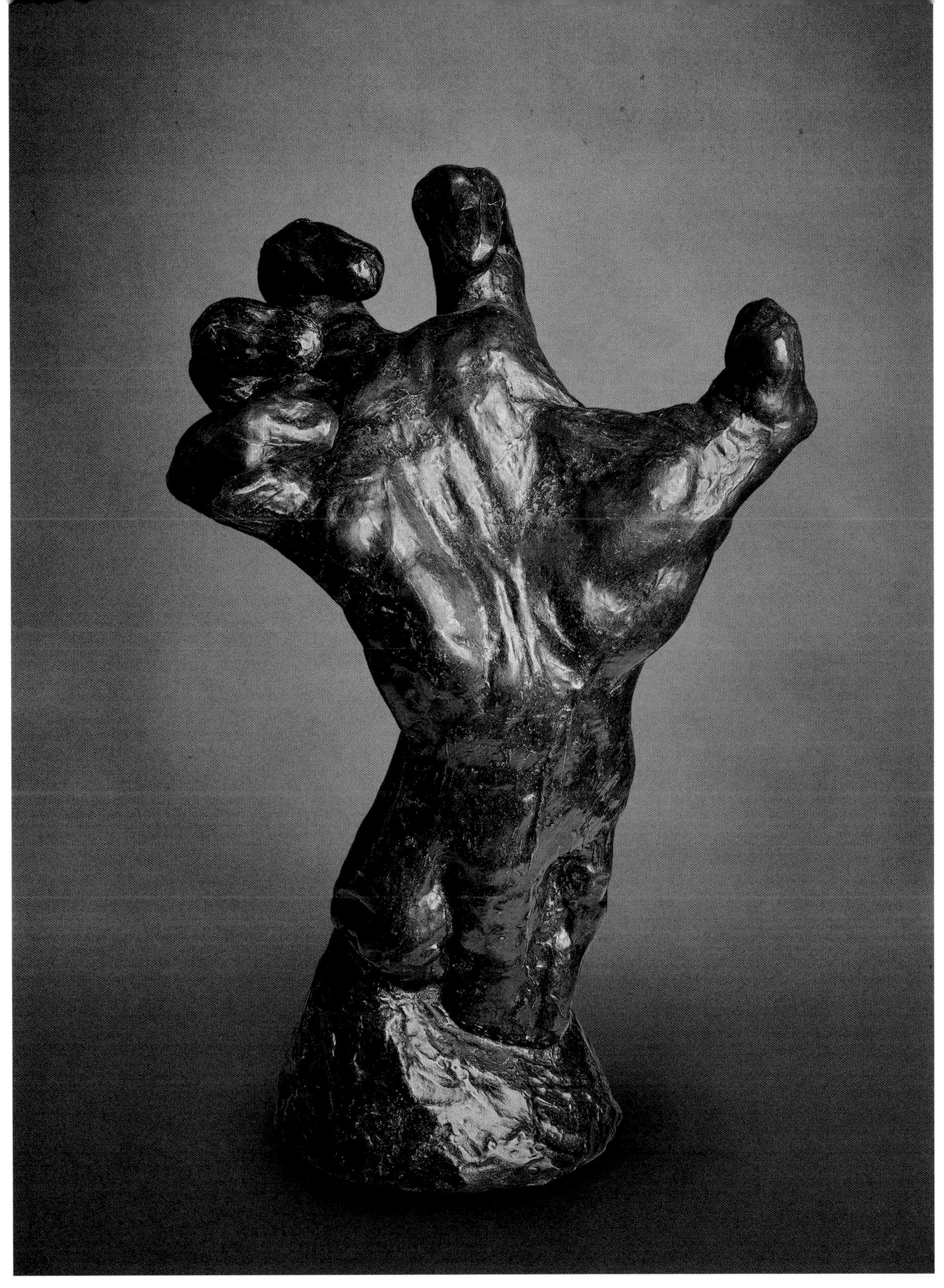

48. *The Mighty Hand* or *Clenched Right Hand,* 1880s (enlarged ca. 1910, cast 1913).
Bronze, 18 x 12 ⅜ x 7 ⅝ in. (45.7 x 31.4 x 19.2 cm).
Inscribed: *A. Rodin* and *ALEXIS. RUDIER / FONDEUR. PARIS.* Gift of Alma de Bretteville Spreckels, 1942.39

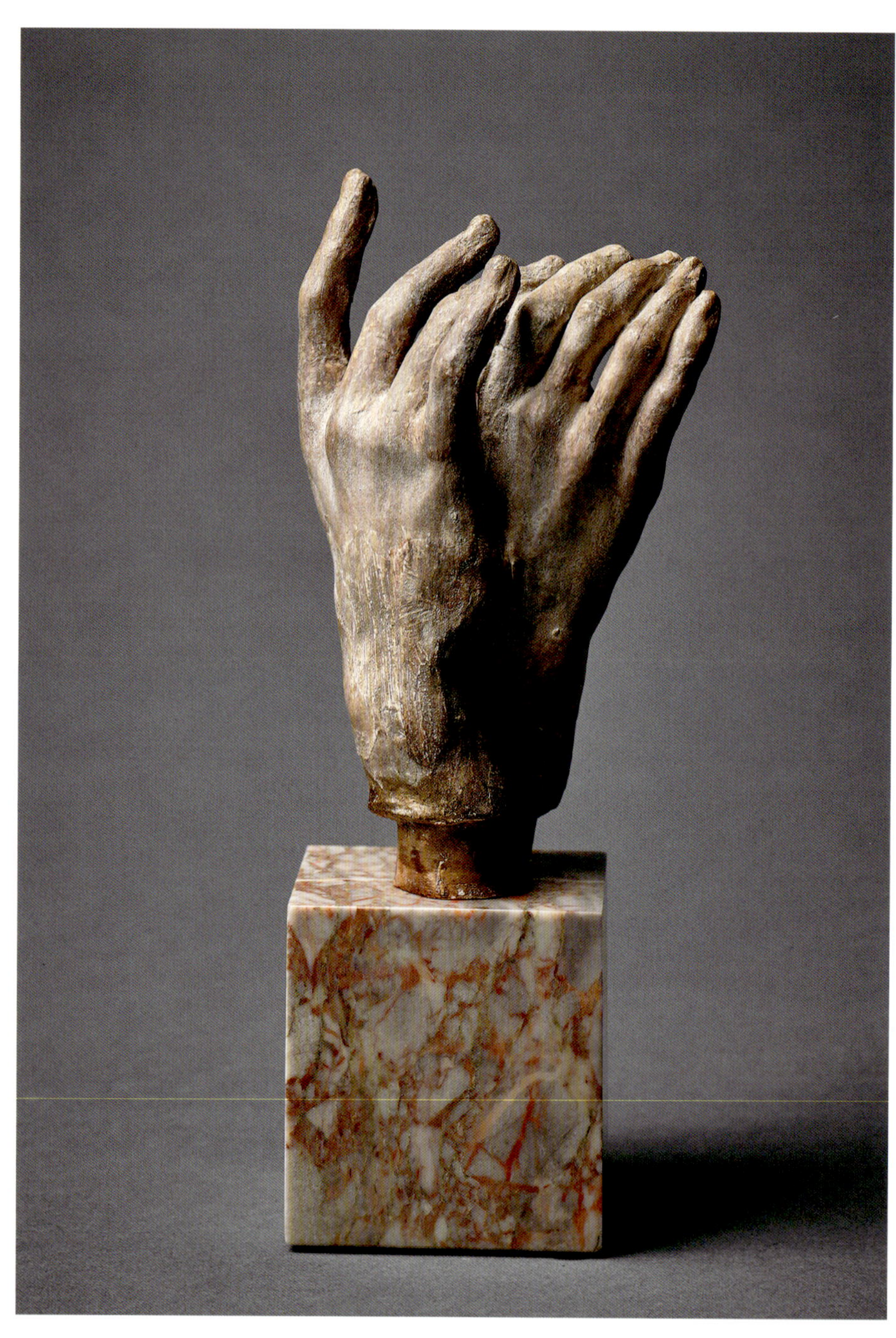

49. *Two Right Hands*, date unknown. Plaster on marble base, 4 ⅛ x 3 x 2 ¼ in. (10.5 x 7.6 x 5.7 cm).
Gift of Adolph B. Spreckels, Jr., 1933.12.12

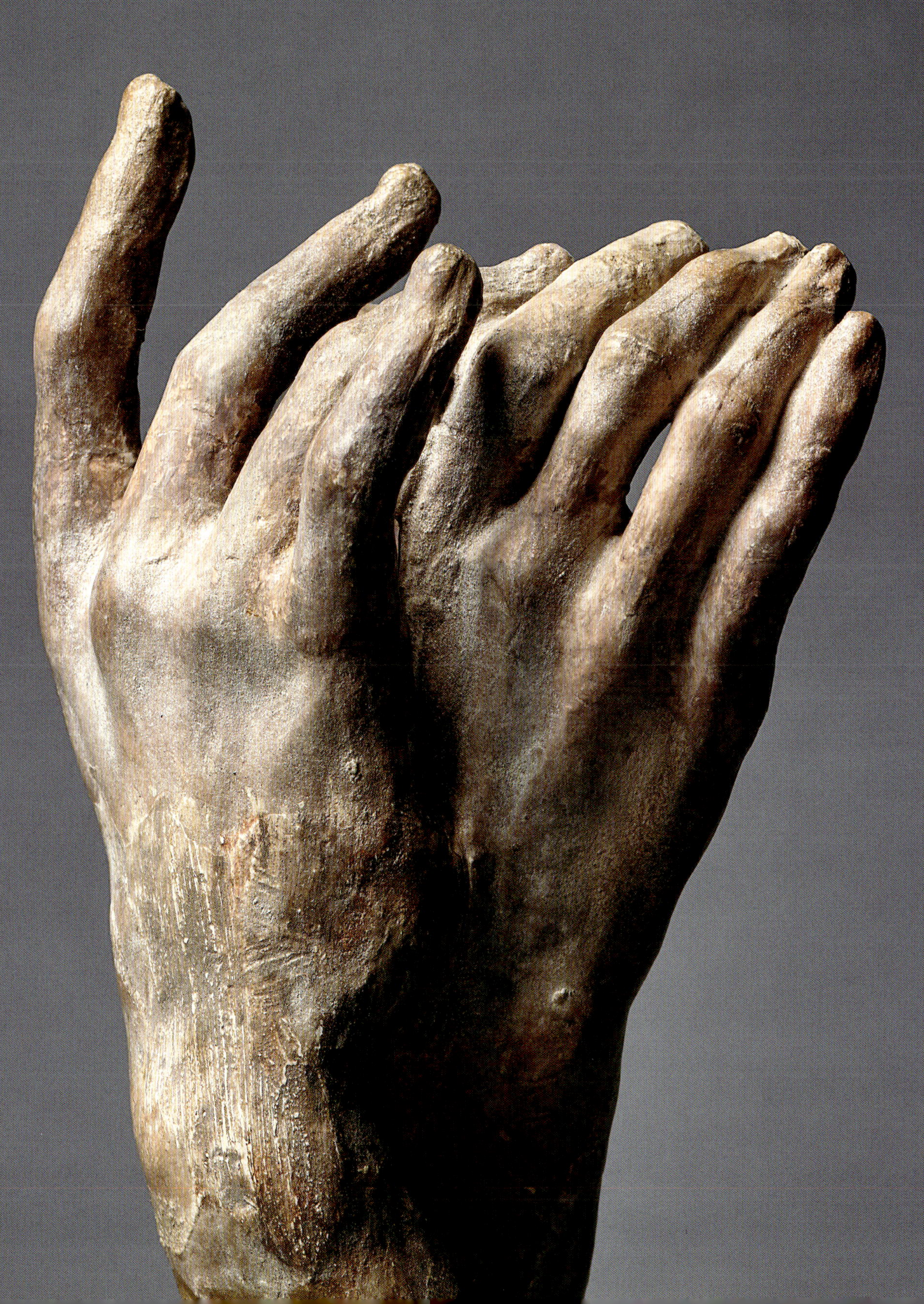

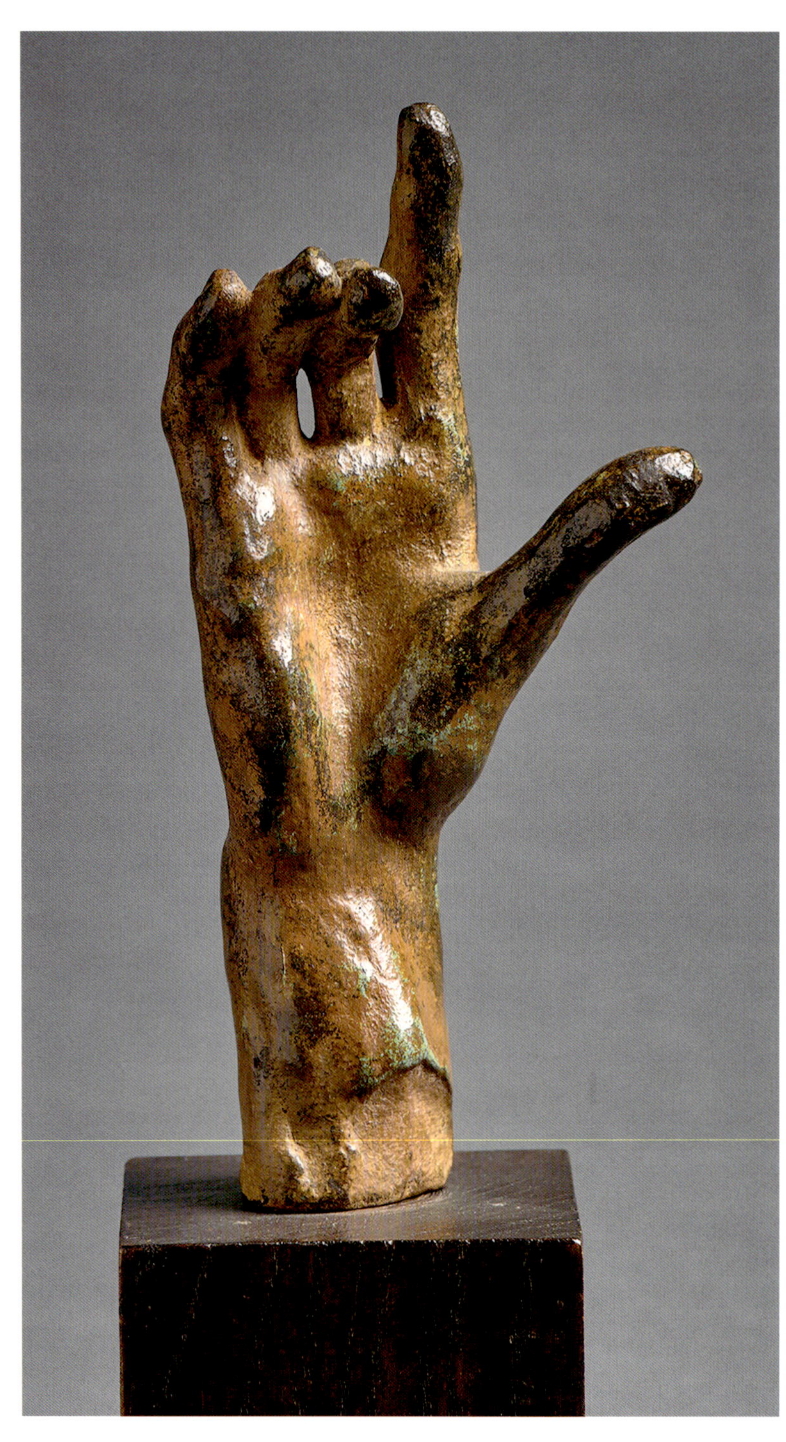

50. *Right Hand with Index Finger Extended*, date unknown. Bronze on wood base, 4 x 2 x 1 ⅛ in. (10 x 4.9 x 2.9 cm).
Inscribed: *A. Rodin*. Gift of Alma de Bretteville Spreckels, 1962.25

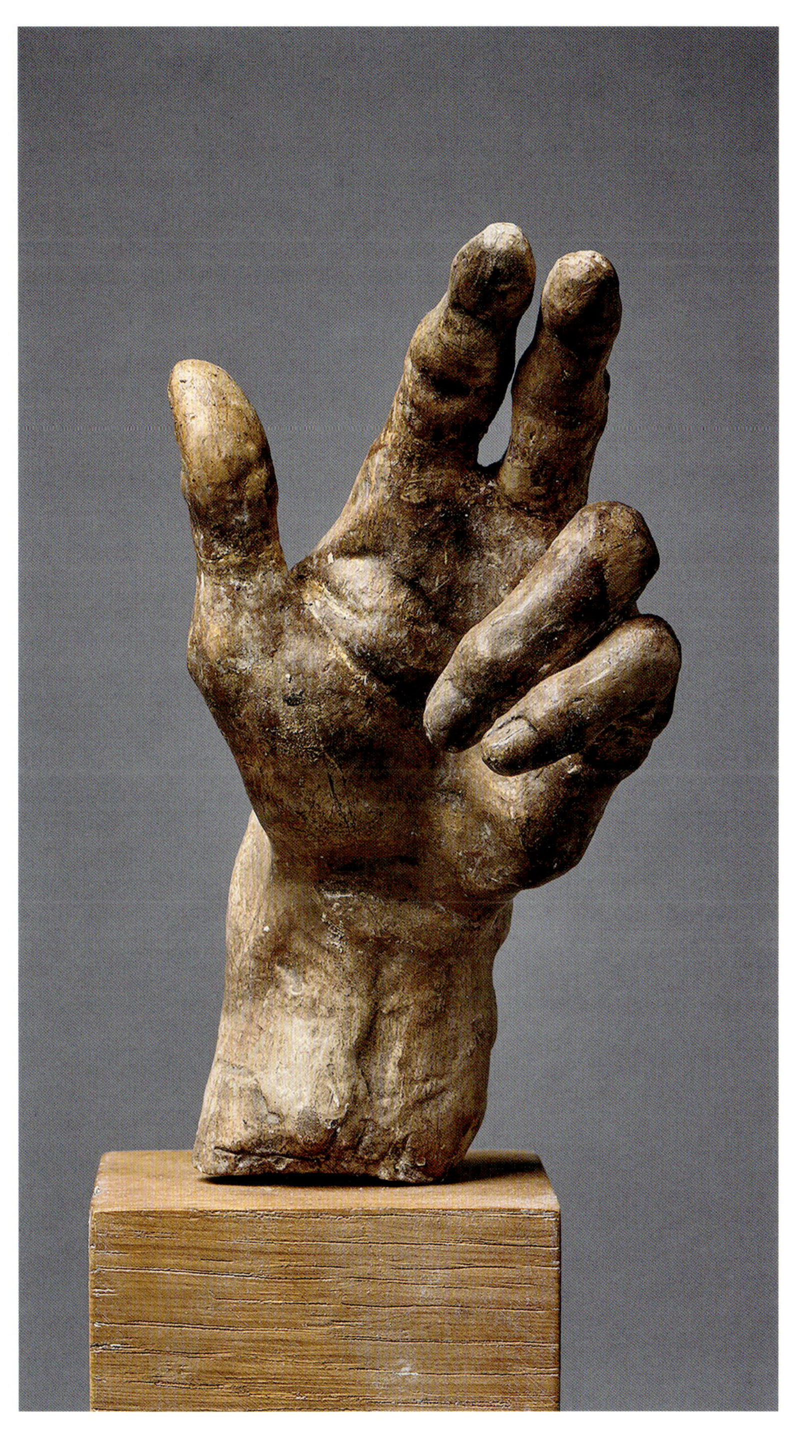

51. *Study of a Small Left Hand*, ca. 1895? Plaster on wood base, 5 ⅞ x 3 ¼ x 1 ⅞ in. (14.9 x 8.3 x 4.8 cm). Gift of Adolph B. Spreckels, Jr., 1933.12.25

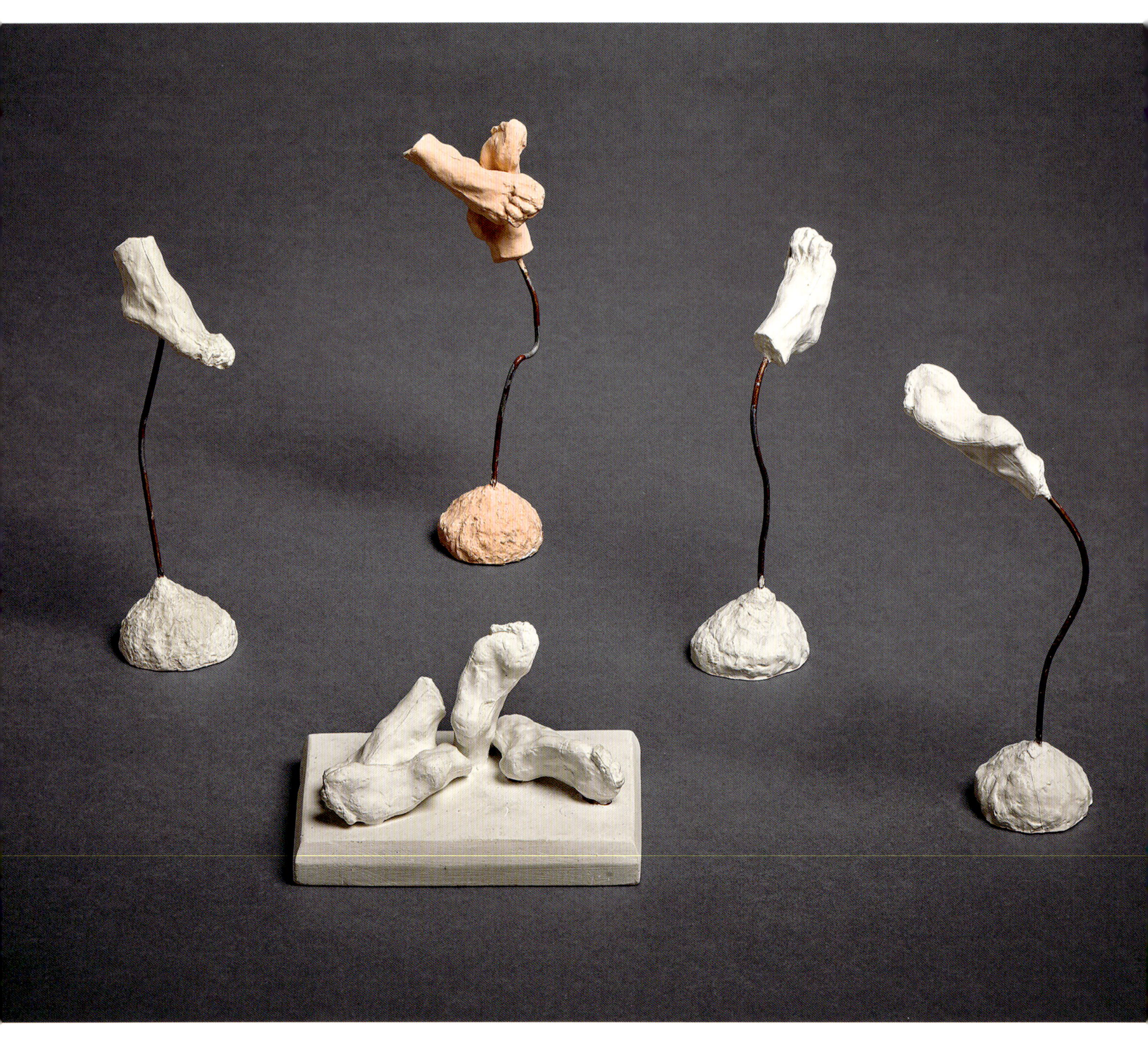

52. *Five Compositions of Right Feet*, dates unknown. Plaster, wire, and clay, variable dimensions.
Gift of Alma de Bretteville Spreckels, 1949.19.14–18

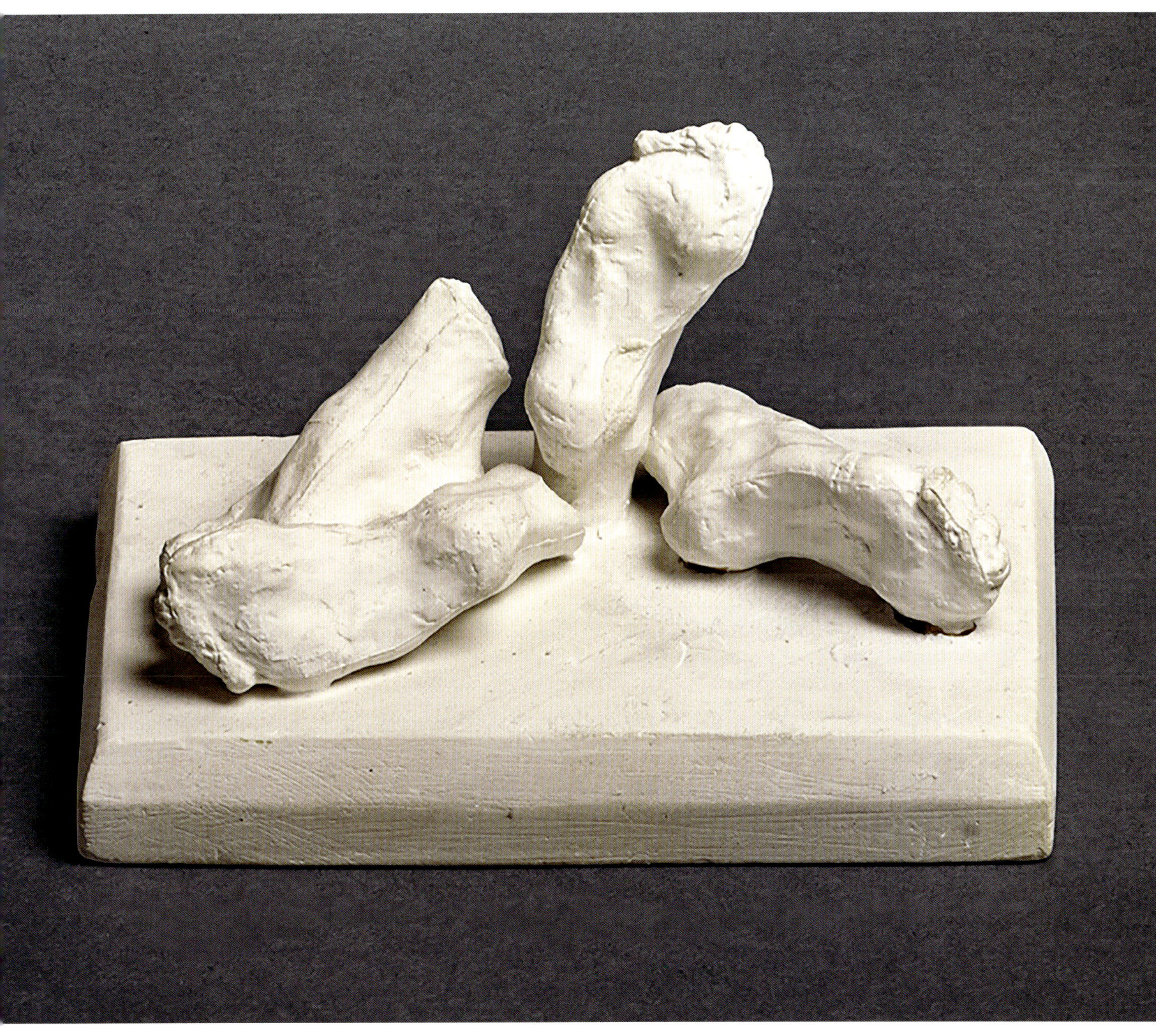

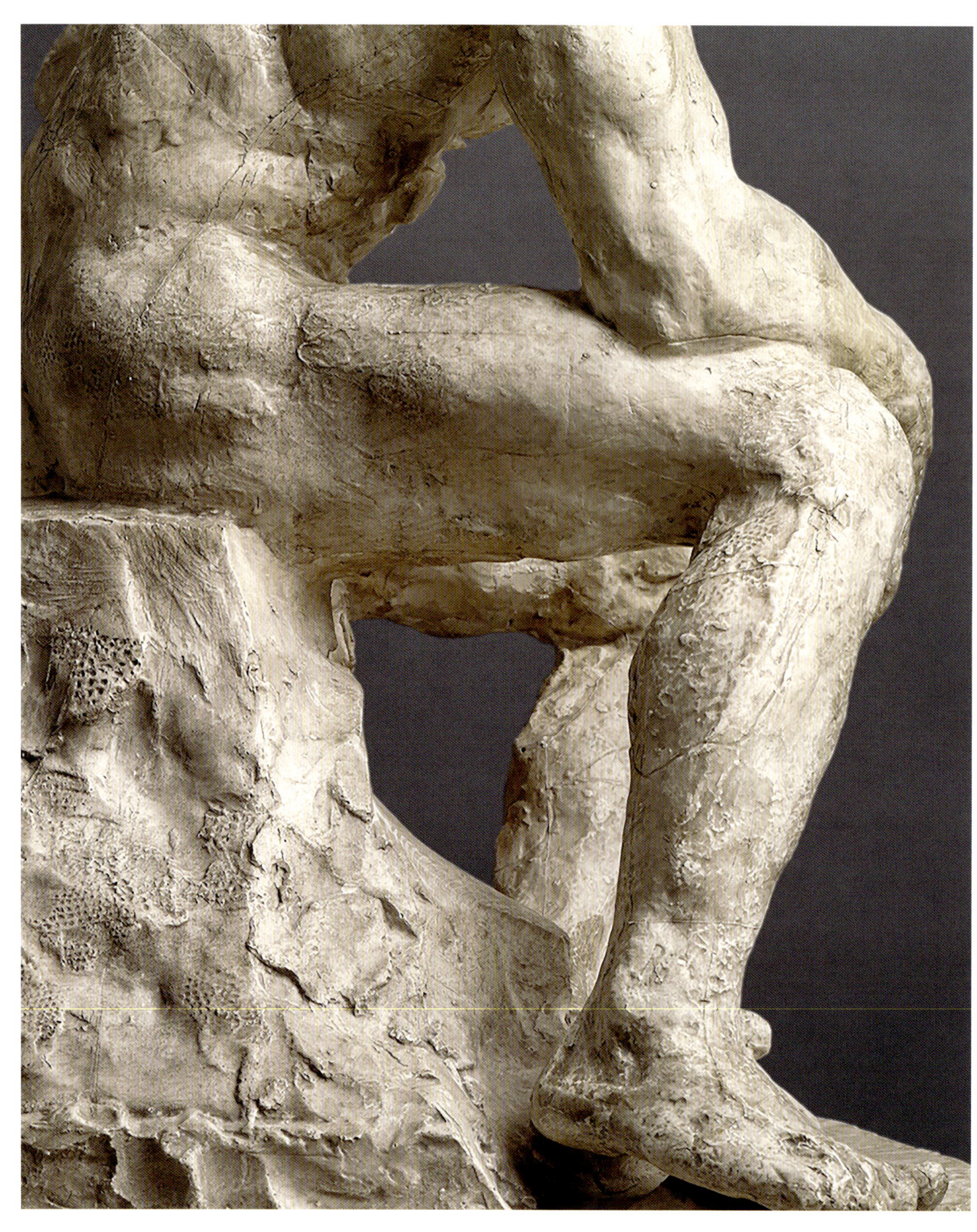

53. *The American Athlete*, ca. 1901 (second model after 1904). Plaster, 18 ⅛ x 13 ¼ x 7 ½ in. (46 x 33.8 x 18.9 cm).
Gift of Adolph B. Spreckels, Jr., 1933.12.9

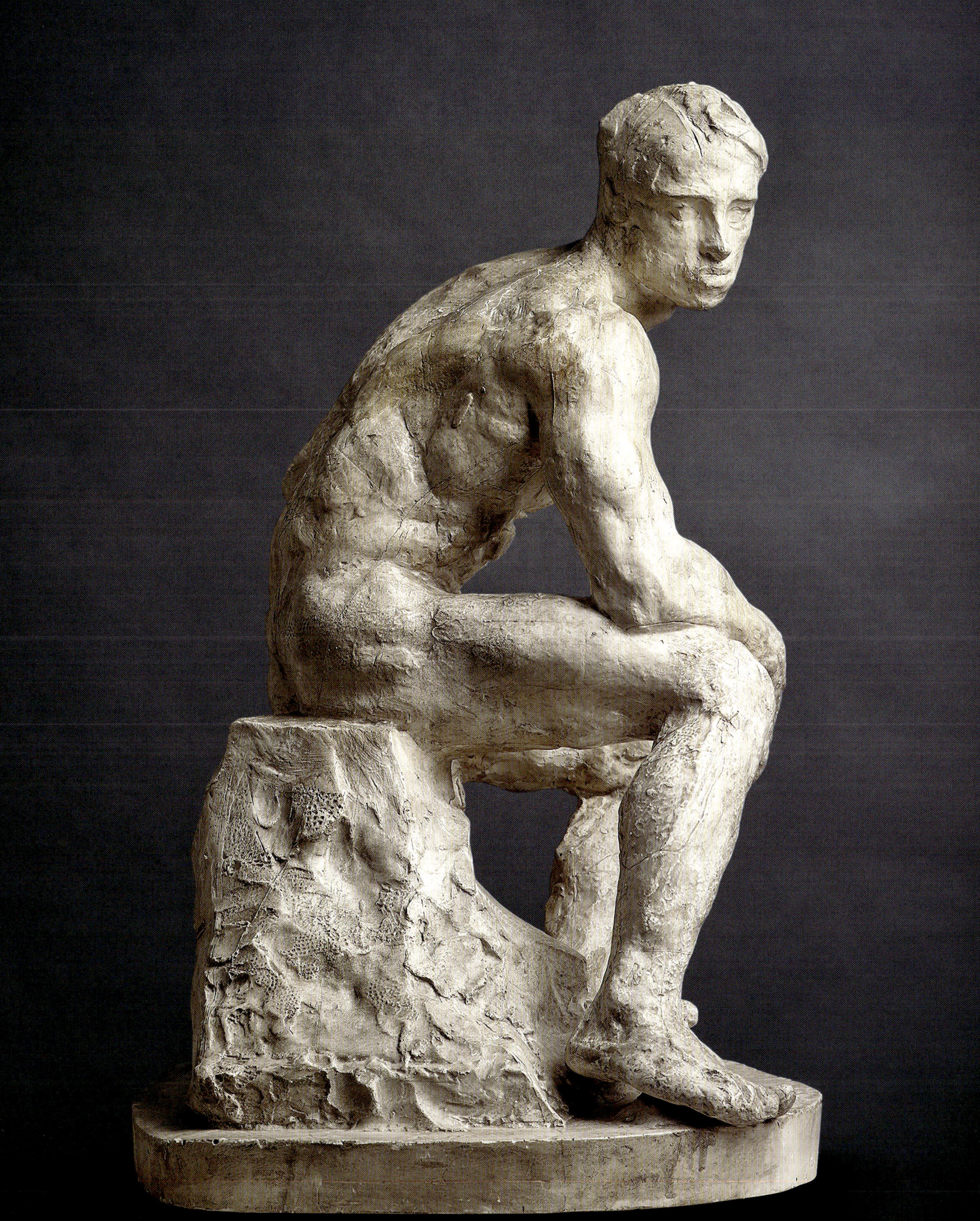

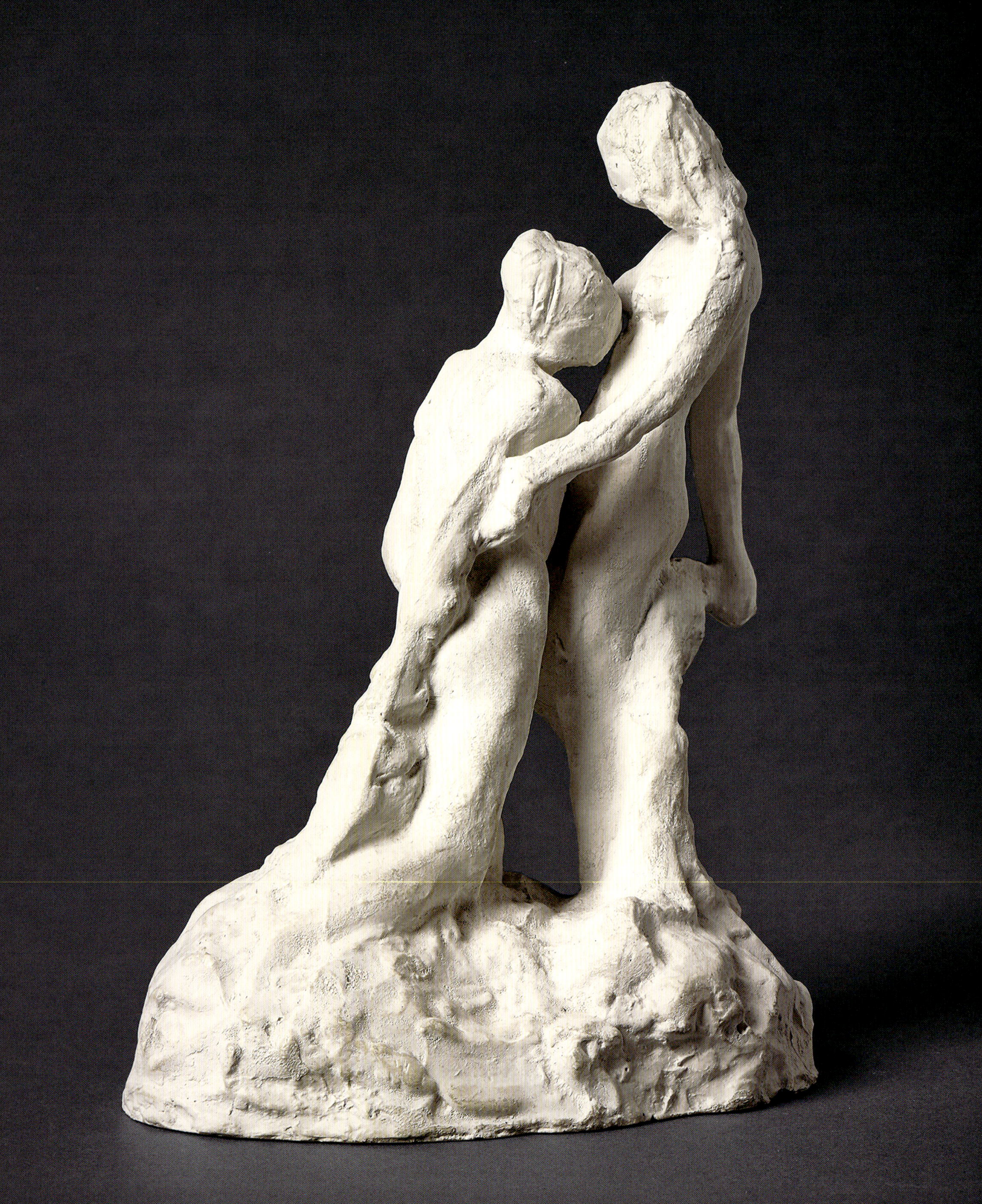

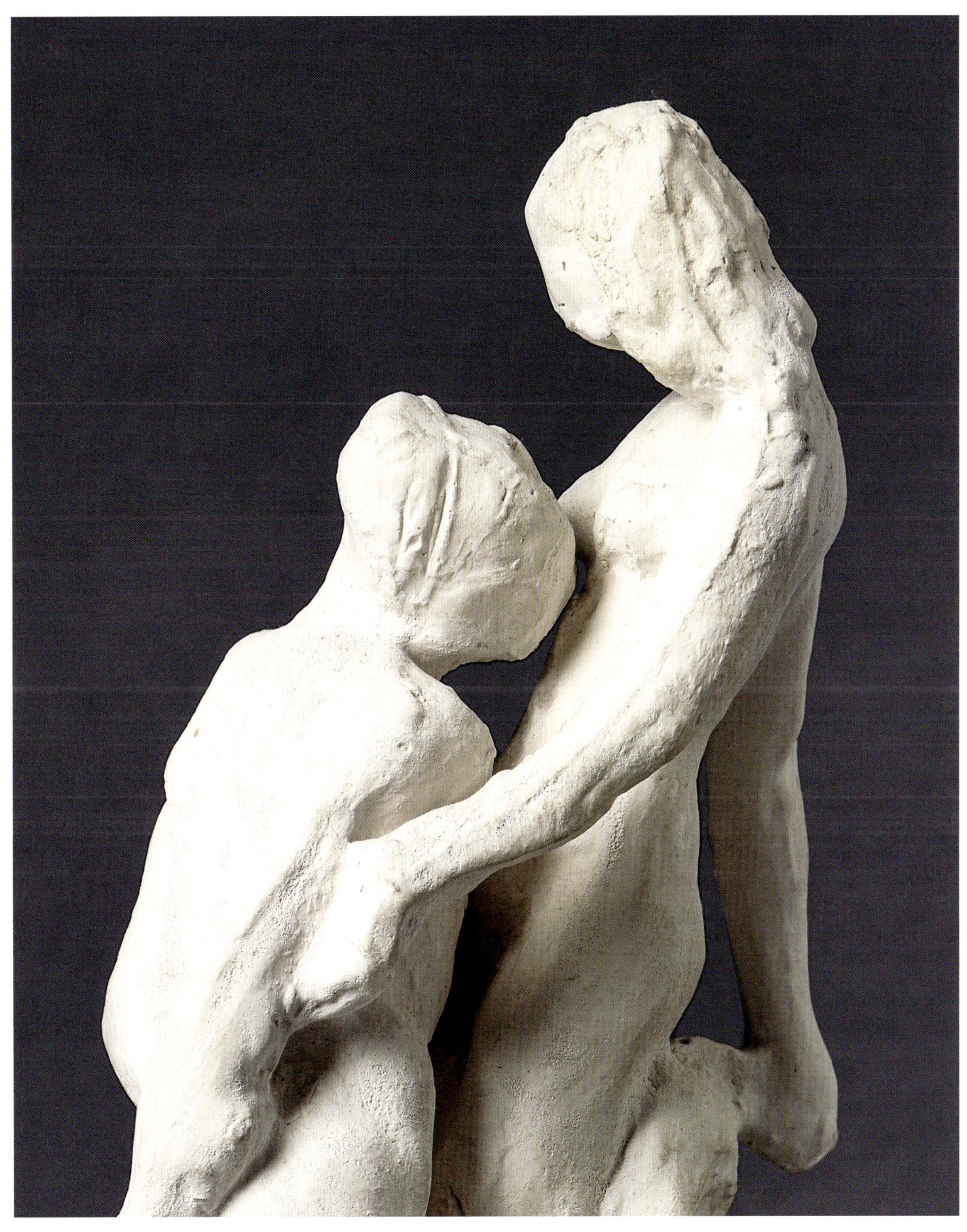

54. *Study for "The Eternal Idol,"* ca. 1891. Plaster, 7 ⅛ x 5 ⅝ x 3 ⅜ in. (18 x 14.2 x 8.6 cm). Gift of Adolph B. Spreckels, Jr., 1933.12.8

NOTES

[i] Ionel Jianou and C. Goldscheider, *Rodin* (Paris: Arted, Éditions d'Art, 1967), 31.

[ii] The unfinished quality of this bust (with the back of its head missing by accident) is found throughout Rodin's oeuvre. He liked to retain accidental elements in his work because they challenged the more highly finished sculpture that were part of the academic tradition prevalent in France during his lifetime.

[iii] Yvon Taillandier, *Rodin* (New York: Crown Trade Paperbacks, 1977), 91.

[iv] This sculpture was perhaps inspired by the figure of Christ in Michelangelo's *Pietà Bandini* (ca. 1547–1555, Museo dell'Opera del Duomo, Florence).

[v] Verdun was one of the First World War's major battle sites between the French and the German forces in 1916.

[vi] *The Age of Bronze* was purchased in 1880. The statue of *Saint John the Baptist Preaching* is now in the collection of the Victoria and Albert Museum, London.

[vii] Young men were commonly used for the modeling of angels since medieval times, so Rodin's angel is exceptional in that it is modeled from a woman.

[viii] Auguste Rodin, quoted in François Dujardin-Beaumetz, *Auguste Rodin, Readings on His Life and Work*, trans. Albert E. Elsen (Englewood Cliffs, NJ: Prentice Hall, 1965), 165–166. See also Albert E. Elsen et al., *Rodin's Art: The Rodin Collection at the Iris & B. Gerald Cantor Center for Visual Arts at Stanford University* (New York: Oxford University Press, 2003), 546, cat. 174.

[ix] The plaster model is held in the collection of the Musée d'Orsay, Paris (DO 1986 4, S 2450). The *Gates* were only cast in bronze after Rodin's death. A bronze version is contained in the holdings of the Iris & B. Gerald Cantor Center for Visual Arts at Stanford University.

[x] Antoinette Le Normand-Romain, *Rodin* (Paris: Citadelles & Mazenod, 2013), 95, pl. 86.

[xi] The dimensions of the original sculpture are 28⅛ x 17⅛ x 22¼ in. (71.5 x 43.5 x 56.5 cm); the dimensions of the large version are 74⅜ x 38⅝ x 55⅛ in. (189 x 98 x 140 cm).

[xii] Antoinette Le Normand-Romain, *The Bronzes of Rodin, Catalogue of Works in the Musée Rodin*, vol. 2 (Paris: Musée Rodin, 2007), 584–595.

[xiii] Eight lifetime casts of the monumental version are listed in various sources, including Le Normand-Romain, *Bronzes of Rodin*, 587. However, the number of casts made since Rodin's death in 1917 fluctuates according to the source. The Wikipedia *List of* The Thinker *Sculptures* (https://en.wikipedia.org/wiki/List_of_The_Thinker_sculptures) numbers forty-seven posthumous casts, and seventy are described in Jacques de Caso and Patricia B. Sanders, *Rodin's Sculpture, A Critical Study of the Spreckels Collection* (San Francisco: Fine Arts Museums of San Francisco, 1977), 15. However, neither source designates the sizes of these casts. The online research and documentation project for Rodin's enlarged *Thinker*, penseur.org (www.penseur.org), lists twenty colossal casts; Wikipedia *The Thinker* (https://en.wikipedia.org/wiki/The_Thinker) indicates "about twenty-eight" monumental casts; and twenty-two are considered to be "original" by the Musée Rodin, Paris, as cited in Le Normand-Romain, *Bronzes of Rodin*, 587.

[xiv] This enlarged cast of *The Thinker*, paid for by public subscription, is now displayed in the garden of the Musée Rodin, Paris.

[xv] Le Normand-Romain, *Bronzes of Rodin*, 587.

[xvi] De Caso and Sanders, *Rodin's Sculpture*, 139.

[xvii] Jacques de Caso and Patricia B. Sanders, *Rodin's Thinker, Significant Aspects* (San Francisco: Fine Arts Museums of San Francisco, 1973), 19n4.

[xviii] Ibid., 11–12n2.

[xix] De Caso and Sanders, *Rodin's Sculpture*, 216n2.

[xx] Le Normand-Romain, *Rodin*, 50.

[xxi] De Caso and Sanders, *Rodin's Sculpture*, 280.

[xxii] Ibid., 282.

[xxiii] Ronald Alley, *The Foreign Paintings, Drawings, and Sculpture* (London: Tate Gallery, 1959), 219. See also Frederic V. Grunfeld, *Rodin: A Biography* (New York: Henry Holt and Company, 1987), 460. Beckett was a great admirer of Rodin's work and persuaded the artist to make an enlargement of *The Thinker*. "He [Beckett] had recently met Rodin and felt himself to be in the presence of 'a supreme genius'—a philosopher and poet as well as a sculptor. Responding to Rodin's 'full-blooded prodigal abounding force,' he described him as 'the Wagner of sculpture.'" Michael Holroyd, "Marriage or Bust," *The Guardian*, November 5, 2010; extracted from Michael Holroyd, *Book of Secrets: Illegitimate Daughters, Absent Fathers* (London: Chatto, 2010).

[xxiv] Le Normand-Romain, *Rodin*, 324. See also Marion J. Hare, *The Sculptor and His Sitter: Rodin's Bust of Eve Fairfax* (Johannesburg: Johannesburg Art Gallery, 1994), 13. Auguste Rodin to Eve Fairfax, March 18, 1907. Johannesburg Art Gallery archives, letter no. 15. See Hare, *The Sculptor and His Sitter*, 36.

[xxv] Auguste Rodin to Eve Fairfax, January 24, 1906. Johannesburg Art Gallery archives, letter no. 20. See Hare, *The Sculptor and His Sitter*, 35.

[xxvi] Unpublished, undated, and unsigned typed note (Loïe Fuller file, Department of Decorative Arts and Sculpture, Fine Arts Museums of San Francisco). Fuller describes the sculpture as "Carrière in marble," referring to the Symbolist painter Eugène Carrière (French, 1849–1906), who was a close friend of Rodin's.

[xxvii] There were several specialized marble practitioners who worked for Rodin, including Émile-Antoine Bourdelle (French, 1861–1929) and Séraphin Soudbinine (Russian, 1867–1944). "These artisans are literally his hands," remarked Lorado Taft, an American sculptor who visited Rodin's studio in 1900. See Lorado Taft, "Rodin in his studio. Visit to the great sculptor," *Chicago Record*, June 16, 1900. Unfortunately, the craftsmen for the marble works in the Legion's collection are not known. It appears that Rodin did work on some of his marble pieces as is supplied in an account, presumably by Loïe Fuller, about the sculpture *La Nature, Miss Eve Fairfax* (pl. 40). In it, she describes "the Master" working on the marble in 1916 (see pp. 102n29, this volume).

[xxviii] De Caso and Sanders, *Rodin's Sculpture*, 114–116. A marble version of this example, dating from 1917 and carved by Victor Peter, is in the Musée Rodin, Paris (S.1103).

[xxix] Ibid. Judging by the date of 1916, the references to "the Master," and the intimate proximity to the sculptor that is expressed, this note is probably authored by Loïe Fuller and was possibly written for one of her lectures. Furthermore, the sculpture is inscribed *A Loïe / Rodin* and was acquired by Alma Spreckels from Fuller in 1917. See de Caso and Sanders *Rodin's Sculpture*, 303n11. The complete note reads: "Le [*sic*] Nature. With regard to this great marble head, I watched the sculptor day after day putting on the finishing touches and when it was partly finished I found the lines so beautiful that I asked the master to leave it as it is today, so he agreed and left the lines as they are. This was in June 1916. This work inspired E. Fairfax, cousin to Lord Fairfax, of Virginia. It resembles the waves of the sea, it is called 'Out of the Earth'. 'The Spiritual', 'Le Nature' [*sic*], 'Birth of Nature'. Any other artist would have made it symmetrical, but he has left it as it is. (left it with the bump) The natural movement of the marble is not interferred [*sic*] with, in fact it is a beautiful piece of art. Probably if this was done by another artist he would chisel out some of the lines, but it is this that has made it such a work of art. It slurs into the indefinite.—Carriere in Marble. This work is beautiful in spite of itself, as busts are seldom beautiful. A decorative effect."

[xxx] De Caso and Sanders, *Rodin's Sculpture*, 302.

[xxxi] Le Normand-Romain, *Bronzes of Rodin*, 30.

[xxxii] Ibid., 31.

[xxxiii] To underscore this point further, *Mother and Child* is also inscribed "*modele pour le Bronze*."

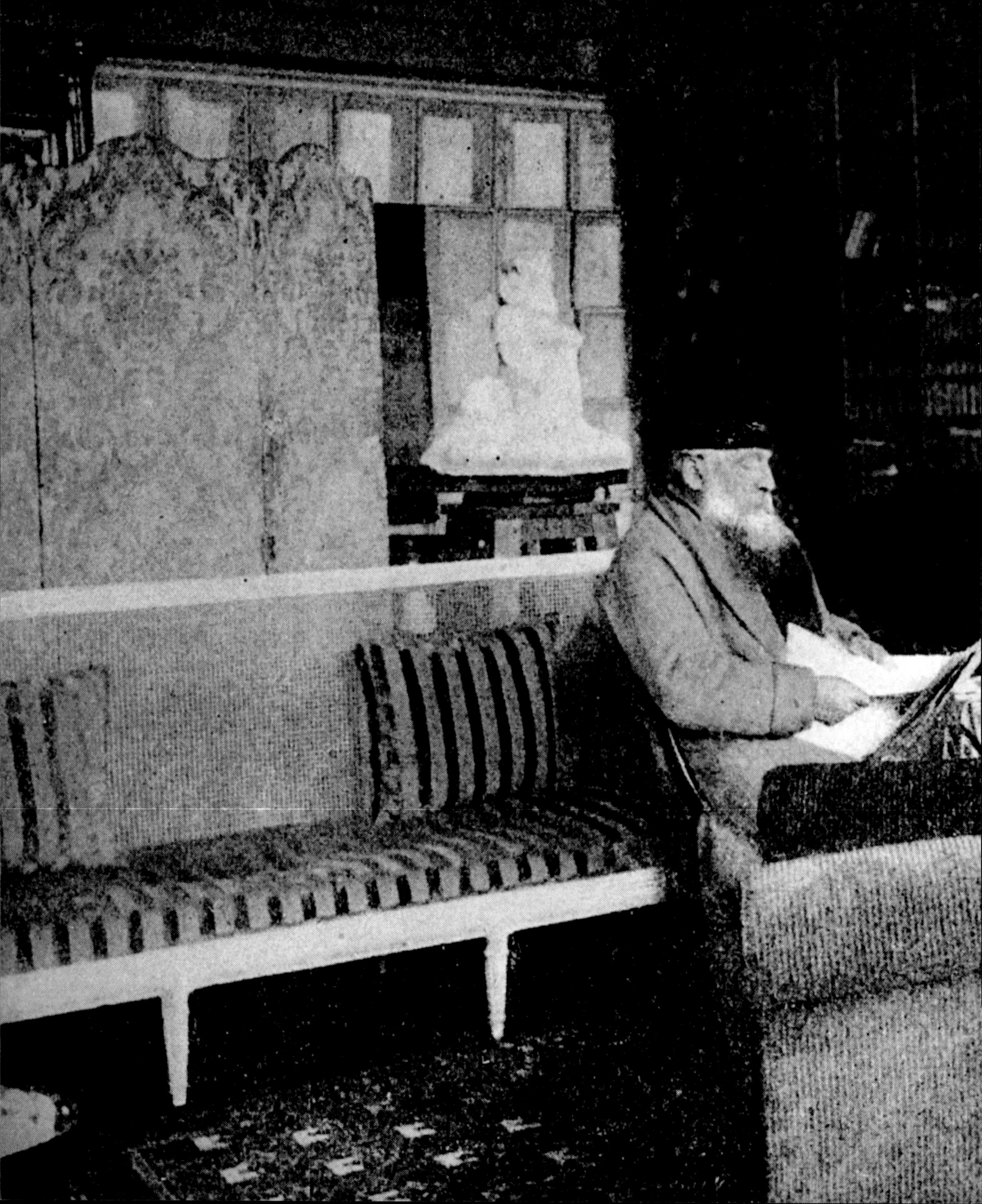

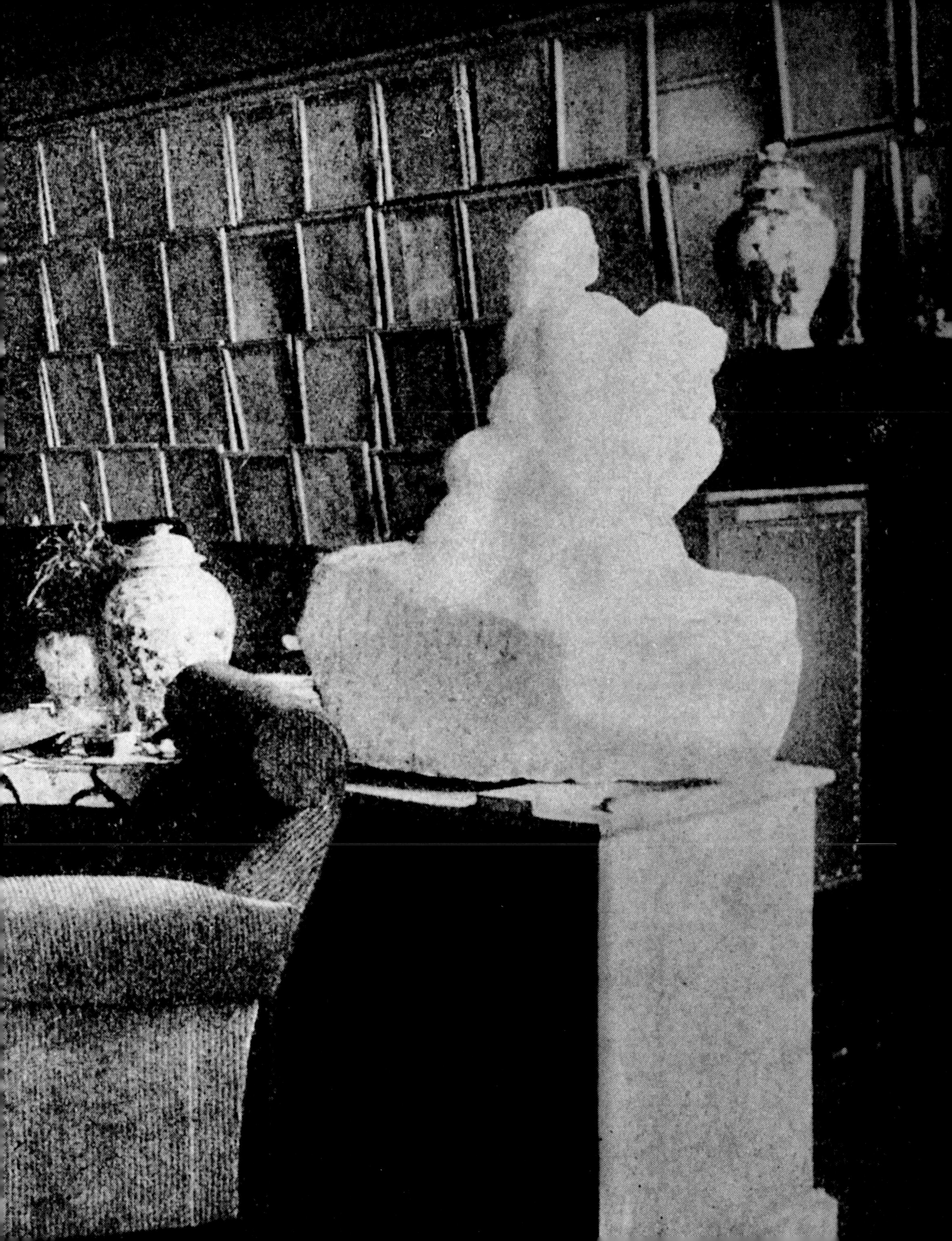

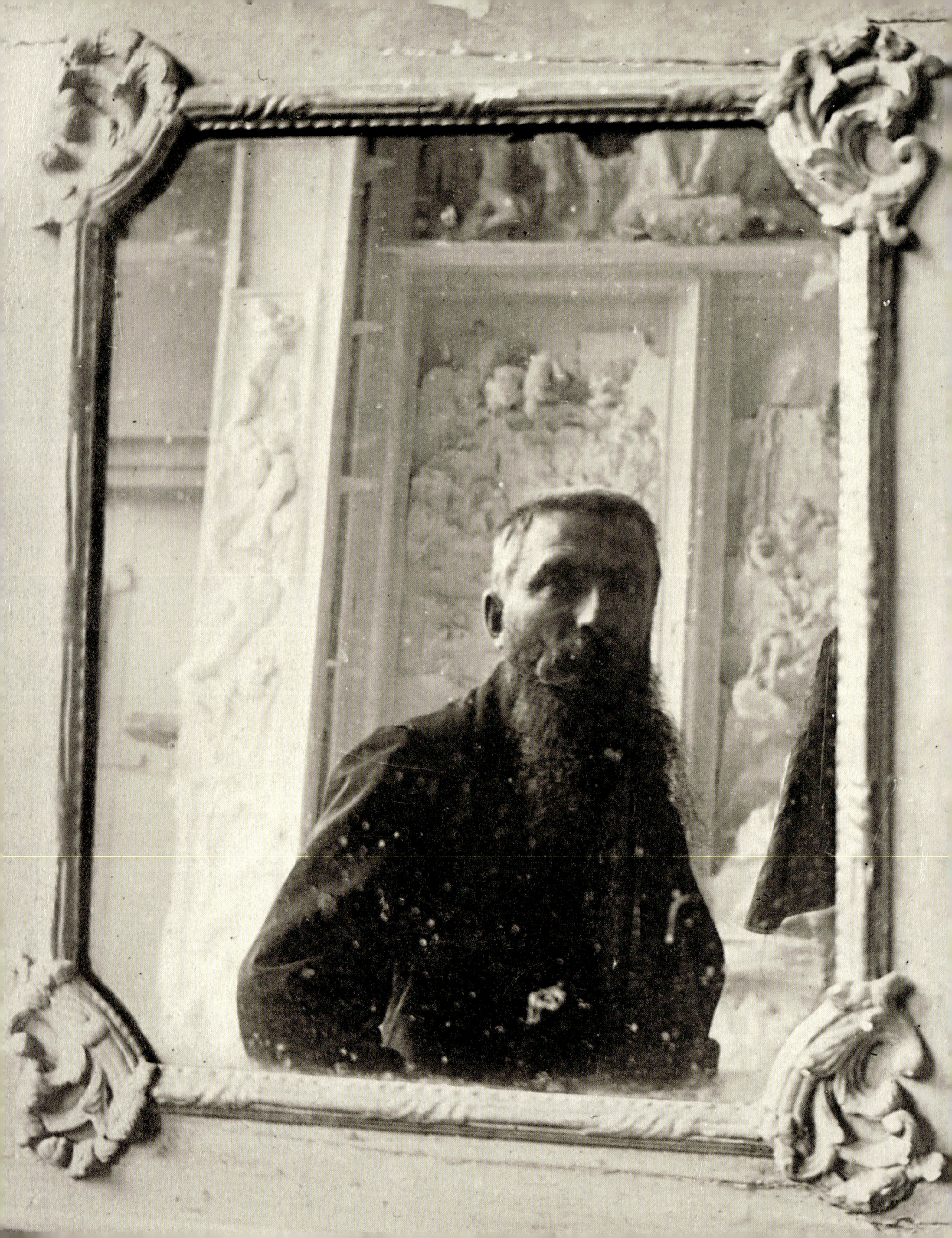

A BRIEF BIOGRAPHICAL TIMELINE OF
AUGUSTE RODIN

1840   Auguste Rodin is born in Paris on November 12 to an inspector of the police and a former seamstress.

1854   Begins studies at the École Impériale et Spéciale de Dessin et de Mathématiques, Paris, known as "La Petite École."

1864   Starts to work for the sculptor Albert-Ernest Carrier-Belleuse. Meets Rose Beuret (pl. 31) who becomes his lifetime partner.

1865   His early work *Man with the Broken Nose* (pl. 3) is rejected by the Paris Salon.

1871   Moves to Brussels to work with Carrier-Belleuse.

1876   Visits Italy, where he sees the work of Michelangelo and Donatello in Florence and Rome.

1877   Exhibits *The Age of Bronze* (pl. 1) in Brussels and at the Paris Salon.

1879   His statue *The Call to Arms* (pl. 2) is submitted to a competition for a monument to the defense of Paris.

1880   *Saint John the Baptist Preaching* (pl. 4) is exhibited at the Paris Salon. *The Age of Bronze* is acquired by the French state collections. Begins a commission for the *Gates of Hell* (figs. 14 and 15), a portal for the future museum of decorative arts in Paris.

1882   Creates *The Thinker* (pl. 12) and *The Kiss* (pl. 13) for the *Gates of Hell*.

1883   Works on the bust of the writer Victor Hugo (pl. 33).

1885   Receives a commission for the monument for the burghers of Calais (pls. 23–30).

1889   Receives commissions for *Monument to Claude Lorrain* in Nancy, France, and *Monument to Victor Hugo* for the Panthéon, Paris.

1891   Works on a commission from the Société des Gens de Lettres for *Monument to Balzac*.

1898   His sculpture *Balzac* (fig. 24) is rejected by the Société des Gens de Lettres. Exhibits a marble version of *The Kiss* at the Salon. Meets the American dancer Loïe Fuller (fig. 2).

1900   Exhibits at the Paris Exposition Universelle in a pavilion at the Place de l'Alma.

1902   Exhibits in Prague and visits Vienna. Receives a British subscription for *Saint John the Baptist Preaching*.

1904   Monumental versions of *The Thinker* are exhibited in London and Paris.

1906   *The Thinker* is installed in front of the Panthéon (fig. 19). Meets Japanese actress "Hanako" (pl. 39).

1908   Rents rooms at the Hôtel Biron, Paris, to serve as a studio.

1912   A gallery devoted to Rodin's work opens at the Metropolitan Museum of Art, New York.

1914   Meets the San Francisco arts patron and collector Alma de Bretteville Spreckels (fig. 1) through Loïe Fuller.

1915   Rodin sculptures are exhibited at the Panama-Pacific International Exposition, San Francisco. Alma Spreckels and her husband, Adolph, acquire their first Rodin sculptures.

1916   Donates his collection to the French state for a future museum in the Hôtel Biron.

1917   Marries Rose Beuret in January. Dies November 17 at Meudon, outside of Paris.

1919   Musée Rodin opens in the Hôtel Biron.

1924   The California Palace of the Legion of Honor, San Francisco, opens on November 11 with *The Thinker* in the Court of Honor (fig. 4).

2017   On the one-hundred-year anniversary of Auguste Rodin's death, a special presentation of his work is mounted at the Legion of Honor to commemorate the sculptor's life and achievement.

SELECTED BIBLIOGRAPHY

Barryte, Bernard, and Roberta K. Tarbell, eds. *Rodin and America: Influence and Adaptation 1876–1936*. Exh. cat. Stanford, CA: Cantor Arts Center in association with Silvana Editoriale, 2011.

Bondil, Nathalie, with Sophie Biass-Fabiani, eds. *Metamorphoses: In Rodin's Studio*. Exh. cat. Montreal: Montreal Museum of Fine Arts, 2015.

De Caso, Jacques, and Patricia B. Sanders. *Rodin's Sculpture, A Critical Study of the Spreckels Collection*. San Francisco: Fine Arts Museums of San Francisco, 1977.

De Caso, Jacques, and Patricia B. Sanders. *Rodin's Thinker, Significant Aspects*. San Francisco: Fine Arts Museums of San Francisco, 1973.

Dujardin-Beaumetz, François. *Auguste Rodin, Readings on His Life and Work*. Translated by Albert E. Elsen. Englewood Cliffs, NJ: Prentice Hall, 1965.

Elsen, Albert E. et al., *Rodin's Art: The Rodin Collection at the Iris & B. Gerald Cantor Center for Visual Arts at Stanford University*. New York: Oxford University Press, 2003.

Grunfeld, Frederic V. *Rodin: A Biography*. New York: Henry Holt and Company, 1987.

Hare, Marion J. *The Sculptor and His Sitter: Rodin's Bust of Eve Fairfax*. Johannesburg: Johannesburg Art Gallery, 1994.

Jianou, Ionel, and C. Goldscheider. *Rodin*. Paris: Arted, Éditions d'Art, 1967.

Le Normand-Romain, Antoinette. *The Bronzes of Rodin, Catalogue of Works in the Musée Rodin*, 2 vols. Paris: Musée Rodin, 2007.

Le Normand-Romain, Antoinette. *Rodin*. Paris: Citadelles & Mazenod, 2013.

Scharlach, Bernice. *Big Alma: San Francisco's Alma Spreckels*, 2nd ed. San Francisco: Scottwall Associates, 1990; San Francisco and Berkeley: Fine Arts Museums of San Francisco and Heyday, 2014.

Taillandier, Yvon. *Rodin*. New York: Crown Trade Paperbacks, 1977.

ABOUT THE AUTHOR

Martin Chapman is curator in charge of European decorative arts and sculpture at the Fine Arts Museums of San Francisco. His recent publications include *Marie-Antoinette and the Petit Trianon at Versailles*, *Royal Treasures from the Louvre: Louis XIV to Marie-Antoinette*, and *The Salon Doré from the Hôtel de La Trémoille*. He also wrote an introduction to the revised edition of *Big Alma: San Francisco's Alma Spreckels*.

ACKNOWLEDGMENTS

We wish to extend our gratitude to the many contributors who have made the Rodin centenary exhibition and its accompanying curatorial and scholarly programming possible. First and foremost, we acknowledge the donors who have helped to bring this presentation to fruition. Our heartfelt thanks are extended to John A. and Cynthia Fry Gunn, our presenting sponsors.

At the Fine Arts Museums of San Francisco, we thank the Board of Trustees and Diane B. Wilsey, president, who have supported the presentation in so many ways. Gratitude is extended to Martin Chapman, curator in charge of decorative arts and sculpture, for overseeing all aspects of this endeavor. We also thank Julian Cox, founding curator of photography and chief curator; Krista Brugnara, director of exhibitions; Deanna Griffin, director of registration and collections management; Stuart Hata, director of retail operations; Tomomi Itakura, head of exhibition design; Susan Klein, director of marketing and communications; Daniel Meza, chief designer and art director; and Claudia Schmuckli, curator in charge of contemporary art and programming. We are further appreciative of all of the staff for their hard work to make this presentation possible.

This catalogue was edited and overseen by Leslie Dutcher, director of publications, with the assistance of Diana K. Murphy, editorial assistant, who researched much of the archival imagery. Sue Grinols, director of photo services, oversaw the new photography campaign, and Randy Dodson, head photographer, created and prepared the stunning new imagery of Rodin's works in our collection. Appreciation is also given to Ryan Butterfield, chief preparator; Egle Mendoza, assistant registrar; Ellie Ohara, assistant objects conservator; and Colleen O'Shea, our Mellon fellow in Objects Conservation, for their careful assistance in preparing the various objects for photography and public viewing. I am also grateful to Yolanda de Montijo and Frank Kofsuske of Em Dash for their fresh design. Pat Goley and Jane Messenger of Professional Graphics are acknowledged for their skilled prepress work on the image files. Pauline Hisbacq, Jérôme Manoukian, and Véronique Mattiussi at the Musée Rodin, Paris, are thanked for their help in preparing for us some of the historical photographs and documents from the museum's archive. And further gratitude is extended to Mary DelMonico, publisher of DelMonico Books • Prestel, and her colleagues for their wonderful partnership to distribute this book into the trade. This catalogue is published with the assistance of the Andrew W. Mellon Foundation Endowment for Publications.

Other colleagues around the world have assisted us in the research for this project. We wish to thank Jacques de Caso and Patricia B. Sanders for their prior work on this collection; Catherine Chevillot, director of the Musée Rodin, who has been so helpful with various aspects of this project; Antoinette Le Normand-Romain, former curator of sculpture at the Musée Rodin, for her deep knowledge and advice; and Helen Marraud, curator of sculpture at the Musée Rodin, for hosting Martin Chapman's visit to Rodin's studio at Meudon.

Max Hollein
Director and CEO
Fine Arts Museums of San Francisco

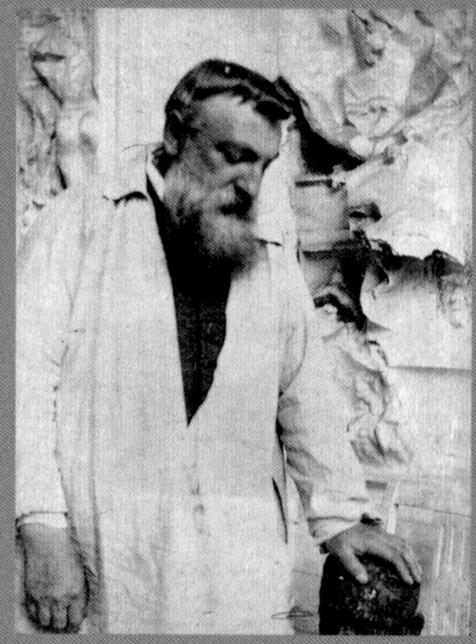

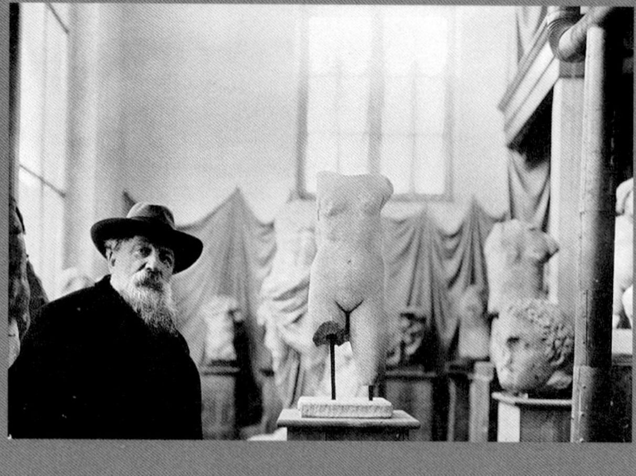

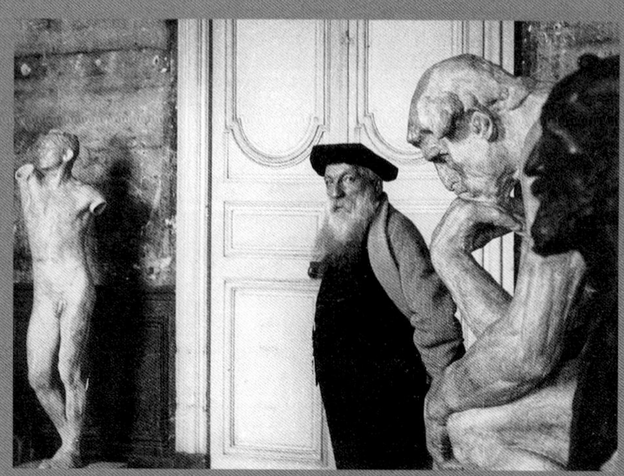

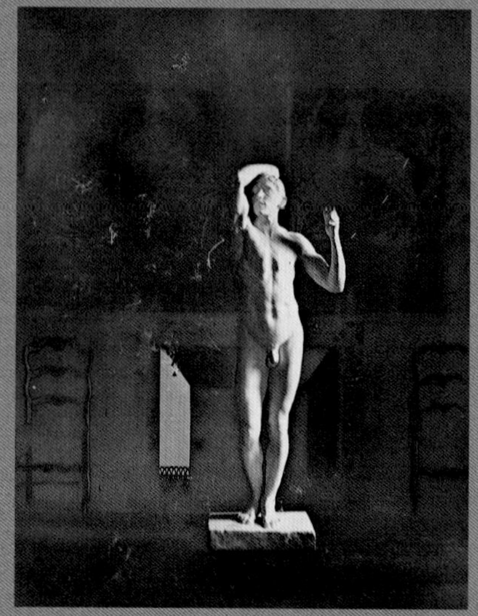

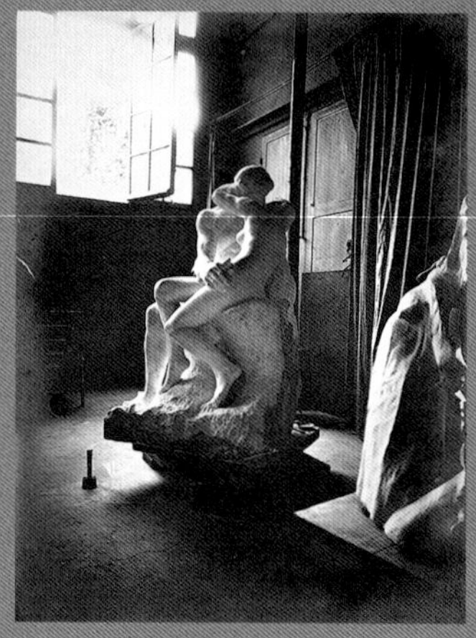

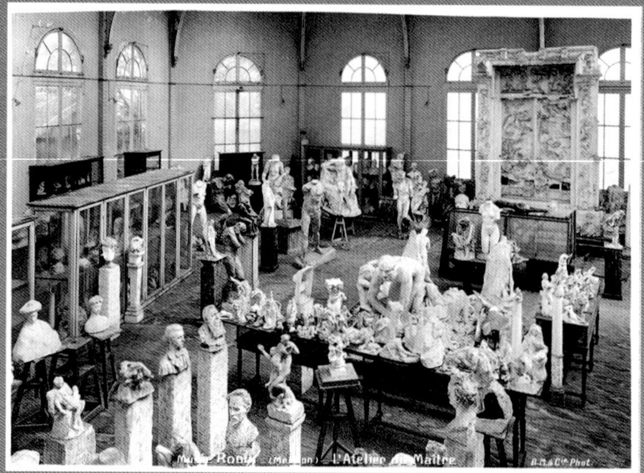

---

1   Gertrude Käsebier, Rodin in front of the *Gates of Hell* (pls. 12–22) in the studio in Meudon, his hand on the bronze head of *Baron d'Estournelles de Constant*, 1905. Gum bichromate print, 27 x 21 ¾ in. (68.6 x 55.1 cm). Musée Rodin, Paris, Ph.249 (p. 4)

2   Albert Harlingue, Rodin in his studio in Meudon, 1910 (pp. 8–9)

3   Rodin with plasters of *The Age of Bronze* (pl. 1) and *The Thinker* (pl. 12), ca. 1910 (pp. 18–19)

4   Eugène Druet, *The Age of Bronze* (pl. 1) in plaster, ca. 1898. Gelatin silver print, 7 ⅛ x 9 ⅜ in. (18 x 23.8 cm). Musée Rodin, Paris, Ph.1875 (p. 20)

5   Eugène Druet, *The Kiss* (pl. 13) in marble in the studio of the Dépôt des Marbres, Paris, ca. 1898. Gelatin silver print, 15 ¾ x 11 ¾ in. (40 x 30 cm). Musée Rodin, Paris, Paris, Ph.373 (p. 32)

6   Bernes & Marouteau, Pavillon de l'Alma (Rodin's studio), Meudon, with the *Gates of Hell* (pls. 12–22) in the background, after 1917. Musée Rodin, Paris, Ph.9001 (p. 52)

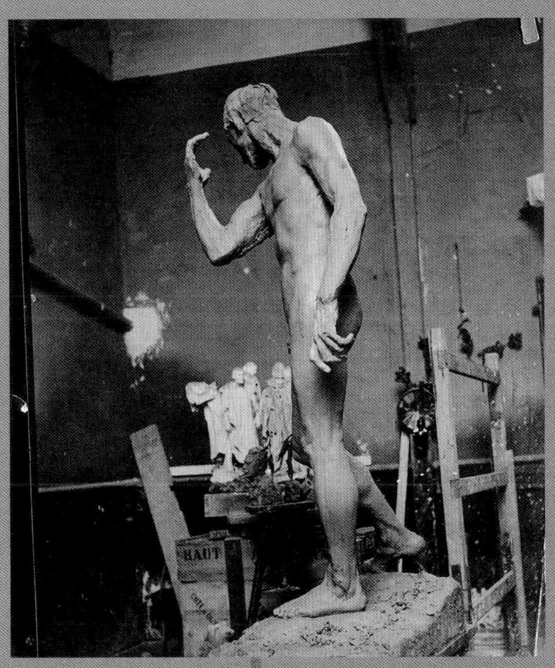

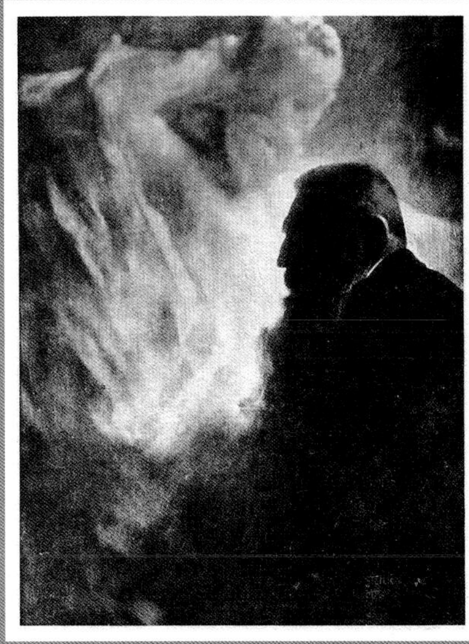

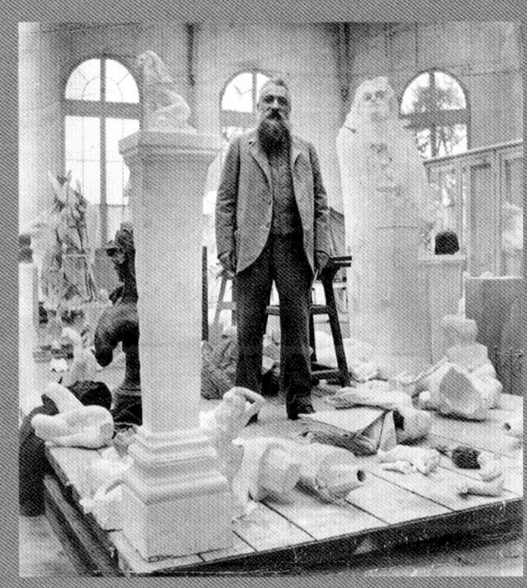

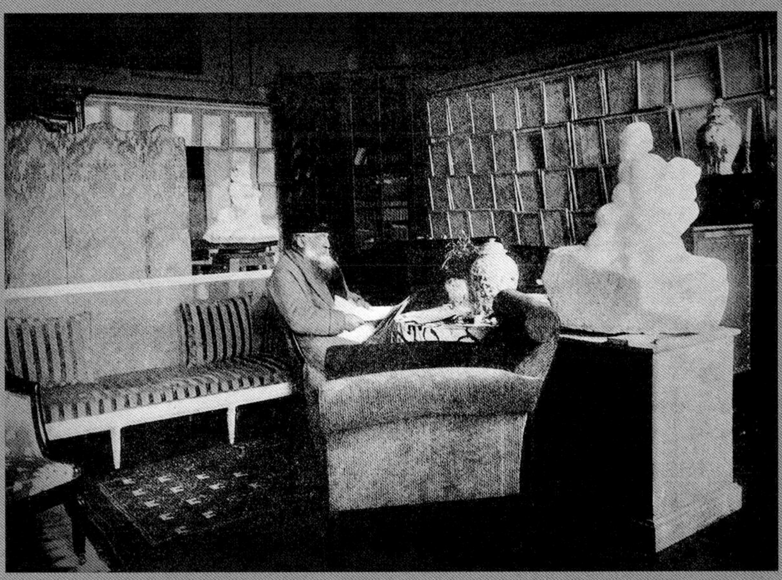

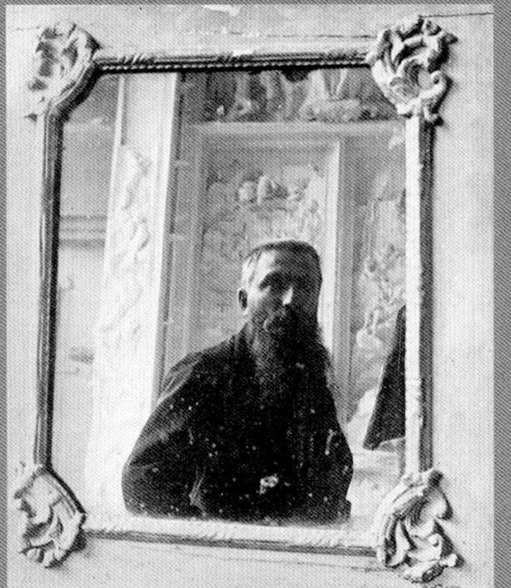

7   Charles Bodmer, *Pierre de Wiessant* (pl. 26), nude clay version, in the studio on 177 Boulevard de Vaugirard, Paris, ca. 1886. Gelatin silver print, 9 ½ x 8 ½ in. (24 x 21.5 cm). Musée Rodin, Paris, Ph.321 (p. 82)

8   Edward Jean Steichen, *Rodin* [showing *Bust of Victor Hugo*, pl. 41], I of a series of VIII photographs published in *Camera Work*, no. 2, April 1903. Photogravure, 8 ⅜ x 6 ⅜ in. (21.2 x 16.1 cm). Fine Arts Museums of San Francisco, Museum purchase, Achenbach Foundation for Graphic Arts Endowment Fund and George Fuchs Memorial Fund, 1994.86 (p. 98)

9   Eugène Druet, Rodin among his works and fragments in the Pavillon de l'Alma, Meudon, ca. 1902. Gelatin silver print, 10 ⅛ x 9 ⅞ in. (25.6 x 25.2 cm). Musée Rodin, Paris, Ph.203 (p. 124)

10   Rodin among his books at the Hôtel Biron, 77 rue de Varenne, Paris, ca. 1900 (pp. 152–153)

11   William Elborne, Mirror reflection of Rodin in front of the *Gates of Hell* (pls. 12–22), plaster version, 1887. Albumen print, 5 ⅛ x 4 ¼ in. (13 x 10.7 cm). Musée Rodin, Paris, Ph.1442 (p. 154)

This catalogue is published in 2017 by the Fine Arts Museums of San Francisco and DelMonico Books • Prestel to mark the centenary of Auguste Rodin's death with a series of special rotations of the Museums' collection of the sculptor's work at the Legion of Honor, San Francisco, January 28–December 10, 2017.

Presenting Sponsor
John A. and Cynthia Fry Gunn

This catalogue is published with the assistance of the Andrew W. Mellon Foundation Endowment for Publications.

Fine Arts Museums of San Francisco
Golden Gate Park
50 Hagiwara Tea Garden Drive
San Francisco, CA 94118-4502
www.famsf.org

Leslie Dutcher, Director of Publications
Danica Michels Hodge, Editor
Jane Hyun, Editor
Diana K. Murphy, Editorial Assistant

Edited by Leslie Dutcher
Proofread by Susan Richmond
Picture research by Diana K. Murphy
Designed and typeset by Yolanda de Montijo, Em Dash
Production management by Luke Chase and
  Karen Farquhar, DelMonico Books • Prestel
Color separations by Professional Graphics, Inc.
Printed in China

DelMonico Books, an imprint of Prestel, a member of Verlagsgruppe Random House GmbH

Prestel Verlag
Neumarkter Strasse 28
81673 Munich

Prestel Publishing Ltd.
14–17 Wells Street
London W1T 3PD

Prestel Publishing
900 Broadway, Suite 603
New York, NY 10003

www.prestel.com

ISBN: 978-3-7913-5633-4

Library of Congress Cataloging-in-Publication Data
Names: Legion of Honor (San Francisco, Calif.), author. | Chapman, Martin (Curator), author.
Title: The Sculpture of Auguste Rodin at the Legion of Honor / Martin Chapman.
Description: San Francisco: Fine Arts Museums of San Francisco–Legion of Honor, 2017. | Includes bibliographical references.
Identifiers: LCCN 2016044560 | ISBN 9783791356334 (Rodin)
Subjects: LCSH: Rodin, Auguste, 1840–1917—Catalogs. | Sculpture—California, San Francisco—Catalogs. | Legion of Honor (San Francisco, Calif.)—Catalogs.
Classification: LCC NB553.R7 A4 2017 | DDC 730.92—dc23 LC record available at https://lccn.loc.gov/2016044560

A CIP catalogue record is available from the British Library.

Front cover: Auguste Rodin, *The Thinker* (pl. 12), 1888 (enlarged 1904, cast ca. 1914). Bronze, 74 3/8 x 38 5/8 x 55 1/8 in. (189 x 98 x 140 cm). Fine Arts Museums of San Francisco, Gift of Alma de Bretteville Spreckels, 1924.18.1. Photograph by Randy Dodson, © Fine Arts Museums of San Francisco

Back cover: Edward Jean Steichen, *Rodin* (detail, pp. 98 and 159), I of a series of VII photographs published in *Camera Work*, no. 2, April 1903. Photogravure, 8 3/8 x 6 3/8 in. (21.2 x 16.1 cm). Fine Arts Museums of San Francisco, Museum purchase, Achenbach Foundation for Graphic Arts Endowment Fund and George Fuchs Memorial Fund, 1994.86. © 2016 The Estate of Edward Steichen, Artists Rights Society (ARS), New York

Endpapers and p. 10: The Spreckels collection of Rodin works assembled at 2080 Washington Street, San Francisco, ca. 1920–1940. Photograph by Gabriel Moulin. © Moulin Studios

pp. 2–3: *The Thinker* (pl. 12) in the Court of Honor at the Legion of Honor, 2013. Photograph by Henrik Kam, © Fine Arts Museums of San Francisco

p. 6: *The Age of Bronze* (pl. 1) in the Rotunda at the Legion of Honor, 2016. Photograph by Randy Dodson, © Fine Arts Museums of San Francisco

For captions for other opening photographs, see the Picture Gallery (pp. 158–159).

Photography credits

All photographs are by Randy Dodson, © Fine Arts Museums of San Francisco, unless otherwise noted.

Pages 2–3: photograph by Henrik Kam, © Fine Arts Museums of San Francisco; 4, 20, 32, 52, 82, 124, 154: © Musée Rodin, Paris; 8–9: Hulton Archive / Stringer / Getty Images; 10: © Moulin Studios; 18–19: adoc-photos / Getty Images; 98: © 2016 The Estate of Edward Steichen / Artists Rights Society (ARS), New York; and 152–153: Print Collector / Getty Images.

Figures 1, 4, 5: California History Center, San Francisco Public Library; 3: California Historical Society; 6, 8: © Moulin Studios; 7: © Moulin Studios, courtesy The Bancroft Library, University of California, Berkeley; 9: photograph by Henrik Kam, © Fine Arts Museums of San Francisco; 11, 19, 22, 23: © Musée Rodin, Paris; 12: © Universal Studios; 14: © RMN-Grand Palais / Art Resource, NY; 15: Musée Rodin, Paris, France / Bridgeman Images; 16: Scala / Art Resource, NY; 18: Photo: Martine Beck-Coppola, © RMN-Grand Palais / Art Resource, NY; and 24: © 2016 The Estate of Edward Steichen / Artists Rights Society (ARS), New York.

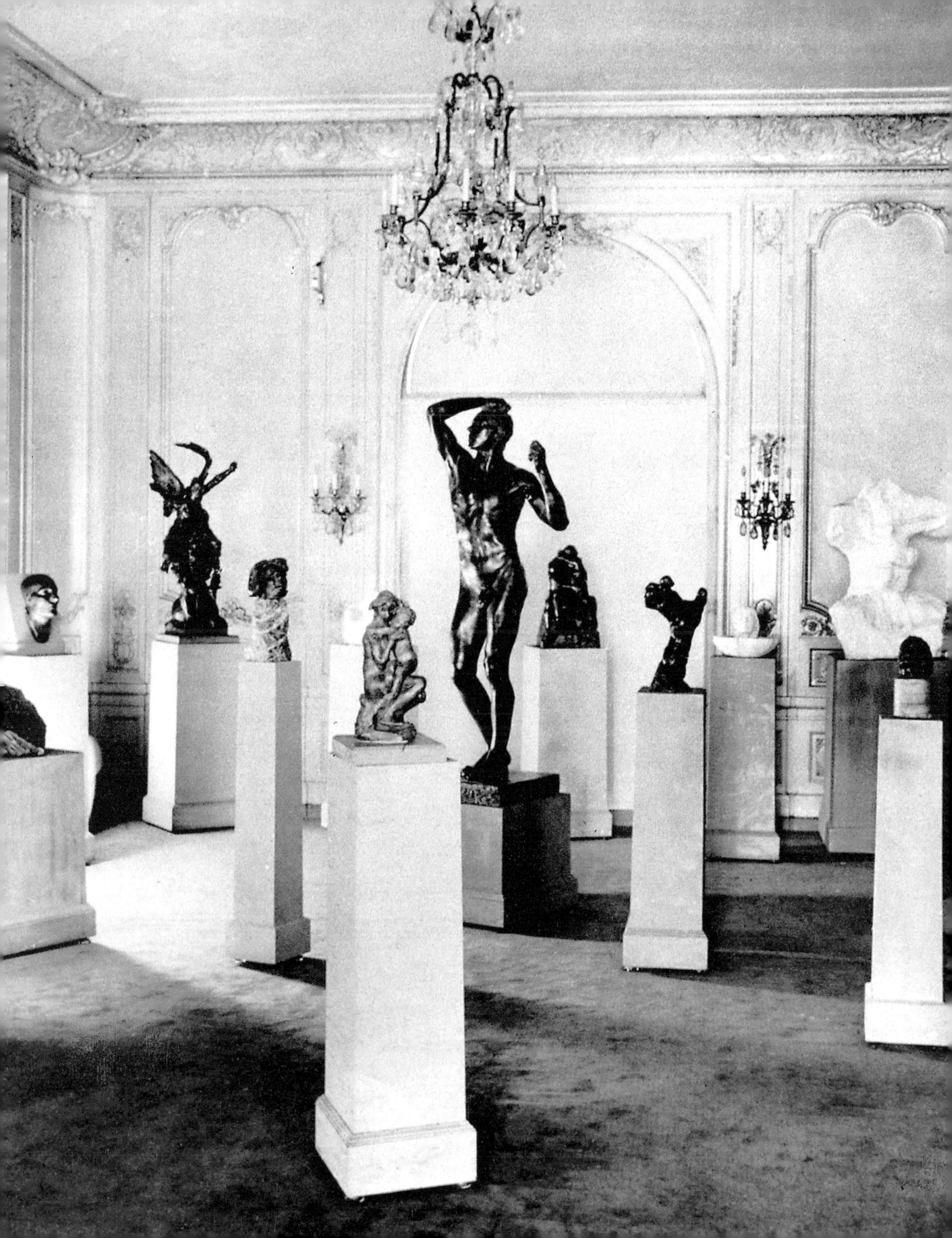

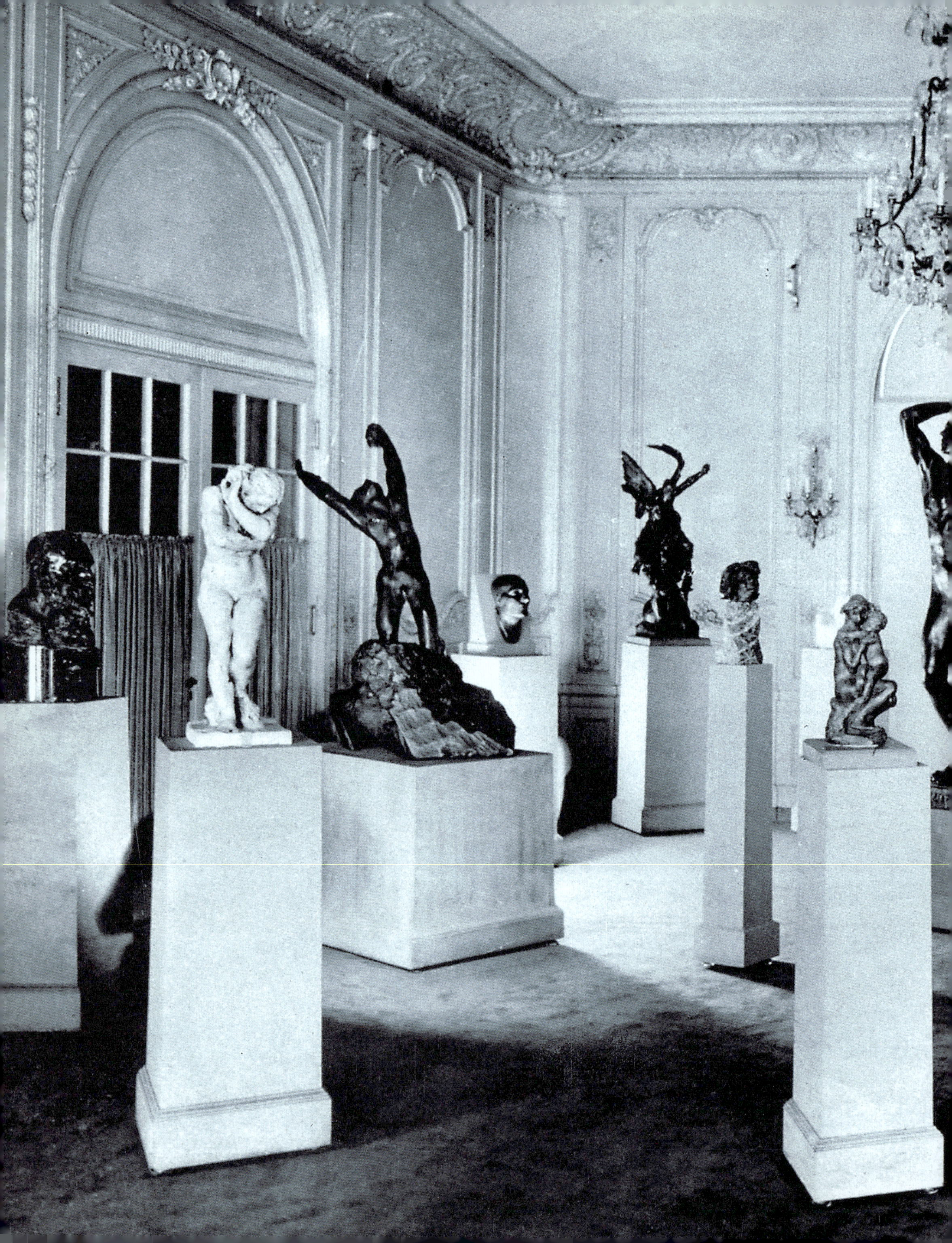